MW00653111

Beyond the Pulpit

PITTSBURGH SERIES IN COMPOSITION, LITERACY, AND CULTURE

David Bartholomae and Jean Ferguson Carr, Editors

BEYOND THE PULPIT

Women's Rhetorical Roles in
the Antebellum Religious Press

LISA J. SHAVER

UNIVERSITY OF PITTSBURGH PRESS

Published by the University of Pittsburgh Press, Pittsburgh, Pa., 15260
Copyright © 2012, University of Pittsburgh Press
All rights reserved
Manufactured in the United States of America
Printed on acid-free paper
10 9 8 7 6 5 4 3 2 1

Library of Congress Cataloging-in-Publication Data
Shaver, Lisa J.
Beyond the pulpit : women's rhetorical roles in the antebellum religious press / Lisa J. Shaver.
p.   cm. — (Pittsburgh series in composition, literacy, and culture)
Includes bibliographical references (p.   ) and index.
ISBN 978-0-8229-6169-7 (pbk. : alk. paper)
1. Women in the Methodist Church—United States—History—19th century.   2. Meth-
odist women—Religious life—United States—History—19th century.   3. Methodist
Church—United States—Periodicals—History—19th century.   4. Methodist women—Press
coverage—United States—History—19th century.   5. Women and journalism—United
States—History—19th century.   6. United States—Church history—19th century.   I. Title.
BX8345.7.S53 2012
287'.608209034—dc23   2011039632

For my parents, Roy and Ann Shaver,
who introduced me to the Methodist Church

Contents

Acknowledgments

I am indebted to so many people for their assistance and encouragement throughout this project. First and foremost is Kate Ronald, who willingly waded through early drafts and provided valuable responses and sage guidance since the inception of this project. I am certain she never expected to spend so much time with so many Methodist women but I am so glad she did. I am also grateful to Sarah Robbins for her generative feedback, suggestions, and expertise in literacy studies and nineteenth-century women's literate practices. I am honored and privileged to have these two women as my mentors.

I also want to thank those individuals who provided feedback on drafts and portions of this book. These include Carla Pestana, Morris Young, and Whitney Womack, whose suggestions provided important early guidance on this project. Portions of chapter 2 originally appeared in my article, "Women's Deathbed Pulpits: From Quiet Congregants to Iconic Ministers," published in *Rhetoric Review* 27, no. 1 (2008). Vicki Tolar Burton and Jan Schuetz provided valuable feedback on this article, and Vicki Tolar Burton's scholarship on Methodism has long been a source of inspiration for my work. Portions of chapters 4 and 5 appeared in my article, "Stepping Outside the 'Ladies' Department': Women's Expanding Rhetorical Boundaries," published in the September 2008 issue of *College English* (Copyright 2008 by the National Council of Teachers of English. Used with permission). I am thankful to John Schilb and the anonymous reviewers at *College English* for their thoughtful feedback on this article. I am also grateful to Patricia Bizzell, Jane Donawerth, Shirley Wilson Logan, Roxanne Mountford, and all the participants in the "Women's Religious Persuasion and Social Activism in America 1780–1940" workshop held at the Rhetoric Society of America Summer Institute at Penn

State University in 2009. I received insightful feedback and a jolt of enthusiasm from this wonderful group of scholars and the important work they are pursuing. Additionally, I want to thank Deborah Meade, Joshua Shanholtzer, Alex Wolfe, and the anonymous reviewers at University of Pittsburgh Press for their suggestions and support of this work.

This project has also benefited from generous institutional support. I received two summer sabbaticals from Baylor University as well as a grant from Baylor's Arts and Humanities Faculty Research Program. I also want to thank my research assistant at Baylor, Julie Ooms, who helped me gather and peruse issues of the *Ladies' Repository*. I received a "Women in United Methodist History Research Grant" from the United Methodist Church's General Commission on Archives that enabled me to do research at the Methodist Archives and History Center at Drew University. Miami University also supported my initial research with a fellowship.

On a personal note, I want to thank my friends and colleagues in the English Department at Baylor University, the University Writing Program at the University of Notre Dame, and the wonderful graduate community in the English Department at Miami University. I am especially grateful to my dear friends Cristy Beemer, Sarah Bowles, Jen Cellio, and Liz Mackey. I cannot fathom making this "road trip" without them. I also want to thank my pastors, teachers, and many friends at the five Methodist churches where I have been a member: First United Methodist Church in Neosho, Missouri; Trinity United Methodist Church in Little Rock, Arkansas; Peachtree United Methodist Church in Atlanta, Georgia; Oxford United Methodist Church in Oxford, Ohio; and Austin Avenue United Methodist Church in Waco, Texas.

I especially want to thank my family—my parents, Roy and Ann Shaver, my sisters, Beth and Susan, and my brother, Mike. They have always been a constant source of encouragement and support; and one will not find a more enthusiastic publicist than my dad. Finally, I believe everyone should begin a big writing project by adopting a dog. Wylie has been my faithful mascot. When I was stuck or discouraged, we just needed to take a walk.

Beyond the Pulpit

Looking Beyond the Pulpit

The contributions of women to Methodism were significant but more often assumed than acknowledged.

—Dee Andrews,
The Methodists and Revolutionary America, 1760–1800

A small group of Methodist women brought Ruth Short back to life. Long before she died, my grandmother disappeared behind the shroud of dementia, and I had somehow forgotten the lively woman she once was. Following her funeral, some women from the church prepared a bereavement dinner for our family. My grandmother had not attended that small, red brick church in Hartford, Arkansas, in several years, but the faces of the women who served the dinner were still familiar to me from all the Sundays we had accompanied Grandmother to church. One of the women sang a solo during the funeral service, and when my sister and I told her how much we appreciated it, she explained that the first time she sang that song, Mrs. Short had approached her after the church service to ask if she would sing it at her funeral. Surprised by the request, the woman said, "Mrs. Short, I have never sung at a funeral." To which my grandmother responded, "Well, I've never died, but I guess that won't stop me." That story about my grandmother prompted another and another until this small group of women with their casseroles, compassion, and wonderful recollections performed a miracle; they had resurrected the outspoken, loud-laughing, devout-Methodist woman who was my grandmother.

In a way, I guess I have been studying Methodist women all my life, but it was just a few years ago that I encountered them in the academy. I distinctly remember the day when I first learned about female Methodist ministers in eighteenth-century England while reading Patricia Bizzell and Bruce Herzberg's "Intro-duction to Nineteenth-Century Rhetoric" in *The Rhetorical Tradition*. Their introduction directed me to Vicki Tolar Collins's article "Women's Voices and Women's Silence in the Tradition of Early Methodism."[1] Following this dis-covery, one of my friends gave me a copy of *Adam Bede*, so in a way, it was George Eliot's fictional Dinah, along with Mary Bosanquet, Margaret David-son, Sarah Crosby, and Ann Tripp, who piqued my curiosity about women in the early American Methodist church and helped forge in my mind the con-nection between women, American Methodism, and rhetoric.[2] Hailing from a long line of Methodist women, the connection made perfect sense to me.

Initially, I turned my attention to the pulpit. In her book *Strangers and Pilgrims: Female Preaching in America 1740–1845*, historian Catherine Brekus meticulously identifies the names of fourteen women preachers and exhorters in the Methodist Episcopal Church (MEC), the first Methodist church estab-lished in the United States. Brekus also acknowledges nine women who were preachers in the African MEC and five women who preached in other Meth-odist denominations that emerged from the MEC, including the Reformed Methodists, Wesleyan Methodists, Primitive Methodists, and the Methodist Protestant Church.[3] Among this list, women such as Julia Foote, Jarena Lee, Fanny Newell, Hannah Pearce Reeves, and Phoebe Palmer have increasingly garnered scholarly attention.[4] However, in a church overwhelmingly com-prised of women, and in a movement that rapidly swelled to the largest de-nomination in nineteenth-century America, this small group of courageous female ministers offers a limited glimpse of women during the American Methodist movement's dramatic expansion in the first decades of the nine-teenth century, especially considering that women preachers and exhorters were frequently viewed as radicals and barred from many Methodist pulpits.

I began to consider my own experience growing up in the Methodist church. I was an adult before I heard a sermon delivered by a female minis-ter, and it was 2002 before I belonged to a Methodist church where a woman presided as the senior pastor. In *The Gendered Pulpit: Preaching in American Protestant Spaces*, Roxanne Mountford shares a similar experience growing up in another denomination. She writes, "As a child, I never saw a woman preach; the only women who stepped before the pulpit gave announcements, led hymns, or told tales of missionary work in Third World countries."[5]

In my own childhood, even though women were absent from the pulpit, I had always perceived that women ran the church. My Sunday school teach-ers and summer Bible school teachers were primarily women. Women raised money for the church's foreign missions; women populated prayer networks;

women prepared the bereavement dinners and comprised the altar guild, which seamlessly changed the colors of the altar cloths during Advent, Christmas, Epiphany, Lent, Easter, and Pentecost. On Monday mornings, women counted, recorded, and deposited the money taken up during "Sundays" offerings, wrote personal notes to visitors, and faithfully visited members in the local hospital. Consequently, I decided to search for Methodist women where I had always found them—beyond the pulpit.

This book examines additional rhetorical spaces in antebellum churches in order to recover a more accurate history of American women's rhetoric. Scholars' ongoing efforts to recover women's rhetoric seek to acknowledge women's rich, expansive rhetorical legacy. By charting the rhetorical roles assumed by and ascribed to women in the Methodist church's popular and widely disseminated antebellum periodicals, this book claims a broader definition of women's rhetorical roles within churches. While a few examples drawn from these periodicals present African American and Native American women, the overwhelming majority present white women from middle and lower socioeconomic classes.

For most of these women, the church and church-affiliated organizations were the first organizations they participated in outside of the home. However, women's activities were usually voluntary and were often excluded from formal institutional records and historical accounts. Methodist periodicals offer glimpses of women's influence within the powerful antebellum Methodist movement. By looking at the periodicals produced by the church and read by its parishioners, I am not only recovering women's rhetorical roles, I am also examining the rhetoricity of the press—how the religious press both supported and circumscribed women's roles. Whether Methodist periodicals are reporting roles assumed by women or roles that they are ascribing to them, the layer of the press is always there. Documenting women's expanding rhetorical roles through the religious press also demonstrates how the burgeoning interdisciplinary field of periodical studies provides fruitful territory for recovering women's rhetorical history. Driven by the rapidly expanding availability of digital archives, periodical studies consider texts that are important cultural artifacts representative of their social and political contexts.[6] Periodicals provide another avenue for encountering individuals excluded from formal institutional histories.

Beyond the Pulpit examines the spaces where women appear in *Methodist Magazine* (*MM*; established in 1818) and the *Christian Advocate* (*CA*; established in 1826), the two most popular general-audience periodicals produced by the antebellum Methodist church, and concludes by discussing the church's creation, in 1841, of a women's magazine, the *Ladies' Repository* (*LR*).

The primary space for women in *MM* was memoirs, more akin to modern-day obituaries than the texts we refer to as memoirs today. Hence, this book charts a progression for the presence of women in the church's publications: from admittance into the text most often through death to the church founding a magazine just for women. In between, I identify numerous rhetorical roles assumed by and ascribed to women in the church's periodicals, including iconic ministers, domestic evangelists, models of piety, benefactors and fund-raisers, benevolent organizers and advocates, Sunday school administrators and teachers, missionary assistants, and assistant ministers. Identifying the discursive and spatial locations in which women appear in these periodicals delineates women's movement beyond their prescribed domestic borders. It also reveals women performing powerful rhetorical roles within their homes, assumed to be private spaces, but which through publication and mass distribution became public spaces. Instead of focusing on achievements of female rhetors, this study attends to the everyday descriptions of women's activities included on the pages of Methodist periodicals. In doing so, it offers insight into the more "regular" and persuasive work of ordinary women and the religious press.

Methodist periodicals are important sites for studying antebellum women's rhetoric, because it is only here that we begin to see many of the important rhetorical roles women played in this vast nineteenth-century institution. Even when women kept diaries, wrote letters, or prepared meeting minutes and reports of their activities, these works were seldom considered valuable, thus, most have been lost to later generations. Methodist periodicals also depict the dramatic growth of the Methodist church in antebellum America. Spurred by the Second Great Awakening, Methodism exploded across the United States during the early nineteenth century, increasing from less than 3 percent of all church membership in 1776 to more than 34 percent by 1850. By midcentury, one out of every fifteen Americans belonged to the Methodist church, and by the start of the Civil War, Methodists occupied more than twenty thousand places of worship across the country. The Methodist church became by far the largest religious body and the most extensive national institution in the United States outside of the federal government.[7]

Founded by John Wesley as a revival movement inside the Church of England in the first half of the eighteenth century, Methodism was initially carried to America by English, Scottish, and Irish immigrants. Wesley did not dispatch itinerant ministers to America until 1769. Prior to this, one of the immigrants who brought Methodism to America was a woman named Barbara Heck, later hailed as the mother of American Methodism. According to the legend, Heck discovered a group of men playing cards in her kitchen. She scooped the cards into her apron, threw them into the fire, put on her bonnet and went to see her cousin Philip Embury, who had been a Methodist class leader and local minister in Ireland, pleading with him, "Philip, you must preach to us, or we shall all go to hell together, and God will require our blood on your hands."[8] Having no place to preach and no congregation, Embury was reluctant, but Heck encouraged him to hold services in his own home, insisting that she would provide the congregation. The first meeting at Embury's house consisted of Heck, her husband, their African American servant, and John Lawrence, one of the reformed card players. This meeting in 1766 represented the beginning of the first Methodist society in New York, and the motivating force was a woman operating persuasively outside of the pulpit.

Formally established as the Methodist Episcopal Church in America in 1784, Methodism gained popularity at a time when America was redefining the relationship between church and state by eliminating all vestiges of state-supported churches. As the Methodists rapidly assumed numerical dominance among America's Protestant denominations, the church reshaped religion in the new republic. Methodism aligned well with America's democratic impulse and optimism. In his examination of Methodism's influence on American culture, historian Nathan Hatch notes that Methodists stressed three themes that resonated with Americans: God's free grace, the liberty to accept or reject that grace, and dynamic religious expression, which was encouraged among women and all classes of individuals. Methodism's focus on free will and free grace contrasted with Calvinistic doctrines of limited grace or predestination common to Presbyterians and Congregationalists. Moreover, Methodism was a voluntary movement that drew members by choice rather than tradition. With this practice, Hatch suggests that Methodists "embraced the virtues of pluralism, of competition, and of marketing religion in every sphere of life."[9] Methodists introduced a less formal, vernacular expression of Christianity that was more accessible, enthusiastic, and extemporaneous.

Methodism grew because of its missionary zeal, which motivated its itinerant ministers to travel wherever there were people. Methodist clergy conducted worship in homes, barns, fields, and at camp meetings and sought all classes of individuals in cities as well as rural and frontier regions. Historian John Wigger provides an illustrative example of one Methodist family that moved from Kentucky to Butler County, Ohio, in 1806. Wigger notes, "At that time, Butler County was an 'almost unbroken forrest' containing so many wolves that shortly after their arrival the family's two large dogs opted to return to Kentucky, swimming both the Miami and Ohio Rivers, on the way."[10] Out of this dense, wolf-ridden forest, the first visitor to appear on the family's doorstep was a Methodist itinerant minister traveling the area on horseback. Historian Nancy Hardesty similarly notes that Frances Willard became a Methodist because a Methodist circuit rider provided the only form of organized religion in the "wilds of Southern Wisconsin" where her family lived.[11]

Ultimately, Methodism offered an egalitarian form of religion that "empowered ordinary people by taking their deepest spiritual impulses at face value rather than subjecting them to the scrutiny of orthodox doctrine and the frowns of respectable clergymen."[12] As a progressive force, Methodism chipped away at traditional patterns of deference such as class; professional clericalism; and conventional boundaries of gender, ethnicity, and education. Methodists recognized religious expression by all individuals—including women.

Local Methodist societies organized around gatherings that provided religious forums for individuals to preach, exhort, testify, pray, and encourage each other. In addition to Sunday worship, members and prospective members attended small group gatherings called class meetings. Up until the middle of the nineteenth century, Methodist societies often required members to attend class meetings, which were led by an appointed class leader who was responsible for overseeing the spiritual progress of class members. During these meetings, individuals opened their spiritual experiences and salvation to discussion, examination, and prayer. Methodists in good standing were also invited to participate in quarterly circuit-wide love feasts. These meetings brought together all the parishioners along one circuit to address administrative matters and share worship. Additionally, Methodists came together for large revivals and camp meetings. In each of these forums, men and women were encouraged to share their testimonies and discuss their spiritual triumphs and failures.

As with most religious institutions of the era, the Methodist church was overwhelmingly composed of women. However, few records of early Methodist women can be found in the main Methodist archives (located at Drew University in Madison, New Jersey). It is not until the latter half of the nineteenth century, when the church's Woman's Foreign Missionary Society, established in 1869, began dispatching women missionaries that women begin to emerge in the archives. Moreover, in their own recovery efforts, religious historians have often narrowly defined women's rhetorical roles within antebellum American churches. Historian Ann Braude claims that most studies of church histories have "perpetuated the contention that the views of one man in the pulpit are more important than those of the many women in the pews."[13] A similar inclination exists in studies of women's rhetoric, which frequently emphasize the pulpit as the sole rhetorical space within churches.

This emphasis on the pulpit excludes the vast majority of women's influence within antebellum churches and the church's role in these women's rhetorical development. In recent years, many scholars—including Patricia Bizzell and Bruce Herzberg, Nancy Hardesty, Catherine Brekus, Susan Lindley, and Karlyn Kohrs Campbell—have mapped the relationship between antebellum churches, women's social activism, and their rhetorical development, yet much of this research has centered on a small group of "extraordinary" women and their efforts to access or subvert church pulpits. Through these recovery projects, we are becoming better acquainted with these early public speakers and religious activists. Pulpit debates are an important chapter in women's rhetoric that warrant continued research, especially since, as Roxanne Mountford argues in the *Gendered Pulpit*, and as my own experience growing up in the Methodist church attests, the pulpit remains an often-contested, gendered space today. However, *solely* focusing on the pulpit in antebellum American churches stresses women's lack of institutional power and overlooks other spaces where "ordinary" women exerted influence within the church and how the church provided sites for women's rhetorical development. In her study of women in the Black Baptist Church in the late nineteenth and early twentieth centuries, historian Evelyn Brooks Higginbotham similarly stresses the need to move beyond studies of early women preachers in black churches, claiming that these discussions alone marginalize women's roles.[14] Higginbotham's desire to provide a more representative portrait echoes other scholars, including Joy Ritchie and Kate Ronald and Barbara Biesecker who have warned against limiting women's rhetoric to the study of a few canonical figures. Ritchie and Ronald, for instance, acknowledge that charting women's rhetorical history by describing the courageous efforts of a few brilliant women could keep "'recurrences' or the 'traces' of the emerging tradition invisible."[15]

The importance of identifying these traces is especially evident in the case of the Methodist church; if rhetorical historians rely on the pulpit as the primary gauge of women's roles, we limit ourselves to a small group of daring female preachers or a half century beginning with women's formal ordination in 1956.[16] Furthermore, emphasizing the pulpit highlights the tendency to assess women's rhetorical power in terms of prominent public roles, which reinscribes the same standards that historical women faced during their own lives and ultimately erases or downplays other women's contributions. I believe that studies of women's rhetoric need to travel both paths—examining the most ardent activists as well as the nameless women who exerted influence through women's organizations, conventional women's roles, and evangelical sites such as the religious press. Combined, these paths will present a more accurate picture of women's rhetorical history and legacy.

Women were often the first in their communities to become Methodists. "As a movement," John Wigger claims, "Methodism was created as much by women as it was by men." He notes that Wesley's heart-religion, with its intimate group meetings and emphasis on religious community, initially attracted female converts.[17] Many came to the church on their own or in the company of other women, and they often joined the church even if their fathers or husbands did not. Although their participation in the fledgling Methodist movement occasionally provoked ridicule and harassment, women had more freedom to follow their religious convictions and join Methodist societies, whereas men were wary of damaging their positions in the community by associating with an upstart religious sect. Historian Cynthia Lyerly shares an illustrative anecdote about an Anglican priest who traveled from England to Maryland in 1784. The priest was dismayed to discover that some of his local vestrymen supported both the Methodists and the Anglicans. Trying to explain their dual allegiance, one vestryman responded, "Pray sir . . . we cannot divorce our wives and turn our daughters out of doors, because they have joined the Methodists."[18] In addition to leaving their husbands' churches to join the Methodists, women often demonstrated their support by hosting itinerants and religious gatherings in their homes. Women served as critical allies to itinerant ministers—using family members and acquaintances to help these itinerants establish networks throughout their assigned territories. Moreover, women acted as caretakers and counselors—providing lodging, food, and medical aid to traveling clergy, mending and sewing their clothes, advising and encouraging them, and often offering financial assistance. Women also proved to be persuasive evangelists, often convincing their family and friends to join the church, thereby furthering Methodism's primary mission of gaining new converts. However, as the church grew and transitioned from fledgling sect to mainline denomination, a narrative of women being "silenced" emerged.

Throughout religious history, women have tended to lose public voice and power when dissenting religious movements become institutionalized. This silencing occurred within the churches of the Puritans in New England, the eighteenth-century Baptists in America, the early Methodists in England and America, and the African Methodist Episcopal Church. As religious movements become entrenched, they usually replicate secular male hierarchies. In other words, the roles for women inside an established church begin to mirror the roles assigned to women in society.[19] Nathan Hatch and John Wigger claim, "More than any other large-scale religious movement of the time, early Methodists allowed women to speak in their meetings, but not without limits.

By the 1830s and 1840s Methodists had largely turned their backs on lay female preaching and exhorting in search of middle-class respectability."[20]

Portrayals of women's roles within the early American Methodist church often present this type of peak-and-valley narrative—beginning with women's empowerment during the mid- to late eighteenth century and ending with the silencing of women in the early nineteenth century.[21] Catherine Brekus likewise asserts that the early Methodist church encouraged women to "shout, sing and testify in public," but as the church embraced an ideology of domesticity, it deprived women of the liberty to speak, "urging them to 'keep silence in the churches.'"[22] In his historical monograph on Methodists in America, Wigger similarly acknowledges women's liberty to publicly preach, exhort, and pray, as well as their roles as class leaders and deputy preachers in the early Methodist movement. However, Wigger claims that as the movement matured, Methodists increasingly concluded that women should not forsake their domestic roles of wife and mother to pursue what they conceived as masculine, public roles.[23] In her examination of early Methodism in the Middle Atlantic region, historian Dee Andrews also points to female class leaders and women who counseled and guided itinerant ministers. Yet, she later claims that women's consignment to the domestic sphere removed them from the "public domain of America's fastest-growing religious movement."[24] I view the valley in this peak-and-valley narrative as one of the gaps often found in the history of women in rhetoric that needs to be filled. As rhetoric and composition scholar Andrea Lunsford laments, the history of women in rhetoric is a story full of gaps, silences, and erasures.[25]

By identifying "little narratives"—the brief everyday descriptions of women's activities included on the pages of the church's periodicals, I am using Beth Daniell's term. Drawing on Jean-Francois Lyotard's conception of overarching "grand narratives," Daniell posits postmodern "little narratives" as a means of challenging broad narratives that often exclude women.[26] By attending to little narratives, we hear voices that are otherwise silenced. During the antebellum period, when women had limited opportunities to speak publicly, texts were especially important to them; hence, the Methodist church's mass-produced and distributed periodicals represent valuable artifacts for recovering women's rhetorical roles. This book also attempts to complicate the spatial correlation of the church with voice and the domestic sphere with silence, as well as the underlying implication that the most meaningful religious voices reverberate from the physical church, particularly the pulpit, during formal worship.

My identification of women's little narratives in Methodist periodicals not only looks at texts written by women, but also texts written about women or directed at women. I have included these latter two groups because they provide valuable evidence of women's participation in public discourse. For instance, recognizing a woman's efforts to collect money for the church's missions provides evidence of her public advocacy for the church. At the same time, when a church periodical assigns a certain role to women either through a depiction or through advice it directs at women, the press has in some way prescribed, inscribed, or sponsored women's rhetorical activities. Here I am referencing Deborah Brandt's concept of sponsors of literacy, which she defines as "[A]gents, local or distant, concrete or abstract, who enable, support, teach, and model as well as recruit, regulate, suppress or withhold, literacy— and gain advantage by it in some way."[27]

Because representations of women in the church's periodicals were often presented for ideological reasons, I believe it is important to acknowledge that women assumed certain roles, such as becoming Sunday school teachers or participating in benevolent organizations, while others were assigned to them, such as iconic deathbed ministers or holy mothers. Altogether, the little narratives found in Methodist periodicals offer insight into women's contributions to this influential and dynamic religious movement and illuminate women's active and symbolic roles in American Christianity more generally. Moreover, these narratives highlight how the church and women's participation in the church-supported efforts expanded women's rhetorical skills and boundaries.

American Methodists inherited their commitment and many of their approaches to publishing from John Wesley, who believed that the printed word and literate practices such as reading, writing, and hymn singing promoted spiritual growth.[28] The American church officially established the Methodist Book Concern in 1789, just five years after the church was established. Using their press to spread evangelical values and to build their denomination, Methodists became publishing pioneers in America. The church continually experimented with different genres, packaging, distribution, marketing strategies, and correspondence with their book agents and customers. The minutes from the 1796 General Conference, the governing body of the church,[29] confirm the important evangelical role early Methodists assigned to publishing. The General Conference stipulated, "The propagation of religious knowledge by the means of the press is next in importance to the preaching of the gospel," and asserted that supplying parishioners with "pious and useful books" so that they "may fill up their leisure hours in the most profitable ways, is an object worthy of the deepest attention of their pastors."[30] Throughout the nineteenth century, churches competed with and railed against what they considered "pernicious" reading, which included romance novels, trivial fiction, and treatises about deism or other works that would have been considered antireligious.

Methodists believed that preaching and the press were intertwined; itinerant ministers both preached and distributed printed materials for the Methodist Book Concern along their circuits. In a practice dating back to Wesley, itinerant ministers were commissioned as both preachers and colporteurs. Selling Bibles, books, tracts, pamphlets, and hymnals produced by the Methodist Book Concern not only assisted itinerant ministers in spreading the gospel, but also helped them supplement their meager incomes because the church gave ministers a percentage of each sale. For instance, in the Ohio conference in 1816, the average book bonus for itinerant ministers was $75, which is noteworthy when compared to their $100 annual salary.[31] This average sum also suggests that these ministers likely pushed the books.

With the addition of periodicals—multigenre publications issued serially at regular intervals—ministers/booksellers also assumed roles as roving reporters. Initially, the Methodist Book Concern did not employ writers, so most of the original content printed in the church's periodicals came from either the ministers who served as the periodicals' editors or itinerant ministers in the field. In the roles of editors and contributors, ministers exerted tremendous influence over the content of the church's periodicals. Indeed, most viewed their writing as an extension of their ministerial duties, which is understandable, considering that the church's periodicals were intended to minister, educate, and indoctrinate.[32] In their interpretation, arrangement, and retelling of stories, ministers often cast incidents and individuals into a religious context or pursued a particular rhetorical purpose, thus transforming people and events into evangelical appeals.

"Virtually nonexistent in 1800," Nathan Hatch claims, "religious periodicals had, by 1830, become the grand engine of a burgeoning religious culture, the primary means of promotion for, and bond of union within competing religious groups."[33] Furthermore, Benedict Anderson suggests that the act of reading a mass-produced periodical can instill a sense of unity or belonging. As individuals imagine others reading the same piece, they begin to conceive of themselves as part of a larger community, which explains how print could be used to cultivate a denominational identity.[34] However, the pervasiveness of Methodist periodicals was more than imagined. The Methodist church's widely disseminated *CA* boasted the second-highest subscription list for any periodical in 1829.[35] Periodicals also provided a timely forum for connecting Methodists across the country and creating textual communities that cast women into new institutionally sanctioned roles, established different sacred spaces, and ultimately transferred religious authority beyond clergy in the church on Sunday morning to family, home, and the publications themselves.[36]

These textual communities effectively converted women into rhetorical agents for the church, extending their influence to audiences beyond their local congregations and communities. This agency is evident in the following excerpt from an article published in an 1832 issue of the *CA*: "From my early youth I have felt a predilection for the employment of teaching; this sentiment strengthened as I advanced in years, and when, through the mercy of God, I was led to obey the requirements of the Gospel, and give to him my heart, a new impulse was given to my desires, and I resolved to engage in the work, and seek to become instrumental in planting the seeds of virtue and piety in the minds of youth." Filled with conviction and confidence, the young Methodist woman who penned these words made a perilous journey with her sister by sea and land from Boston to Tuscumbia, Alabama, to provide religious instruction to the town's youth at a Sabbath school there. According to the young woman, unnamed in the paper, the Sabbath school opened before her "a scene of labor" to which she hoped with "earnest wishes and prayers that my feeble efforts might be blessed of God." Despite what she described as the "difficulties attendant upon settling in a new country," the "languid state" of the Sabbath school, the "low state" of religion she found in the local community, and the tremendous "exertions" required, the young woman claimed, "I have spent some of the happiest hours of my life with my Sabbath charge, and I find in the performance of this duty much satisfaction." This young woman considered her work in the Sabbath school an important part of Methodism's mission to ignite religious zeal in a community that she feared was more focused on secular pursuits than salvation. In fact, the young woman's efforts to spread the gospel were acknowledged by the title "Female Missionaries" that the newspaper attached to her letter, which was originally addressed to her minister in Boston but reprinted in the Methodist church's popular newspaper eight months after she wrote it.[37]

Institutionally, Methodists in the early nineteenth century rarely recognized single women as missionaries in their own right, yet in print, the *CA*'s editors elevated this woman and her sister to the roles of missionaries and religious models. In an introduction to the letter, the editors extol, "The spirit which led, and the motives which influenced these young ladies, were those of the cross of Christ. They left their friends, and a part of the country where they might have had good employment, for a new and distant part, that they might be more useful." Embedded in these editorial comments is an evangelical emphasis on Christian action, usefulness, and placing religious concerns ahead of financial or familial comfort. The editors also transformed these women into religious exemplars for their male and female readers, asserting, "There are calls from thousands in the southern and western parts of our country to females as well as males, to engage in the instruction of youth; and in this work they may cultivate the wilderness and the solitary place, and greatly help forward the cause of God."[38] Emblematic of rhetorical conventions repeatedly employed in Methodist periodicals, particularly gendered depictions that construct women as religious models, this article highlights the roles antebellum women chose to assume as well as those roles assigned to them in print.

Motivated by their religious conviction, these two young sisters journeyed to Alabama to assume professions as teachers and purveyors of the gospel. Under a religious mantle, these antebellum women radically expanded their field of labor and influence, and under a religious masthead, their roles and influence were further expanded by the Methodist church. Through the acts of rhetorical accretion, publication, and dissemination to a broad audience, the *CA*'s editors transformed these women into religious models for emulation. In this instance, the paratexts[39]—the editorial comments and the title affixed to this letter—framed these sisters' actions as spiritually inspired and anointed these women as religious examples. Based on her study of the widely disseminated memoir of British Methodist Hester Ann Rogers, Vicki Tolar Collins refers to this act as "rhetorical accretion, a process which respeaks and redefines the original speaker," often with male voices "talking over" a woman's text instead of talking through it.[40] Scrutinizing the depiction of women in these publications can expose how male ministers—who wrote, collected, and edited most of the texts appearing in Methodist periodicals—purposefully converted women into pious models, which sometimes had the collateral effect of elevating antebellum women to ministers or missionaries, offices they were otherwise precluded from holding.

Also evident in the example of these missionary sisters is the liminal space between private and public spheres that church work and church publications provided women. Arguments against the conception of separate spheres, which limited nineteenth-century white, middle-class women to a narrowly circumscribed domestic sphere, are certainly nothing new. However, the church, which is typically conceived as part of women's prescribed sphere of activity, is often assumed to operate as conservative and limiting. By showing how church work and church publications operated as empowering rhetorical sites for women, *Beyond the Pulpit* contributes to our understanding of how antebellum women's public and private boundaries were often blurred.

The conception of separate spheres carried a prescriptive domestic ideology based on the idea that while nineteenth-century white, middle-class men worked in the marketplace pursuing commerce, their wives and mothers preserved the religious and moral foundation of society through their domestic roles. Readily apparent in these gendered-spatial assignments is the inequitable distribution of power. At the same time that men achieved a firmer grasp on economic, legal, and political power, women's subordinate roles as wives and mothers became more clearly prescribed. Cultural geographer Gillian Rose acknowledges that feminists have long recognized the ways in which spatial assignments have been used to maintain male power.[41] Consequently, feminist scholars have continually debated whether, in its nineteenth-century context, domestic ideology oppressed women or empowered them. Some scholars have depicted domestic ideology to be confining, some have shown it as liberating, and some have suggested ways in which it was both. By plotting the church and its periodicals as a liminal space between separate spheres, my work here further interrogates that concept as well as the strict boundaries it assumes.

Taking into account the rise of capitalism and secularization, some scholars locate the nineteenth-century church, along with the home, in the private sphere because of its irrelevance to materialistic production. Yet the work of the church was not tied to any specific locale but rather part of a vast middle ground often described as "civil society," "the social," or the "informal public."[42] As both a private and public space, the church became an important liminal zone in which women could expand their sphere of operation while maintaining social respectability. Cultural geographer David Sibley labels these liminal zones "zones of ambiguity" because they mark uncertain boundaries between two spheres that offer the opportunity for change.[43] In her classic work, *The Feminization of American Culture*, Ann Douglas similarly focuses on this liminal space as she describes an alliance between Protestant churches and women's sentimental culture that emerged during the nineteenth century as both groups sought new means of wielding influence. Although Methodists were not included in Douglas's examination, I believe an alliance between the Methodist church and women can be seen in the church's periodicals. Because the church and church-supported activities were located in an indeterminate realm—between domestic activities and market enterprise—church work ultimately provided white, middle-class women with a sanctioned rhetorical borderland from which they could step beyond the domestic sphere while still maintaining social mores of the era. At the same time, church work often increased women's moral authority inside the home.

While depicting women as pious models and religious instructors inside their homes, Methodist periodicals also mapped women's migration outside of the home by reporting their participation in social programs and religious missions. Consequently, the Methodist church sanctioned, publicized, and in some instances even encouraged women's movement beyond domestic boundaries. In her study of women's print culture in American Christian foreign mission movement in the late nineteenth century, Sarah Robbins notes the power that missions' publications had on their audiences. Both the creation and the consumption of these texts tied women to the larger movement and reinforced their commitment.[44]

Similarly, the little narratives in these Methodist periodicals bound women together, strengthened their commitment, and ultimately helped the women conceive of new identities for themselves. For example, a report from the Methodist Annual Conference of 1831, written by men and printed in the *CA*, directly addresses the members of the Asbury Female Mite Societies, calling them "respected sisters." The report encourages women's fundraising efforts for superannuated preachers and preachers' widows and young children, stating: "[Y]our labour of love has afforded a sum, if not sufficient to supply every want, yet enough to cause the tears of affliction and poverty to give place to those of gratitude . . . and we exhort you to use your best endeavors to provoke others to love and good works, that from each of our stations and circuits a rill may flow into the fund of the Asbury Female Mite societies until every necessity is relieved."[45] This little narrative, which is directed at women, offers evidence of women's effective public advocacy for the church through their fundraising. It also emboldens women in their efforts by asking them to encourage others to pursue good works. Ultimately, evidence of women's rhetorical roles and activity such as this can easily be overlooked. Uncovering traces of ordinary women's rhetoric often requires us to listen hard, imagine, and revalue the texts in which they appear. Literary scholar Jennifer Sinor acknowledges that feminist and cultural studies research has already begun questioning the "arbitrary line separating the high from the low, the public from the private, and the personal from the political," which is often used to distinguish which texts are valued and which are not.[46] Newspapers and magazines, which are quickly discarded today, were valued by antebellum audiences who had limited access to printed texts. Methodist periodicals were deemed important by the church that produced them and the readers who consumed them. These periodicals were often saved, reread, and sometimes even bound; they were also passed among friends, neighbors, and members of congregations. Thus, it is important for us to situate these texts within their historical context.

For me, uncovering women's rhetorical roles in the antebellum Methodist church simply became a matter of *looking* for them in the church's periodicals and also reconsidering traditional female roles which are too often overlooked because they were deemed proper "feminine" occupations. For instance,

Catherine Brekus asserts: "As ministers' wives, Sunday school teachers, home and foreign missionaries, and charitable workers, women found outlets for their talents that did not require them to overstep the boundaries of acceptable female behavior. Many seem to have concluded that it would be easier to channel their religious ambitions into more 'feminine' activities than to face public ridicule or clerical sanction."[47] While Brekus's characterization is accurate, I believe it is incomplete because it does not acknowledge the way these acceptable roles became sites for women's rhetorical development and expanded rhetorical activity. By acknowledging women's influential roles as Sunday school teachers, missionary assistants, minister and missionary wives, and benevolent organizers and fundraisers, I am building on the work of Anne Boylan, Patricia Hill, Julie Roy Jeffrey, Lori Ginzberg, and other scholars who have ventured beyond the pulpit to explore additional rhetorical spaces for women in antebellum churches. In doing so, I am contributing to the argument that the church provided an empowering rhetorical space for innumerable women. For them, marrying ministers, teaching Sunday school, and joining benevolent organizations opened new rhetorical opportunities and broader spheres of influence. These religious "careers" offered women ways to enact their faith; in other words, women drew meaning and identity from this work.

By undervaluing that which has been deemed "women's work," our remapping efforts have frequently concealed and diminished the significance of these initial steps that women took beyond their prescribed domestic boundaries. The church did not initially view Sunday school teaching and benevolent work as female pursuits; however, the status of these roles seemingly declined when women predominately entered them. Moreover, women's rhetorical roles in the church and the role of the church as an important site for women's rhetorical development are frequently concealed by pervasive stereotypes in the academy and the reluctance to study religious sites. Roxanne Mountford acknowledges that feminist scholars and the humanities have generally ignored religious women and religious subject matters, no matter how culturally significant. "In our secular age," Carol Mattingly further suggests, "scholars tend to disregard women associated with evangelical or religious causes not considered progressive by today's standards."[48] Women were drawn to religion and religious institutions from a variety of motivations; in addition to cultural expectations and the desire to submit to God, women also came in search of individual identities, the desire to join supportive communities, and as a means of self-assertion.[49] However, too often these latter motivations are ignored. Even when scholars discuss the most vocal feminist reformers, their religious motivations, spiritual identities, and conflicted feelings about religion are often downplayed or ignored. Ultimately, this type of revisionist historical mapping expunges the role religion and churches played in sanctioning ordinary women's actions and voices. Indeed, historian Gerda Lerner claims it is in this manner that historians and institutions often use selective memory to exercise the power of forgetting.[50] Acknowledging that history is more a matter of the present than the past, Robert Connors notes that while history doesn't change, our perspective on history does. By looking at historical women, feminist and rhetorical scholars are searching for a legacy or a path of "how we got here."[51] Clearly, the path seems much more direct if drawn from the actions of the most ardent women's rights activists; however, most contemporary American women are more likely to find temperance women, clubwomen, and active church women in their own genealogies, which seem to offer an alternative story about "how we got here." Through its examination of everyday women's rhetorical roles in the largest religious movement in nineteenth-century America, *Beyond the Pulpit* contributes to this more expansive story.

CHAPTER ONE

Dying Well

> After progressing a few years in her religious course, she was ar-
> rested by the hand of death: and as though Providence designed
> her as an example of patience and resignation to her neighbors,
> he permitted the messenger to hold her in affliction for several
> months.
>
> —Memoir of Harriet Neale, *Methodist Magazine, 1822*

arriet Neale led an exemplary life; however, she is memorialized more for the way she died than the way she lived. By dying well, Neale became a holy messenger and a model Christian demonstrating the strength and power of her faith. According to her memoir, when Neale became sick, she knew that her illness would prove fatal. Nonetheless, "she was entirely resigned to the will of Providence, and confidently believed that God would not let her die in doubts and fears." Although she suffered indescribable pain over the course of four months, readers were told that she "never indulged in a single murmur." Instead, "she observed, 'who would not live a life of pain to feel what I now enjoy.'" When her mother remarked how patiently her daughter bore her afflictions, Neale responded, "we can do any thing when assisted by his grace." And when asked by her husband if she was ready to die, Neale is described joyfully assenting, telling her husband to "prepare to meet me in a better world."[1]

For those who surrounded Neale's deathbed and the thousands who were later invited to witness her death through the publication of a four-page memoir in *Methodist Magazine* (*MM*), Harriet Neale became a model of holy dying. More importantly, she was converted into an argument for holy living. In fact, her memoirist stressed the persuasive power of Neale's death, claiming that Neale's example "would have convinced the most cold-blooded sceptic of the efficacy of religion."[2] Memoirs such as Harriet Neale's were not merely intended to celebrate and honor the memory of the deceased, but to motivate and instruct the living. Indeed, memoirs were carefully constructed rhetorical compositions. Unlike the first-person accounts and reflections that constitute contemporary memoirs, the pieces customarily labeled memoirs in *MM* are more akin to modern-day obituaries because they were posthumously composed narratives of another person's life and death. Yet the memoirs in *MM* are far more rhetorical than contemporary obituaries, containing more than the factual accounts of a person's life and accomplishments. *MM* memoirs function as testimonials in which the dead are resurrected to implore the living to seek salvation. Through accounts of their holy deaths, these individuals advocate not only Christianity, but also a distinct Methodist ideology.

The concept of dying well and the publication of exemplary death for the edification of others is a long-standing religious tradition preceding Methodism. Hagiographies, which date back to the primitive church, have for centuries provided models for Christians by recounting the lives of saints who tried to follow Christ's example. Similarly, Puritans produced biographical narratives that attempted to outline the stages of personal spiritual growth.[3] Drawing on hagiographies and other religious biographical traditions, Methodist founder John Wesley began printing and distributing memoirs in his London periodical *Arminian Magazine* in 1781. He outlined his rhetorical intent, writing, "nothing is more animating to serious people than the dying Words and Behaviour of the Children of God."[4] Wesley believed that the most genuine example of one's religious faith came when an individual bravely faced death. Moreover, as Vicki Tolar Burton explains, Wesley's doctrine of perfection stipulated that while few individuals would experience a union with God or spiritual perfection during life, many would experience perfection at the moment life ended. This belief added even more import to the words individuals spoke as they approached death.[5]

Due to the rudimentary medical care of the eighteenth and early nineteenth centuries, individuals like Harriet Neale often suffered slow, painful deaths in their homes. During these struggles, witnessed by family and friends, many believers demonstrated the benefit of their faith as they approached death unafraid. Through the collection, publication, and dissemination of memoirs, the early Methodist church expanded the audience surrounding the deathbeds of Christians in the hope that these accounts would rescue the unrepentant and validate the faithful.

In Elizabeth Prentiss's popular religious novel *Stepping Heavenward* (1869), Katy, the main character, confesses to her diary, "I have read ever so many memoirs, and they were all about people who were too good to live and so died.["6] Katy's diary entry acknowledges nineteenth-century America's obsession with religious memoirs. These renderings of the idealized lives of exemplary Christians were a staple for evangelical Christians—Methodists, Baptists, and some Congregationalists, Presbyterians, and Episcopalians— who emerged from the Second Great Awakening with heightened religious fervor. In many cases, memoirs made their subjects household names. Some of the individuals included among the bestselling religious memoirs in the nineteenth century were Congregationalist David Brainer (1718–1747), Episcopal Archbishop Robert Leighton (1611–1684), Congregationalist Edward Payson (1783–1827), Anglican Henry Martyn (1781–1812), Methodist Hester Ann Rogers (1756–1794), and Baptist missionaries Adoniram (1788–1850) and Ann Judson (1789–1826).[7] These book-length memoirs often combined personal journal entries, correspondence, poems, or other religious writings by the deceased, which were posthumously compiled, framed, augmented, and published by family and friends. Containing the same hybridity and similarly intended to mold Christian character, the smaller memoirs published in *MM*, although often ignored, have as much to tell as these more famous ones.

The 154 memoirs printed in *MM* during its first seven years of publication (1818–1824) were a site where rhetoric and ritual combined to confirm a distinct evangelical and Methodist ideology. The religious press acted as a rhetorical agent by converting the deceased into emissaries for Methodism, and memoirs were simply one element in the church's strategic use of periodicals to evangelize for Christianity broadly, expand the denomination specifically, and create a far-reaching textual community. Memoirs also highlight women in the early American Methodist church, because these little narratives are the primary space where women initially appear in the church's first periodical.

The preponderance of women's memoirs published in *MM* signifies the important rhetorical role assumed by women as well as the rhetorical role assigned and inscribed to women by the Methodist press. Joanna Bowen Gillespie suggests that memoirs also provide insight into the spiritual autonomy women asserted beyond political and social prescriptions.[8] Through their personal meditations and religious writings, women claimed independence outside of these secular realms by maintaining possession of their souls. Jane Tompkins similarly argues that women exert power through their possession of two territories—the soul and the home.[9] However, after death, women's private religious writing and the words they spoke from their deathbeds were often opened for public consumption—elevating women to public evangelical roles.

Soon after its inception, the American Methodist church recognized the importance of periodicals as a means for expanding its membership and connecting individual congregations through an overarching textual community. *MM*'s reintroduction in 1818 actually followed two earlier attempts to launch a monthly religious periodical by the Methodist Book Concern. *Arminian Magazine* (1789–1790), named after Wesley's London periodical, and the first *MM* (1797–1798) each lasted just two years. In fact, because of worries that the unbound tracts would be damaged or lost, *Arminian Magazine* did not actually take the form of a periodical; instead, it was published in two complete bound volumes, which were added to the Book Concern's catalog.[10] Even in its bound state, *Arminian Magazine* was published the same year the American Methodists initiated their own Book Concern, thus placing periodicals among the American church's first publishing priorities.

Six years after the demise of the American *Arminian Magazine*, the 1796 Methodist General Conference requested the publication of a monthly periodical titled *Methodist Magazine*. Underscoring the church's emphasis on disseminating religious models, members of the General Conference prescribed that the periodicals should include "original accounts of the experiences of pious persons."[11] Responsibility for producing the new magazine fell to the first book agent for the Methodist Book Concern, John Dickins. Dickins successfully published issues from January 1797 to August 1798, but during the summer and fall of 1798, yellow fever besieged Philadelphia, the initial location for the Book Concern. While many fled the city, Dickins, who was a preacher first and publisher second, remained in Philadelphia to minister to the plague victims. When he succumbed to yellow fever, *MM* died with him.

Easily overlooked in John Dickins's tenure as book agent is the important role his wife, Betsy, played in the establishment of the Methodist Book Concern. The daughter of a North Carolina gentleman, Betsy sold her dower land to her brother-in-law after Bishop Asbury[12] assigned Dickins to the Wesley Chapel church in New York in 1783. In 1789, when her husband was named book agent, and the couple moved to Philadelphia, proceeds from the sale of Betsy's land were used to establish the book concern. Thus, a woman provided the seed money to establish what would later become nineteenth-century America's most powerful religious press.[13]

After Dickins's death, twenty years passed before the book concern produced another periodical. The 1816 General Conference resolved that it was "necessary and expedient to publish a periodical work" and prescribed that the "work be issued in monthly numbers of forty pages each, in octavo form."[14] Providing smaller, more manageable, affordable, and timely texts was a likely motive. In fact, in an earlier resolution, the conference requested that the managers of the book concern publish shorter books. The early nineteenth-century Methodist church primarily attracted individuals from the middle and working classes with limited disposable incomes and little more than a common school education. Smaller texts and periodicals, which were also easier for itinerant ministers to transport, were a better fit for current congregants and the church's westward expansion.

With a circulation of several thousand, *MM* enjoyed immediate success, prompting the book concern to publish more periodicals and making those texts essential vehicles in Methodism's publishing and church-building strategies. Periodicals gave the church more control over content than books, which were primarily reprints. They also enabled Methodists to establish a distinct denominational identity and to explicate and defend their doctrine. For instance, James Osgood Andrew, a young southern minister and future Methodist bishop, described the enthusiastic reception ministers gave the first issue of the 1818 *MM*, noting, "Up to that time we had not even a thumb paper through which we might converse with one another from Maine to Georgia, or through whose columns we might be able to repel the numerous assaults which were constantly being made upon us."[15] With its magazine, the church connected members and congregations across the country to create a broader textual community.

Methodist periodicals also transmitted and reflected a shared denominational language. Benedict Anderson asserts that language has the "capacity for generating imagined communities, building in effect *particular solidarities*."[16] Indeed, early American Methodist orations and compositions reflect a combination of influences from which Methodist historian Russell Richey has identified four distinct languages. These include: *Wesleyan*, which denoted particular beliefs and practices of John Wesley's Methodist movement such as classes, societies, perfection, and itinerancy; *Episcopal*, which derived from Methodism's emergence out of the Anglican Church and is reflected in organizational titles such as bishop, elder, deacon; *republican*, which was drawn from the ideology of the American Revolution and includes terms such as virtue, liberty, corruption, and reason; and *popular* or *evangelical*, an emotional religious language that Methodists shared with other evangelical movements during the Second Great Awakening.[17] Methodists acquired this unique combination of languages from church publications and by participating in an array of ritual gatherings—society meetings, class meetings, prayer meetings, quarterly love feasts, revivals, and camp meetings—at which they preached, prayed, exhorted, sang hymns, and read Scripture.

While Methodist clergy and congregants enthusiastically received *MM* with its distinct Methodist identity, the Methodist Book Concern's agents, Joshua Soule and Thomas Mason, who bore the burden of producing the monthly periodical, were less enthusiastic in undertaking the venture.[18] Agents of the book concern were already responsible for printing, selling, and distributing religious texts, and the additional responsibility of producing a monthly periodical dramatically altered their roles and significantly increased their workload. Because the General Conference did not provide funds to hire writers or additional staff, whatever was not submitted from ministers and readers or snatched from British Methodist periodicals and other religious publications had to be written by Soule and Mason. One monthly issue of the magazine contained forty text-heavy pages, which rarely included engravings or graphics and no advertisements.

Initially, Soule and Mason arranged the magazine's content into nine sections: "Divinity," "Biography," "Scripture Illustrated," "The Attributes of God Displayed," "The Grace of God Manifested," "Miscellaneous," "Religious and Missionary Intelligence," "Obituary," and "Poetry." This organization continued for seven years (1818–1824). Three of these magazine's nine sections, "Biography," "Grace of God Manifested," and "Obituary," primarily contained memoirs. In fact, during these first seven years of the magazine's production, 779 pages—almost a quarter of the magazine's 3,360 pages—were filled with memoirs.[19] Why was so much space in the Methodists' flagship publication devoted to dead people?

The ready supply of memoirs is one possible explanation. Continually needing to fill forty pages each month, the editors often solicited content for the magazine, and memoirs, primarily written by ministers or family members, appear to be one of the most common submissions. Because book-length memoirs were readily available in this era and widely read, individuals were familiar with this genre, and the formulaic nature of memoirs likely made them less daunting compositions than explications of Scripture or doctrinal discussions. Additionally, ministers and family members were motivated by the desire to elegize their parishioners and loved ones.

Rather than style, usefulness was the quality most valued by evangelical publishers, and memoirs were deemed useful in confirming and increasing readers' piety. In *MM*'s introductory issue, the two editors stressed their desire for the periodical to be "both useful and entertaining," and to act as an "efficient auxiliary" in the "triumph of evangelical truth."[20] John Wesley believed examples of Christianity provided powerful doctrine in and of themselves. He "sought, collected, and published texts describing experiences he considered to be sensory evidence of God's working in individual lives, stating: 'We find by experience, example frequently makes a deeper impression upon us than precept.'"[21] Candy Brown argues that nineteenth-century evangelicals "privileged memoirs because they considered example a powerful tool to mold Christian 'character.'"[22] While well-known individuals such as Calvinist John Elliott; C. F. Swartz, a German missionary in the East Indies; and Dr. Thomas Coke, one of the first bishops of the Methodist Episcopal Church, appear among the subjects memorialized in *MM*, ordinary individuals, especially women, were also converted into exemplars through published depictions of their struggles to lead holy lives and to resign themselves to God during sickness and death.

The amount of space devoted to memoirs in *MM* denotes the composition, collection, distribution, and consumption of memoirs as important rituals for antebellum Methodists. Indeed, transmission and ritual, two communication functions described by journalism scholar James Carey, are both evident in *MM* memoirs. Whereas transmission characterizes the basic sending or imparting of information, ritual implies sharing, participation, or association. Rather than simply conveying information, ritualistic communication is directed at the maintenance of a society through the "representation of shared beliefs."[23] In the sense that they reported a death, *MM* memoirs transmitted information. Yet, because they also framed lives and deaths within an evangelical Christian ideology, memoirs served a much more ritualistic and rhetorical function for the Methodist church and its textual community.

Authors and editors of these memoirs operated as part of an interpretive community—a group whose perceptions and judgments are based on a set of shared assumptions such as belief in God's pardoning grace, free will, and damnation for the unsaved.[24] Thus, the production and consumption of texts became interdependent; in the act of writing and editing texts, authors and editors assumed certain percepts within their readers and relied on readers to extrapolate the significance. Hence, meaning was not contained within the text, but in the reading of it. Consequently, vicariously participating in these holy deaths became a ritual shared among the members of this interpretive community. Rhetorically, memoirs combined praise and persuasion to uphold individuals as Christian models. Memoirs not only ceremonially honored the past life of the deceased, but also persuaded the living with regard to the future.

The memoirs represented in the separate sections of *MM* are delineated by important distinctions but share many similarities that highlight their formulaic nature. Similar to writers of conversion narratives, memoirists, consciously or unconsciously, followed the same general arrangement and employed many of the same rhetorical and ideological conventions. The overarching plot in most *MM* memoirs connects conversion and death—designating these as the two most significant religious events in a person's life. Memoirs intentionally used these two climactic, emotional events to move readers toward increased spiritual commitment. While it might seem odd to identify an "overarching plot" within memoirs, doing so helps to distinguish a person's actual life and death from the rhetorically constructed accounts of holy lives and holy deaths that began appearing in the first issue of *MM* in 1818.

Occasionally, a memoir was introduced by the request for publication that accompanied it, such as the one preceding Thomas Gillam's memoir.

Dear Brother,

A desire to perpetuate the memory of a man of God with whom I have been acquainted for ten years past, and with whose religious experience, an account of which I have often heard in Love-Feast, I have been much edified, induces me to request the insertion of the following memoir in your Magazine . . . By giving it a place in the Magazine, you will gratify numerous friends and relatives; and no doubt your numerous readers will contemplate with pleasure the history of a man, in whom the graces of Christianity shone with peculiar splendour. . . .

I remain yours in Christian love,
John Connell, Washington City, 27th Feb. 1822[25]

Paratexts such as introductory letters were a common convention used in book-length memoirs. Typically, these letters provided authentication. In this instance, the letter validates that the author knew the deceased and could accurately provide a firsthand account of his religious life and death. In fact, this letter alludes to hearing the deceased's oral testimony during church gatherings. Introductory letters also served as recommendations in which the writer suggests that the text has something to teach readers.

Authors of memoirs were not always introduced or acknowledged, but ministers, customarily, wrote the majority, and thus assumed the role of interpreting, arranging, and retelling the lives and deaths of their parishioners. Using rhetorical accretion, ministers sometimes layered over the original text to accentuate a certain religious ideology. Even when a memoir was composed by a family member or friend, the temptation still existed to present a person's life and death in the best light possible or to embellish in order to improve the odds for publication. Periodical editors represented another possible source of rhetorical accretion. *MM*, like most religious periodicals, was edited by clerics, who conceived of editing as part of their role in ministering. "Since evangelicals viewed memoir subjects as models of emulation," Candy Brown asserts, "editors felt justified in modifying narratives in order to present more worthy models to the public gaze."[26] As a result, a memoir often contains multiple "narrative levels," as Gérard Genette uses the term, including the editor's and author's narratives in addition to those words attributed to the memoir's subject.[27] These narratives help reveal the way memoirs were rhetorically constructed. At the end of this process of gathering, composing, and editing it would be difficult if not impossible to determine how accurately a memoir depicts the actual life and death of a person. Yet as carefully constructed accounts or pieces of institutional rhetoric, memoirs have much to collectively tell us about Methodist beliefs, rituals, and the church's literate and rhetorical practices.

MM memoirs usually followed a uniform thematic arrangement that addressed four general topics: religious upbringing, conversion, holy dying, and the moral of the memoir. Each of these themes served a rhetorical function. Including information about individuals' religious upbringing attested to the importance of spiritual inculcation during childhood. Methodists advocated religious education for children, and memoirs usually noted whether the memorialized individual was of pious parentage. Early religious education by devout parents was portrayed as an advantage or blessing that could influence the course of an individual's life. For instance, Reverend Jason Walker's memoir suggested that his early religious instruction helped shield him from sin by "keeping him from those follies and vices to which the youth are strongly inclined."[28] In an excerpt from the Reverend Aurora Seager's journal, included in his memoir, Seager described his own religious upbringing: "I early acquired a predilection for the principles and duties of Christian religion . . . I took much delight in reading the Bible, and was particularly fond of books which described in language suited to my capacity, the character of Christ,—his mission, sufferings, and death,—his ascension . . . the impressions which these subjects made on my mind at that early period will never be erased."[29]

Just as Walker's and Seager's memoirs highlight the benefit of early religious instruction, those individuals who did not receive this influence were depicted at a disadvantage. Because his parents professed no religion, Colonel J. Burrus was described as "destitute of the advantage of religious instruction, in those years when the mind is ready to receive any impression that may first be made upon it."[30] The implied consequence was that Burrus lived a corrupt life until he was forty years old. However, these depictions also demonstrated that God-fearing parents and religious instruction alone did not ensure a person's conversion. Methodists believed that while God reaches out to humans, each individual has the free will to accept or reject God's call. Wesley opposed interpretations of preordination or election, stressing that salvation was available to all people through grace and free will. Methodists believed a religious upbringing might fortify a child against sin or make the child more open to hearing God's call, but afforded no guarantee that the child would heed it.

Washburn Peck's memoir acknowledged that both his parents were pious, and their home was a regular site for Methodist preaching; "but notwithstanding these religious advantages, the salvation of his [Peck's] soul occupied but little of his attention in the early part of his life."[31]

Most memoirs addressed the memorialized person's conversion experience. The refrain "nothing very remarkable occurred during the early part of his or her life" often marked a quick transition to that subject, which underscores the evangelical belief that spiritual life began with conversion. Jerald Brauer defines conversion as "a profound, self-conscious, existential change from one set of beliefs, habits, and orientation to a new structure of belief and action."[32] Antebellum Methodists, along with other evangelicals, believed a crisis-like conversion resulting in regeneration was essential for a Christian. Gregory Schneider claims that accounts of Methodist conversions reveal "a story of death and resurrection, of dying to worldly attachments and disordered living and rising to heavenly affection and well-ordered habits."[33] In this way, I believe, conversion narratives serve as an antecedent genre to memoirs, influencing the way memoirs were structured.

In her extensive study of nineteenth-century conversion narratives, Virginia Lieson Brereton describes a fairly uniform pattern of transformation long recognized by religious scholars. This transformation progresses from the convert's early life to an increasing sense of sinfulness to a climatic conversion that concludes with the fruits of regeneration.[34] These three stages repeatedly described in conversion narratives are often labeled: *awakening, conviction,* and *conversion.*[35] Individuals who were awakened became acutely aware of their sinfulness. In many cases, this awakening was prompted by a religious event or tragic circumstances such as illness or the death of a family member. Dissatisfied with their current lives, individuals often sought counsel and comfort in religious gatherings. This discontent then led to conviction—a period accompanied by tremendous guilt and agitation as individuals abhor themselves and their sins and begin to fear eternal damnation. Generally, memoirs described conviction as a time of extreme anguish. Individuals usually turned their focus inward, and it was through this introspective examination of their souls that believers were prepared for a regenerating conversion. John Mann's memoir offers a typical account of this progression from awakening to conviction to conversion.

> Under his [Reverend Stringer's] preaching it pleased the Lord to awaken
> him to the sense of the awful state he was in. He immediately forsook
> his follies and sinful companions, and attended stately on the means of
> grace. His mind at the time was filled with keen anguish, and bitter re-

flections on his past life, the misery he had brought upon himself, and distress upon his family and connexions. He was made to feel sensibly the plaug of his own heart, and was penetrated with a consciousness of his miserable condition as a sinner before God. His convictions were deep and lasting, nor could he rest satisfied until the healing balm of a Saviour's blood was applied to his guilty conscience.[36]

As in this instance, conversion is presented as a consoling pardon in which believers felt their guilt removed.

By stipulating that conversion was available only through divine grace, Methodists believed that humans could submit to God's will, but they could not control their conversion experience. Hence, part of the drama surrounding conversion was timing; when would the climactic conversion occur? Ancient Greeks had two concepts of time: *chronos* or continuous, linear, measurable time, and *kairos* a more situated or opportunistic time.[37] In the context of conversion, whereas chronos might be referred to as human time, kairos can be viewed as God's time. In a sense, conversion became a kairotic event as the progression from awakening through heart-wrenching conviction eventually brought a person to that special moment when conversion occurred.

The inability for people to control conversion underscored the sense of individuality inherent in a conversion experience. Conversion forced individuals to acknowledge and examine their own sin and prepare their souls. Even though conversion experiences were celebrated publicly, preparing for conversion was a private act. "Humbling as it was to sound the depths of private wickedness," Christine Heyrman notes, this "plunge into the self also persuaded sinners of the utter singularity of their experience."[38] Moreover, the fact that individuals were asked to provide testimony of their conversion experience, regardless of social status and gender, reinforced the Methodist doctrine of free will and the belief that individual religious experiences were important. While conversion ultimately brought one into the fold, it also cemented a sense of individuality and a personal relationship with God. Thus, paradoxically, submission to God also became an act of independence and recognition of self-worth. This was especially important for women and members of other marginalized groups.

Methodists believed that conversion was a never-ending process in that it marked a continuous struggle to live a holy life. In a journal entry included as part of his memoir, Reverend John Pitts wrote that after his conversion, "I thought that my enemies were all slain, and that I should know war no more. But alas! I soon found there was a tempting devil, and that all who live godly in Christ Jesus shall suffer persecution." While acknowledging that conversion did not end a Christian's toil, Pitts also recognized God as a loyal advocate. "I found him to be a present help in time of need. He still supported me in all my trials and kept me in the narrow way." Similarly, Robert M'Elheny's private journal entry, which was included in his memoir, conceded that M'Elheny experienced periods of pain, trial, and doubt. Yet, he overcame these by acknowledging his dependence on God and praying for assistance.[39]

Methodists believed that the fruits of this spiritual pilgrimage became most evident when an individual faced death. The three stages of conversion—awakening, conviction, and conversion—mirror the stages preceding a person's death as described in most memoirs. Becoming aware of possible or impending death resembled the awakening stage as individuals faced their own mortality. The period in which a person suffered physical and emotional pain and restless doubts was similar to the conviction stage. And, resignation to God's will and a person's actual death resembled conversion itself. In the same way that conversion required submission to God, believers facing death also had to resign themselves to the will of God. Submission did not, in either case, eliminate suffering, but it did provide the individual with a measure of peace, comfort, and patience.

To evangelicals, death represented a pivotal point between heaven and hell; thus, a victorious or triumphant death was usually perceived as the culmination of a good Christian life. In the introduction to a memoir he wrote in 1819, Coles Carpenter asserted, "The infidel may die in a state of insensibility, the philosopher submit in silence to his fate, and the hero rush thoughtlessly into eternity; but the Christian conquers as he falls, and proves a victor in the arms of death."[40] Rather than insensibly, silently, or thoughtlessly rushing to death, Methodists in their memoirs present a consistent deathbed ritual in which a dying person, surrounded by family and friends, made final preparations for death. In the pulpit and in print, nineteenth-century evangelicals attempted to take the dread out of death by converting it into a victory that believers could prepare for throughout their spiritual lives.

Methodists did not believe in shielding individuals from death. Even if persons did not sense the seriousness of their medical conditions, Methodists felt an obligation to inform them, so that they could prepare. This exchange was part of the rich dialogue that occurred between a dying person and the people surrounding the deathbed. According to Spicy Meek's memoir, when her physician reluctantly told her, "Madam, you must prepare for death," she immediately replied, "Sir I am prepared."[41] While individuals like Meek were depicted approaching death completely at peace, others often suffered through periods of restlessness and doubt. The source of this doubt and anguish varied. Often this suffering was physical, due in part to crude medical care. In the late eighteenth and early nineteenth centuries, Americans lived with the constant threat of illness and death. Women frequently died in childbirth, many children did not reach adulthood, and even the common cold carried the threat of death. On average, white persons in the early nineteenth century only lived to the age of forty; as a result, individuals, families, communities, and church congregations frequently witnessed suffering and loss.[42] Some of the primary purveyors of death repeatedly mentioned in memoirs were severe colds and fevers, cholera, dysentery, consumption, pleurisy, and bilious fever. Medical treatments for these illnesses in the early nineteenth century were primitive, at best. If the illness did not kill a patient, the cure just might. Family members and physicians, who had little understanding of disease, relied on crude treatments, including bloodletting, tonics, and plasters.

This rudimentary medical care, combined with descriptions of excruciating suffering, made a strong appeal for individuals to reach out to heaven for bodily as well as spiritual comfort. In fact, memoirs often depicted individuals dealing with their pain by comparing it to Christ's suffering on the cross. According to Mary Douglas's memoir, when one of her sisters, sitting by her bedside, expressed sympathy for her pain, Douglas replied, "These pains are nothing compared to what my Saviour endured for me." Similarly, Reverend Jason Walker's memoirist wrote that he wanted his parishioners to know that, "I suffer, but Christ's sufferings were greater—I sweat, but Christ sweat great drops of blood—Let them think what Christ has done for them."[43] Not only did dying persons gain comfort from the comparison, but their empathy and the compassion they inspired brought about a closer identification with Christ's crucifixion in readers.

In addition to physical suffering, there were also persons who suffered tremendous anxiety because they felt they were not spiritually prepared to die. Some were also distressed about the loved ones they were leaving behind. In each case, resigning oneself to God's will was repeatedly depicted as the key to achieving peace while facing death. In essence, death became a test as well as a witness of one's faith. In Hannah Lathrop's memoir, her husband observed, "Her mind, amidst great distress of body, seemed to be exercised about the future welfare of her family, but more especially for the cause of God. She watched every symptom of approaching dissolution with a kind of submissive anxiety, and every evidence of her departure, as a welcome friend."[44] This focus on heaven is also evident in Mary Douglas's memoir. Readers are told, "Her affection seemed to be unglued from earthly objects and set on things above; she would kiss her little babes and calmly resign them to the arms of her husband and the protection of God."[45] Such moving acts of separation and resignation made a powerful pathetic appeal, demonstrating the strength of dying believers' faith.

This reprioritization of heaven above earth is especially evident in the emphasis placed on the state of the soul rather than the body. The soul, generally viewed as an immaterial entity that according to Christian teaching becomes a disembodied spirit at death, was a central focus for memoirs. Memoirs frequently presented an antithesis between the weakening body and the strengthening soul. James Banks's memoir noted, "while his body was sinking to its mother dust, his soul was rising to its father God."[46] According to philosopher Douglas Walton, whereas secular death is conceived as "total and irreversible extinction of consciousness and sensation," including the termination of the individual personality, Christian death "postulates actual survival of the individual personality and continuation of postmortem consciousness and sensation."[47] In that sense, holy dying can be viewed as an argument for this Christian conception of death.

Deathbed inquiries, another element repeatedly found in memoirs' depictions of holy dying, underscore this Christian conception of death. Taking many forms, deathbed inquiries dealt with the question of whether individuals were confident in their salvation. Sometimes, individuals surrounding the deathbed asked this question and in other instances, the dying person provided an answer without prompting. These inquiries were intended to provide loved ones, ministers, and readers with the consolation that the dying person was at peace and confident in God and heaven. As Reverend Richard Emery approached death, his memoirist wrote that he turned to his wife, saying, "Betsy, I leave you in the hands of God; let this be your consolation, I am happy. The Lord is good, he has been with me and comforted me in all my distresses; he has not left nor forsaken me."[48] Providing ample evidence of consolation to the immediate audience as well as the secondary audience reading the memoir was a crucial element in the deathbed drama.

There was tremendous anxiety in not "knowing" if someone died at peace, because it called into question that person's eternal status. The author of John Wesley Bond's memoir expressed this discomfort, noting, "We trembled lest in this state of mind he should be deprived his senses, and be carried off without leaving us the only consolation . . . that of an assurance, that he died in peace." In the case of Reverend Edward Paine, who drowned, the author of his memoir attempted to provide consolation that Paine was spiritually prepared to die by reporting that Paine had often told his wife "that for him death had no terrors, that he was no more afraid to die than he was to fall asleep." Sarah Wood, according to her memoir, was so worried about providing adequate consolation that she asked the group surrounding her bed, "if I should say no more, have I given you sufficient evidence that I have gone to heaven?" Similarly concerned about offering consolation, Sally Agard and her husband designated a signal where she would raise her finger as a sign of her "happiness in God" if she was unable to speak at the end of her life.[49]

A description of the deceased person's countenance was another sign of consolation that memoir writers frequently provided as evidence of a happy death. The assumption was that facial expressions provided some insight into a person's soul by revealing that person's level of comfort or peace at death. The author of Elizabeth Ackerman's memoir wrote, "So strong were her consolations in death, that her countenance evinced all who saw her, that she sweetly slept in Jesus." Likewise, Robert M'Elheny's memoir claimed that as his death neared, "the most perfect tranquility reigned in his countenance."[50] Offering the hope of a heavenly reunion was another way dying individuals tried to console their families. Indeed, Methodists often pointed to the love of family as evidence that there was life beyond current existence and that faith was the key to maintaining those familial bonds in eternity.[51] Hannah Howe's memoirist wrote that she told the group around her deathbed, "I hope we may all meet in heaven where parting can never come."[52] The desire for a heavenly reunion provided a further appeal for family and friends to prepare for heaven. The dying person's last words were the final means of consolation presented in memoirs. Memoirists recorded these words because they believed they were imbued with meaning. According to their memoirs, "Come, Lord Jesus, come quickly," were Hannah Lathrop's, and "Lord receive my precious soul," were John Thomas's.[53] Most of these last words resemble prayers, thus serving as a final affirmation of these believers' steadfast faith and their holy deaths.

The Methodist belief in free will meant that every person ultimately made the essential choice between eternal life and damnation. In her journal, Elizabeth Peck described seeing one of her school friends die with the "horrors of a guilty conscience." She wrote, "We found him just expiring in the most frightful appearance . . . the awful scene so alarmed me that I awoke."[54] The experience of watching this unredeemed classmate die awakened Peck to her own unrepentant state. Indeed, memoirs often alerted survivors to their own mortality and helped to wean them from worldly to heavenly concerns. This warning is especially evident in memoirs containing the common narrative of eleventh-hour conversions, or desperate pleas emanating from the deathbeds of reluctant believers. In introducing Thomas Garside's memoir, his memoirist asserted, "I am no advocate of the sick bed repentance when the fear of death seems to be the only cause of sorrow for past offences." This author goes on to suggest that many of those who repent at the eleventh hour may ultimately be found at the left hand of God—prohibited from entering the gates of eternity. Unlike most of the memoirs in *MM*, eleventh-hour narratives are not included as examples for emulation, but more as cautionary tales. Instead of elegizing the dead, they usually deliver a parable to the living. Indeed, Garside's memoir concluded with the warning, "Surely this is a brand plucked out of the burning."[55] Similarly, Frances Cook's memoirist concluded by reiterating the lesson of Cook's life and death: "Thus gloriously terminated the life and sufferings of sister Frances Cook, who was happily reclaimed from the paths of vice, and brought back to the fold of Christ by the rod of affliction. . . . Let all who have forsaken the fountain of living water, be encouraged to return again to the Lord, that they may in their last moments find the same comforts and support and breathe out their lives in the full assurance of happy and blessed immortality."[56] By noting that she was reclaimed, Cook's memoir affirms the Methodist belief that conversion is an ongoing pursuit. Just because an individual was converted in the past does not mean that person remains converted in the present; there was always the possibility of backsliding. Hence, like Cook's memoir, eleventh-hour narratives stress the urgency for believers to resume the righteous path so they will be prepared when death approaches. Most of these last-minute appeals emanate from a deathbed after an illness, which may even be presented as a blessing because it has prompted that person to prepare for eternal life. John Newton's memoir attributed his illness to God, noting that "he was visited with the pulmonary consumption, which he soon recognized as from the hand of the Lord."[57]

Although the individuals in eleventh-hour narratives ultimately achieve triumphant deaths, their memoirs were usually filled with fear and the frenzied efforts of the dying trying to attain some level of peace; many of these individuals plead for more time in order to prepare themselves to die. In a series of rhetorical questions, the author of James Horton's memoir outlined what he considered both the purpose and the emotional appeal of eleventh-hour narratives, "Who can behold a fellow creature, not only worn down with pain and affliction of body, but also groaning under the weight of sin, and all the horrors of an awakened conscience, without sympathizing with, and praying for the sufferer? Who can withhold the sympathetic tear, when they see an aged father and mother, watching with parental solicitude, over the body of an affectionate and languishing son, torn with disease, and weeping for his sins?"[58] The emotional appeal is powerful. Situated among other memoirs that overwhelmingly portrayed devout believers at peace and prepared to die, these eleventh-hour narratives stood in stark contrast and rhetorically heightened the call for readers to shore up their faith.

By suggesting that it is never too late to seek salvation, the successful conclusion of these eleventh-hour narratives might appear to undercut the over-riding message to get on the righteous path. The idea that one can always turn to the Lord is clearly one of the central messages conveyed in these narratives; however, this message is tempered by the tremendous anxiety these individuals experienced as well as their warnings to others not to wait. According to William Cole's memoir, when a young woman who was unacquainted with religion walked into the room where Cole lay dying, he cried out, "O Catherine, prepare for death! Put it not off until it is too late; for I am one out of ten thousand to experience religion, and obtain mercy at such a time as this." A similar sense of urgency and regret was evident in the depiction of Eliza Akers, who bemoaned, "if she had her time to live over again, she would devote it all to God," and exhorted her friends and relatives "to seek the Lord while they had opportunity."[59]

Similar to these cautions conveyed from those converted at the eleventh hour, the last theme addressed in most memoirs was some sort of concluding moral, which typically outlined how the author wanted readers to use the memoir. In some instances, memoirists listed the deceased's virtues that were worthy of emulation. Lydia Leavitt's memoir, for example, praised her "intimate knowledge of doctrines," "precepts of religion," and "uniform spirit and practice of piety."[60] With such lists, memoirists pointed out traits that they believed provided entry into heaven. Frequently, memoirs concluded by appealing to readers to remember the dead and hold them up as examples. For instance, Eliza Higgins's memoirist implored, "I have only to add my earnest prayer that while Eliza lives in her death, and flourished from her tomb, her bright example excite many, especially the young to be a virtuous emulation."[61] Referencing Hebrews 11:4, "for he being dead, yet speaketh," the author of Jeremiah McDaniel's memoir emphasized influence beyond the grave.[62] Further stressing this idea of remembrance, Anna Nickerson's memoir referenced Psalms 112:6, "The righteous shall be in everlasting remembrance."[63] Likewise, Revelations 14:13, "Blessed are the dead which die in the Lord," and Numbers 23:10, "let my last end be like his," were repeatedly evoked in memoirs. Incorporating Scripture not only added the weight of God's word but also further exalted the individual as a model worthy of emulation.

It is ironic that the subjects portrayed in memoirs rarely die. The act of dying was almost always conveyed through heightened figurative language that renamed death. Indeed, this is a practice continued in contemporary obituaries. More than fifty different tropes are used to convey death in *MM* memoirs. By giving death another signifier, memoirists accorded death a different significance. Metaphorical phrases such as "the spirit took its flight" or "her ransomed soul ascended to the regions of the blessed"[64] present death as an ascent from earth to heaven. This ascension mirrors Christ's ascension.

Many representations of death followed the structure of Tamzey Causey's memoir, which said, "she breathed out her soul into the hands of her gracious God."[65] In Scripture, breathing is a common means of transferring a person's spirit or the Holy Spirit. In fact, the illustration of individuals breathing out their spirit to God represents the reverse of the creation story in Genesis 2:7, in which the Lord formed man out of dust and breathed life into him. Thus, breathing out one's spirit enacts a reunion with the creator. Sleep and rest were two other themes that emerged from the tropes used to convey death. Phrases such as "fell asleep in the arms of Jesus"[66] describe death as a soothing and peaceful end to suffering, which contrasts starkly with the physical suffering that often preceded death. Jesus often cradles the deceased in a maternal manner, and personifications of death such as "he sunk into the arms of death without a struggle or groan" and "death has entered our dwelling" offer a comforting rather than frightening image of death.[67]

Several of the metaphors used to convey death in memoirs showed human bodies as earthly tenements, such as "his spirit had taken leave of its cumbrous clay, we doubt not to inhabit a more glorious mansion."[68] As well as cueing readers to several scriptural passages, these references reinforced the temporal nature of the body compared to the eternal nature of the soul. Overall, the tropes used to rename death conveyed the Methodist belief that death was nothing to fear for Christians.

For the individuals described in *MM* memoirs, death marked a beginning instead of an end. Through the composition, dissemination, and consumption of their memoirs, deceased individuals were resurrected. Depictions of their holy lives and holy deaths, as well as their own voices, were used to instruct and motivate the living and to cultivate a textual church community. Examining the common tropes used in *MM* memoirs as well as their formulaic arrangement highlights their rhetorical and ideological functions. Much more than mere descriptions of death, these little narratives were intended to both elegize and persuade.

CHAPTER TWO

Women's Deathbed Pulpits

She was so enlivened in prayer, that while her lips were stiff with
death, she smiled, (looking at each other in the room) and faintly,
though with great vehemence, said, "Make it your business to get
to heaven."
—Memoir of Sarah Tomlinson, *Methodist Magazine*, 1818

sing both the ethos and pathos of her deathbed, Sarah Tomlinson
stressed the "necessity of conversion" and warned her visitors "not to
persecute religion as she had done."[1] While her exhortations were directed at family and friends, who stood vigil by her bedside, through the publication of her memoir in the April 1818 issue of *Methodist Magazine* (*MM*),
the audience surrounding Sarah Tomlinson's deathbed was expanded, and a
woman customarily silenced in the antebellum Methodist church was granted
an extensive institutional voice.

Although memoirs were occasionally authored by family members (Sarah
Tomlinson's was written by her sister), the memoirs appearing in *MM* were
principally written by male clergy, who visited and comforted their dying congregants. In the hands of these clerical authors and the ministers who edited
MM, women whose spiritual voices were limited in life were broadened after
death. Through these persuasive testimonies projected in women's published
memoirs, the deathbed became a far-reaching pulpit for female adherents like
Tomlinson, elevating them to the role of minister, a position they were excluded from during their lives.

This postmortem promotion by the church is particularly evident in the
memoir of Hannah Howe, written by her husband, a Methodist minister.
When Hannah was thirty, the loss of one of her children prompted a serious

decline in her already weakened health. Her husband wrote that Hannah's "complaint, which proved to be the consumption, became more alarming and her dissolution drew near." During this time, Reverend Howe said she was "much engaged with God in prayer for resignation to his will, and often expressed a wish that she might die shouting, and have an easy passage over the Jordan of death." Throughout his wife's illness, Reverend Howe portrayed Hannah as expressing her fullest confidence in God. Her husband even claimed to be awakened out of a deep sleep one evening by her fervent prayers. He recalled that "her language was the most feeling, and enough to move the hardest heart. She rejoiced in God her Saviour, and shouted aloud for joy; and witnessed that the Lord was good to her amidst all her afflictions." Remarking on her anticipation of death, Reverend Howe overheard Hannah tell one woman at her bedside, "I often thought when I came so near death, it would appear gloomy, and awful, but glory be to God, it appears pleasant." In fact, shortly before her "soul took its flight," Reverend Howe described his wife's visual confirmation of heaven, noting that Hannah "appeared to be conversing with invisible guests, and was distinctly heard to say, 'Glory! Glory! Angels, Angels, Jesus loves me.'"[2]

Howe's deathbed experience is emblematic of rhetorical conventions repeatedly employed in women's *MM* memoirs. Communing between those in heaven and those on earth, Hannah Howe ascends beyond the role of pastor's wife. In her memoir, she becomes an iconic minister. I use the terms *icons* and *instruments* to describe the different representations typically assigned to men and women in *MM* memoirs.[3] Both representations exert transformative power; however, individuals who act as instruments transform others through official institutional roles, while individuals who act as icons transform others through their real or perceived holiness. Although these two functions can overlap, laymen and clergy in memoirs are primarily described as instruments of God outwardly exerting transformative power in their official capacities as clergy, class leaders, and church administrators. Women, on the other hand, are mainly cast into iconic roles in which they symbolically exert transformative power through their inner sanctity. In memoirs, authors direct both instrumental and iconic action toward the same end, moving readers to pursue greater holiness; it is the way in which instruments and icons operate rhetorically that distinguishes them.

While it is not surprising that clergy and laymen's memoirs repeatedly recognize men for their official roles serving the church, it is surprising that women's memoirs depict their subjects assuming roles on their deathbeds far different from their roles in everyday life. Through women's words delivered from their deathbeds many women clearly assumed ministerial roles. At the same time, the Methodist press accentuated and carefully shaped this subject position. Male ministers, who primarily wrote and edited the texts appearing in the *MM*, transformed women's deathbed experiences into powerful, far-reaching, rhetorical appeals—often converting the women into iconic ministers. In the hands of authors, editors, and publishers, ordinary women's painful deaths often became ritualistic, religious affirmations.

In her examination of the British Methodist church's initial (1793) and subsequent publications of *The Account of Hester Ann Rogers*, a spiritual journal by an early female British Methodist leader, Vicki Tolar Collins describes the ideologically laden act of religious publishing. Specifically, Collins notes how production and distribution decisions affected women's *ethos* in published texts.[4] Through composition, production, and distribution, women's memoirs became powerful testimonials in which dying women implore the living. Sarah Tomlinson and Hannah Howe's memoirs, for instance, were not intended to honor the memory of the deceased as much as they were meant to motivate the living. Likely, because of the superior piety often assigned to nineteenth-century women, *MM* editors used female religious models to motivate readers to seek salvation. At the same time, the deathbed ministry depicted in many women's memoirs can also be viewed as an example, albeit fleeting, of women erupting out of the silent, subservient roles prescribed to them by society and the church. As they approached death, the ministers who sat next to women's deathbeds and the ministers who wrote and edited women's memoirs recognized the rhetorical force of women's experiences. Interestingly, they did not silence or restrict these women's voices. If anything, the clergy who observed and edited women's memoirs accentuated their appeals and ultimately elevated women as iconic ministers in deathbed pulpits. The ministers who composed and edited women's memoirs not only used, but were also unable to contain the rhetorical force of women's deathbed experience and thus unable to contain women in their conventional roles as quiet congregants.

One factor in the powerful, persuasive force of women's memoirs is that the deathbed operated as both a sacred and a feminized space. Although women were excluded from certain sacred spaces such as the pulpit, too often their roles in other holy spaces are overlooked. From its emphasis on memoirs and ministers' responsibility to confirm dying persons' preparedness for eternity, the Methodist church recognized the deathbed as a sacred and powerful rhetorical space. In her book *The Gendered Pulpit: Preaching in American Protestant Spaces*, Roxanne Mountford suggests that the common trope, "a woman's place," highlights the correlation between space and roles traditionally assigned to women. Mountford contends that one of the reasons women were banned from preaching was because preaching primarily takes place in the public sphere. Further, she argues that cultural traditions, homiletics, and architecture combined to make the church pulpit a masculinized space.[5] The expectation was that strong, confident, masculine bodies would fill church pulpits. Conversely, the deathbed was occupied by a weak, inferior body—the often-accentuated characterization of women's bodies. Moreover, women have traditionally supervised the sickroom, and the deathbed was usually contained in a bedroom, one of the most private spaces within the domestic sphere and one typically embellished with handmade quilts, bedding, and decorative handiwork. Hence, the deathbed pulpit from which women delivered powerful exhortations was a feminine space, and through the publication of deathbed scenes, women's voices and actions resonated far beyond their homes and the intimacy of family and friends. By their inclusion in church periodicals, women's voices and actions not only became public, but were also institutionally sanctioned as models for emulation. Consequently, women's deathbed pulpits call into question the traditional private/public divide and undermine the exclusive authority often granted to the lone man who speaks from the pulpit during formal worship.

Setting aside religious and secular distinctions, death would appear to be the great equalizer; whatever a person's gender, race, class, education, age, or legal rights, everyone dies. However, a person's actual death and an account of that death are two distinct events. The language authors choose both arbitrates the initial experience and constructs an experience of its own. Even choosing to write a memoir represents an important choice, especially for women. For many women, who did not have the literacy or leisure to record their own spiritual experience in letters or journals, memoirs became a way to preserve and share their religious lives and experiences.

By calling attention to certain aspects of an individual's life and death, memoirs encourage a particular interpretation. Memoirs, which are often constructed to perform a ritualistic function, uphold and encourage Methodist beliefs about conversion, death, the afterlife, and appropriate gender roles. Within this frame, authors decide what to remember or record, and in the acts of composing, revising, and editing, authors and editors decide what to include, what to exclude, how to arrange the material, and what to emphasize or embellish.

Embedded in all of these choices are particular religious ideologies and rhetorical motives. For instance, Hannah Howe's memoir, written five years after her death, alluded to its rhetorical intent in its introduction. Hannah's husband, Reverend Howe, wrote, "Agreeably to the request of the Conference I shall attempt to give you a short, though it may be somewhat imperfect account of the Experience and Death of my beloved wife."[6] Presumably, the local church conference asked Reverend Howe to compose and submit a description of his wife's death to *MM* because Reverend Howe had shared oral accounts of Hannah's death during religious gatherings and the conference recognized the rhetorical force of this deathbed narrative. Hence, through oral performance, her husband's written account, and the church's publication of her memoir, Hannah Howe was resurrected into a religious archetype—intended as a model of faith for Methodists. Ultimately, the identities and rhetorical roles assigned to memoir subjects were intricately tied to the memoir's persuasive force and function as well as the individual's gender and occupation.

Of the 121 memoirs of American Methodists published in the magazine from 1818–1824, 50 honor women, 47 honor ministers, and 24 honor laymen. Clearly, in terms of being memorialized, women align more closely with ministers than laymen. Ascribing particular gender identities and behaviors to women was common practice in antebellum conduct books, women's magazines, and even sentimental novels. In fact, the woman on her deathbed was a popular literary trope. "As every reader of popular fiction knew in the early nineteenth-century," writes historian Barbara Welter, "woman was never more truly feminine than when on her deathbed, the innocent victim of male lust or greed, she forgave her cruel father, profligate husband, or avaricious landlord."[7] The deathbed depictions of women in *MM*, primarily written by men, seem to anticipate female novelists' didactic acquisition of the deathbed pulpit later in the century, such as little Eva's dramatic death in Harriett Beecher Stowe's *Uncle Tom's Cabin* (1852). Jane Tompkins, in her study of nineteenth-century women's sentimental novels, claims that Eva's death was intended as the supreme Christ-like act of heroism. Her death "enact[s] a philosophy, as much political as religious, in which the pure and powerless die to save the powerful and corrupt, and thereby show themselves more powerful than those they save."[8]

Preceding most of these popular fictional accounts by thirty years, *MM* cast real women into the roles of spiritual heroines as a means of persuasion. Like these later fictionalized heroines, Methodist women not only comforted, but also boldly exhorted those around them.

For women, "dying well" was an accomplishment for which they were recognized, exalted, and held up as models. According to religious historian Jean Miller Schmidt, "Women became the exemplars of the good, righteous, victorious Christian death for the community of faith; it was a final act of faithfulness."[9] *MM* used women's perceived symbolic power to present specific women as pious models to redeem the unregenerate. Although Methodist books had previously transformed women such as British Methodist Hester Ann Rogers into models of piety, the majority of these books honored well-known men—primarily ministers.[10] Likely, the books relied on their subjects' notoriety to assist in their sales. However, by providing a medium that was more current and affordable than books, the monthly *MM* provided a space where ordinary women could be memorialized in print.

A memoir's rhetorical purpose, which was linked to its subject's gender, usually determined where memoirs were placed within *MM*. During the magazine's first seven years of publication, memoirs appeared in three different sections: "Obituary," "Biography," and "Grace of God Manifested." Although no strict criteria for determining the section in which a memoir would be placed emerges, some general patterns are evident. For instance, memoirs in the Obituary section typically reported deaths, providing the facts of who died, when, where, and how. Averaging one page in length, Obituary memoirs were also much shorter than the memoirs printed in the Biography and Grace of God Manifested sections, and they were timelier, usually appearing in the magazine within six months of a person's death.

In the Biography section, timeliness and reporting the facts tended to be less important. On average, Biography memoirs were printed twelve months after the person's death. They often omitted details such as the date of death and the age of the deceased, they averaged a longer six and a half pages, and typically provided detailed descriptions of a person's conversion, occupation, and death. The two memoirs written about Reverend Aurora Seager by two different authors highlight these distinctions. One of these memoirs, published in the February 1820 edition of the magazine, appears in the Obituary section just two months after Seager's death. Less than a quarter of a page in length, the memoir primarily served as a death announcement. Conversely, another memoir about Seager appears in the Biography section of the October 1821 issue of the magazine, almost two years after his death. Filling nineteen pages, this memoir described in detail Seager's upbringing, conversion, preaching career, and holy death. Seager's Obituary memoir primarily transmitted or reported information, while his Biography memoir served a much more ritualistic purpose, strengthening and affirming readers' faith or persuading them toward a Christian worldview.

Memoirs placed in the Grace of God Manifested section were even less concerned with reporting and timeliness. Published almost two and a half years after the subject's death, these memoirs also served a ritualistic function, emphasizing the deceased individual's conversion and the events leading up to the person's death. However, unlike Biography memoirs, the Grace of God memoirs rarely discussed occupation, which highlights two important differences between the Biography and Grace of God sections—gender and clerical status. The Biography section primarily contained memoirs about men (twenty-seven out the thirty-five, or 77 percent), and all but four of these men were ministers. Conversely, the Grace of God Manifested section primarily contained memoirs about women (twenty-seven out of the thirty-eight, or 71 percent), and only one minister's memoir.

Not surprisingly, women's memoirs do not include discussions of occupation. Presumably, most of the women did not have occupations outside of the home. Conversely, ministers' memoirs primarily focused on their ministerial careers, and laymen's memoirs typically emphasized their religious roles, such as class leader, Sunday school superintendent, church trustee, and spiritual head of household. For men, memoirs emphasized their participation as God's instruments through official roles within the church. However, these roles were not open to women. Although some women served as class leaders in the late eighteenth century, in the nineteenth century class leadership increasingly became a role designated solely for men.[11] Moreover, while women's memoirs often mentioned their conversion and their personal faith during their lives, they primarily focused on women's "victory" in death—usually presenting dramatic deathbed scenes.

Ironically, memoirs represent one of the first textual spaces where American Methodist women appear, yet as Cynthia Lyerly notes in her study of early American Methodism in the South, memoirs usually exclude much of women's "pre-death lives."[12] In memoirs, women's lives are closely cropped and framed simply as a prelude to their deaths. Indeed, Lyerly's characterization of "pre-death lives" underscores not only the exclusion of women's biographies in memoirs, but also the way in which memoirs resurrected women as religious icons through depictions of their deaths, in essence granting them a second existence. While early issues of *MM* seldom noticed women's first existence, the periodical exuberantly acknowledged their second. Simply stated, Biography memoirs recognized men for their lives, and Grace of God memoirs recognized women for their deaths.

By far, laymen's memoirs are the smallest group of memoirs found in *MM*, constituting less than 20 percent. Focusing on their religious lives, laymen's memoirs present their subjects as active instruments for the church. Almost half of the laymen's memoirs list church offices held by those individuals. John Allen, for instance, served as superintendent over a large Sabbath school, and he also served as a leader over two classes.[13] Laymen's memoirs also recognized and upheld men who acted as the spiritual head of their households. For example, John Corry's memoir noted that he led family prayer and strictly observed the Sabbath, and Colonel Joseph Burrus's memoir credited him with converting his wife and establishing family worship.[14] Unlike the women who overwhelmingly made up the majority in most Methodist societies in the

1820s and 1830s, many men had abdicated their roles as spiritual leaders in their communities and households. Hence, these memoirs may be intended to persuade men to resume their roles as religious leaders, or they may simply represent different generations.[15] Increasingly, laymen were closely aligned with their secular pursuits and considered more apt to fall prey to the corrupting influences of business and economic interests. This risk is illustrated by the number of laymen who appear in eleventh-hour conversion narratives frantically grasping for personal salvation as they faced impending death. In these narratives, laymen's focus on earthly concerns rather than eternal matters was blamed for their desperate, last-minute appeals. This comparatively small number of laymen's memoirs may represent their diminishing presence in the church as a whole. Laymen's memoirs also lacked the powerful emotional appeals found in some ministers' memoirs and the memoirs of most women. As a result, they were probably considered less rhetorically useful.

Like laymen's memoirs, clerical memoirs functioned as a rhetorical space in which roles were assigned and accentuated based on the subject's gender and related occupation. Ministers' memoirs that extend beyond mere death announcements tend to depict their subjects as faithful instruments, cataloging their clerical posts, appointments, and talents. While ministers and women's memoirs were constructed in vastly different ways, both delivered strong pathetic appeals—heightening their persuasion and adding to their usefulness. This is especially evident in what I label the "itinerant minister as martyr" narrative. This common narrative found in the memoirs of clergy emphasizes ministers' devotion and sacrifice. Typically beginning with a condensed conversion story, it proceeds to the individual's call to preach. This is followed by a list of preaching appointments and a detailed account of the minister's fatigue or illness combined with his unrelenting perseverance, which ultimately leads to a tragic early death. Unlike the overwhelming majority of Congregationalist ministers, who served one parish for their entire careers, early Methodist itinerants generally changed circuits every one or two years. Along their circuits, they preached in meeting houses and followers' homes. They visited poor houses and preached in streets, open fields, and other public venues in their efforts to rescue the unsaved. These preaching circuits often encompassed hundreds of miles of rural landscape with few roads and many streams in between the scattered collection of Methodist societies. They were called circuits because ministers were expected to circle them every four to six weeks. Maintaining that schedule on horseback along rugged terrain and in every type of weather could wear down the heartiest of men.

Sterling Brown's 1823 memoir offers an example of this narrative. According to his memoirist, shortly after his conversion, a call to ministry manifested itself in Brown's prayers. Answering this call, he was first licensed as a local preacher,[16] and then he was assigned as an itinerant preacher. Brown threw himself into the profession. His memoirist observed, "Our beloved brother Brown may properly be styled a martyr in the work of God. His exertions and labours subjected him to frequent afflictions." At one camp meeting he was said to be almost "reduced to a skeleton," yet once he ascended the pulpit, "the spirit of the Lord was poured out upon him in such a manner, that he forgot his weakness, and his hearers could think of nothing but the subject which he poured onto their souls." Although he persevered, Brown's body eventually gave way; suffering from a violent fever, he was unable to proceed on his circuit. He asked the doctor who attended him to be candid, and when Brown was informed that his prospects for recovery were doubtful, he resigned himself, saying, "I have given myself to the Lord." Brown was twenty-five when he died and had served as a traveling preacher for just two years.[17]

Reverend Thomas Thorp's memoir presents a similar narrative. Soon after his conversion, he felt driven to preach, as "he could not be satisfied to see his fellow men immersed in the pleasures of sin, without warning them of their danger." He served as a traveling preacher for less than two years before he fell victim to a serious fever that "apparently laid the foundation of that disorder which finally terminated his mortal life." Although he suffered throughout the next four years, Thorp persevered as an itinerant as long as his health permitted. His memoirist contended that he was prepared to go wherever God led him—be that earth or heaven. His memoir concludes noting that Thorp was "arrested in the prime of life and summoned at the age of twenty-six to appear before his judge." Thorp's memoir exhibits his willingness to sacrifice mortal life in order to give others an opportunity for eternal life.[18] In that sense, his memoir not only depicts a martyr, but a Christ-like figure as well.

In both of these cases we see Methodist itinerants who took the church to the people rather than waiting for people to come to the church. In his book, *Taking Heaven by Storm: Methodism and the Rise of Popular Christianity in America*, historian John Wigger claims that early itinerants endured arduous travels because they believed "bringing the lost to Christ was the highest calling," and "their reward in heaven would more than compensate for their sufferings on earth."[19] Not surprisingly, traveling ministry was a young man's profession. After a few years of traveling, most ministers settled in locations or died during their travels. According to Nathan Hatch, over 70 percent of the itinerant Methodist ministers who died between 1780 and 1818 had served less than ten years, and most were under the age of forty, thus accentuating their sacrifice and heartrending depictions of their deaths.[20] Itinerant ministers embodied early Methodism's rabid missionary zeal. Like the stories of early apostles, who often died as martyrs, memoirs elevated many Methodist clergy to the role of religious martyrs by showing their willingness to sacrifice their own lives while acting as instruments for salvation for others. Just as the devotion of these ministers often inspired followers during their lives, so too was the rhetorical intent of memoirs depicting their sacrifices and deaths.

Although *MM* editors usually segregated women's and ministers' memoirs into different sections, many similarities exist between the two. Clerical memoirs frequently recognized ministers for their modesty and meekness as well as affectionate, tender, and unassuming demeanors. Interestingly, these were many of the same traits celebrated as feminine virtues in the nineteenth century. As a result, early Methodism forged a natural alliance between its two most fervent groups of followers—women and clergy. In her foundational text *The Feminization of American Culture*, Ann Douglas argues that liberal northeastern clerics who had lost their economic, political, and intellectual standing by the nineteenth century increasingly turned to moral and emotional appeals—traditional feminine sources of power—thus allying themselves with their white, middle-class, female congregants.

Although Douglas's book does not address evangelical Protestant movements, a similar alliance between clergy and women can be seen in early Methodism. Evangelical Methodists viewed emotion and sentiment as a means of creating a "heart-felt" religious experience for both women and men. From the beginning, virtues such as meekness and gentleness, "once despised as womanly," were celebrated by Methodists as "fruits of the Spirit of Christianity."[21] Opposed to the rituals of traditional patriarchal honor, Methodism's evangelical rituals required individuals to declare themselves weak—ceding all strength to God. By doing so, they were trying to imitate a "self-sacrificing, submissive Christ."[22]

Keeping spiritual diaries and journals as well as examining one's spiritual pilgrimage through written correspondence also appear to be much more common literate practices among women and clergy than among laymen. In her examination of John Wesley's personal literacy practices and those he embedded in the Methodist movement to foster spiritual formation, Vicki Tolar Burton describes Wesley's exhaustive journaling, noting that he believed the practice "helped him to dedicate his days to God, hour by hour."[23] Keeping a spiritual journal was a practice Wesley used for his spiritual self-examination and one he encouraged all Methodists to adopt, and it is a practice that extended to Methodist preachers and laity in America. Jean Miller Schmidt notes that charting one's spiritual development through diaries and letters was not only consistent with Wesley's instruction, but became "for women, an important means of self-construction."[24] Indeed, by including extracts from letters and journals, the memoirs of women and clergy not only offered personal insight into their spirituality, but allowed memorialized individuals to speak for themselves. Even so, authors and editors still controlled which extracts were included in memoirs.

The combined memoir of Lancaster and Harriet Dusinbery demonstrates the common practice of including women's spiritual writing in their memoirs. In this twenty-one-page memoir, which honors a husband and wife who died within weeks of each other, more than ten pages are devoted to Harriet's spiritual life, while less than four pages are devoted to Lancaster's. The memoir recognized both Harriet's and Lancaster's active participation in religious pursuits by listing the church and charitable offices Lancaster held as well as the offices Harriet held in several charitable concerns. The difference in content is primarily the inward spiritual reflection that constituted most of Harriet's depiction and is absent from Lancaster's. To present Harriet's spiritual views and struggles, the memoirist relied on extracts from her diary and spiritual letters.[25] For instance, Harriet's memoir included the following excerpt from her diary to illustrate her struggle between conscience and duty as she approached the communion table: "This day, after many doubts and fears, I ventured to approach the table of the Lord. I drew near with fear and trembling. My heart sunk within me lest I should partake unworthily. I did indeed halt between two opinions. I dared not disobey the pointed and dying command of my Lord and Master; and yet I hardly knew how to obey, feeling such a deep sense of unworthiness. A sense of duty, however, prevailed; and God fed me with the manna of his love." Excerpts like these from Harriet's journal authenticate and provide insight into her spiritual journey. They also show how her personal journal assisted in her spiritual formation by helping Harriet articulate and examine her doubts, motives, and actions. Conversely, this type of introspection is not available for Lancaster. In fact, his memoirist conceded, "We are not able to speak so particularly in regard to the private exercises of his mind, as it respects religious things, as we have of Harriet, as he has no notices of these in writing."[26] Because extracts from letters and journals were more commonly presented in memoirs of clergy and women than in laymen's memoirs, the latter tended to present their outward actions rather than their inner thoughts and reflections. Again, this difference places laymen in an instrumental rather than an iconic role.

Common depictions between clergy and women also occurred in their memoirists' descriptions of deathbed scenes. Both ministers' and women's memoirs converted the deathbed into a site of worship in which dying individuals, along with the crowds surrounding their deathbeds, are presented participating in prayers, devotions, hymn singing, Scripture reading, and praise. For instance, Reverend John Man's memoirist noted, "he sometimes called us into his room to read, sing, and pray."[27] However, while ministers' memoirs elegized their subjects by focusing on their holy lives, the primary focus of women's memoirs were depictions of their holy deaths. In making these compositional choices, memoirists emphasized descriptions of ministers' church appointments and professional activities, believing that these exemplified their faith. Conversely, because women were precluded from the pulpit and other official roles within the church, memoirists turned to the deathbed for evidence of women's faith. As a result, ministers and laymen became religious instruments, and women became holy icons.

Memoirists repeatedly used certain conventions to convert women into iconic ministers, including women's emotion, the depiction of women in a liminal state communing between heaven and earth, and the exigency of the deathbed, which granted women the authority to speak. While emotion is a basic component of all memoirs, in most instances, the emotional appeal derives from the memoir's content and rhetorical situation. In the case of women's memoirs, much of the heightened emotion came from the women themselves. This emphasis on the subject's own emotions in women's memoirs aligned with the Enlightenment's construction of natural gender differences, which stipulated that women were governed by sentiment and emotion. Women felt with their hearts, whereas men who were governed by intellect thought with their heads. Reverend Richard Emery's memoir described him exclaiming in "raptures of joy," and "enraptured with the love of God,"[28] but amplified depictions of rapture, ecstasy, and glory are generally reserved for women's memoirs. For instance, Sally Agard's memoirist described her "in an ecstasy of joy," exclaiming "in rapturous triumph, O precious Jesus! O glorious Redeemer! O glory to God. I am going home! I am glad I have borne the cross, for now I see a crown of glory reserved for me. O glory! Glory! I am going. O Jesus, why do thy chariot wheels delay?"[29] Similarly, Mary Hollowell's memoirist wrote, "Her whole soul seemed wrapt in the mantle of devotion while we were singing: we then kneeled down to prayer, and the display of divine presence was unusual, and many who were present will long remember the solemn, awful and glorious scene."[30] Such heightened depictions of emotion ultimately contributed to the construction of women as religious icons.

These ecstatic descriptions often placed women in a liminal state between earth and heaven, ascending beyond all mortal matters. For instance, the author of Tamzey Causey's memoir acknowledged, "The writer of these lines has more than once beheld her, when her soul appeared filled with the divine afflatus, that, like Moses, her face shone. And so fervently would she look upward, that it seemed as if she had penetrated the veil, and the glories of the eternal world in full view."[31] Thus, women were cast into the role of heavenly scouts, who saw visions and provided those around their deathbed with a glimpse of heaven and the afterlife. In that sense, women assumed the intermediary role between God and mortals—a role primarily reserved for ministers. In women's memoirs, the living were often connected and transported with the dying because of their mutual belief and desire for eternal life. Certainly, this opportunity to catch a glimpse behind the veil of death drew many believers to deathbeds—in person and in print. Describing Susan Wyval's death chamber, her memoirist acknowledged a "divine presence," and later observed, "The day before her departure I called to see her, and found her, surrounded by female friends, in an extacy, pouring out her soul in torrents of praise to God, in language which seemed to be almost more than human."[32] Often, memoirists attempted to portray the depths of women's holiness by describing traces of the divine inscribed on their bodies and souls. At the same time, these depictions signal a distinct, emotionally charged deathbed experience. In essence, women's elevation to icons represents a collaboration between the dying women and their memoirists. The ministers who wrote and edited women's memoirs recognized women's distinct death experience and may have accentuated their depictions in order to persuade others.

Women's powerful exhortations are the feature that most distinguishes their deathbed scenes from those of clerics. Surprisingly, in memoirs, male preachers were far less often depicted exhorting the people around their deathbeds than their female followers. In fact, two thirds (eighteen out of the twenty-seven, or 67 percent) of women's memoirs in the Grace of God Manifested section present women exhorting, whereas only five out of twenty-three (or 22 percent) of ministers' memoirs in the Biography section portray ministers doing so. Generally, the early Methodist movement in America had always offered women more liberty to speak than more established Congregational, Presbyterian, and Anglican churches. Women were encouraged to pray publicly, offer testimony at class meetings and circuit-wide love feasts, reprove sinners, and counsel fellow congregants and clergy. As opposed to formal worship, Methodist class meetings and love feasts were considered social gatherings, yet Catherine Brekus notes that the line between social gatherings and worship occasionally blurred, and laypersons who felt divinely inspired delivered exhortations at such events.[33]

However, early American Methodist women were rarely permitted to preach. Unlike Wesley, who had condoned female preaching in Britain during his life, institutionally the American church did not sanction female preaching. In her study of early female preachers in America, Brekus identifies the

names of twenty-eight women preachers and exhorters in the Methodist Episcopal Church, the African Methodist Episcopal Church, and other Methodist denominations that emerged from the Methodist Episcopal Church;[34] still,
considering the size of the antebellum Methodist movement, this is a small
representation. While some women were recognized as gifted exhorters, they
were rarely licensed. Moreover, John Wigger notes that instances of female
exhorting became increasingly rare in the early nineteenth century as the
Methodist movement matured.[35] So why are depictions of women exhorting
so prevalent in these memoirs? And is exhorting preaching?

The explication of Biblical texts usually delineated preaching from exhorting. Exhortations primarily centered on personal stories of repentance
and salvation, and exhorters were often moved to speak extemporaneously
by the tremendous emotions they felt. In the eighteenth century, exhorters
were identified as "informal evangelists" who urged individuals to repent;
they had no formal authority, were not allowed to deliver sermons, and if they
were in a church, they generally spoke outside of the pulpit.[36] Early Methodist preaching was less formal and predominately evangelistic in intent. Indeed, Wesley stressed preaching from the heart in a common language and
plain style.[37] Instead of prepared and practiced texts, ministers typically delivered plainspoken, extemporaneous sermons. Often, these relied on moving
personal testimonies, illuminating anecdotes, and direct emotional appeals. In
fact, Wigger argues, "Since only a thin line separated much of early Methodist preaching from exhorting, Methodist female exhorters undoubtedly used
their public speaking opportunities to preach what were, in effect, sermons."[38]

However, few of the women in these memoirs were recognized as exhorters prior to their actual deathbed exhortations. Albeit devout Methodist adherents, these were seemingly "ordinary" women. Yet, as the women
approached death, their memoirs assigned them to roles most were not depicted performing during their lives. Moreover, because the church licensed
exhorters, the Methodists clearly viewed it as an important ministerial function that often served as a training post for future itinerant ministers. Thus,
the church's willingness, even eagerness, to publish and disseminate so many
memoirs depicting women exhorting from their deathbeds provides evidence
of the authority posthumously granted to these women. Furthermore, women
who appear in memoirs clearly were not delivering scriptural exegeses, but
by delivering emotionally charged exhortations intended to save the lost they
were performing a role that Methodists usually reserved for ministers. Finally, although Methodism offered women more opportunities than other religious movements to speak publicly, most Methodist women did not do so.

Even in their efforts to prioritize religious concerns over secular ones, female adherents were still products of a society that cautioned women to avoid public display. In *Composition-Rhetoric*, Robert Connors offers an illustrative example showing that even when women were permitted and encouraged to read their college compositions aloud in mixed rhetoric classes at Oberlin College in 1839, they refused to step beyond that societal restriction.[39] Similarly, Methodist memoirs often present women as reluctant public speakers. In her memoir, composed of extracts transcribed from her diary, Margaret Anderson described her fear of public speaking, writing: "It was immediately impressed upon me, that the Lord who had given me a heart to pity the miseries of my fellow mortals, had also given me a tongue to speak in his name. And that I must tell my associates, in plain terms that they must be converted or eternally lost . . . but how gladly I would have excused myself from that duty! Lord, I have neither courage nor ability to pray in public; and if I speak to any they will mock me, and I shall be despised for my pains."[40]

Anderson felt empowered, even obligated, to publicly advocate her faith, yet she was stymied by the fear of being mocked or despised. Women who believed that they were encouraged by God to speak still often remained silenced by patriarchally imposed strictures. Elizabeth Keagey's memoirist described her reluctance to offer public testimony, noting that "joined with her natural timidity of mind, she was led to speak of her religious enjoyments with much caution."[41]

Even when women were presented as confident speakers, memoirists were careful to confirm these women's femininity and acknowledge their equal devotion to family and domestic concerns. For example, Hannah Lathrop's memoirist noted, "She continued to testify of the goodness of God and the work of grace in her soul, from time to time, publicly and privately, with great boldness," but also stressed that "marks of humility" and "female modesty" were clearly evident.[42] Similarly, Anna Nickerson's memoirist, who described Nickerson with "a peculiar gift to speak," was also quick to note that while she "delighted in public and social ordinance and the social means of grace, her religion was not confined to these. How much she cared for her family, and how ardently she laboured for their good, is known and recollected by them."[43]

In their studies of nineteenth-century women reformers, Lindal Buchanan and Nan Johnson highlight this double standard in which women speakers must somehow reassure audiences of their femininity and that they are adequately fulfilling their domestic duties in order to maintain respectability.[44] Even when speaking about religion, women's public speech raised concerns that these women had stepped beyond appropriate feminine boundaries and even shirked their roles as wives, mothers, and quiet congregants. Thus, women's memoirs occasionally provided additional evidence of feminine virtue in order to position women's public evangelism within accepted gender norms.

One way in which memoirs lend further credence to women's speech and their ultimate elevation to ministers is by attributing their emboldened speech to their impending deaths. Drawing from her study of women in early American Methodism, Diane Lobody asserts that women's speech was often bolstered by a "fundamental evangelical conviction that no human authority could be permitted to stand between the believer and God."[45] If spiritual truth was revealed to a woman through experience, prayer, or her reading of Scripture, she was obligated to share it despite ecclesiastical or social convention. However, women appeared more willing to communicate these spiritual truths as they approached death, and the church seemed more comfortable posthumously acknowledging these women's revelations. For instance, the author of Ellenor Everdige's memoir explained "now that she was called to depart, she could confidently speak of her joys and hopes without fear of reproach from her acquaintance, and without any dread of future misery."[46] Mary Douglas's memoirist observed, "she was strongly impressed to witness for her Lord . . . but this duty appeared to her almost impossible," and went on to show how Douglas felt empowered to speak on her deathbed: "She exhorted those that came to see her to prepare to follow her, and faithfully declared that unless they should follow Christ in the humble way of the cross they would never be able to enter in at the strait gate."[47] If these women felt societal constraints loosen as their deaths approached, or if they simply felt a stronger call to warn others, or if these emboldened depictions of women are the result of some measure of editorial license is unclear. However, their memoirs unmistakably elevated these women to a ministerial role that few ever dared to perform before being confined to their deathbeds.

In Nancy Spears's memoir, the author described the young woman exhorting an adult man from her deathbed: "entreating him with more than human energy, to seek the salvation of his soul."[48] A young woman boldly exhorting an older man would have been considered untoward in most antebellum settings, yet in this memoir it is celebrated. When Elizabeth Keagey is described upstaging a minister, her memoir similarly presents what would have been considered an act of impropriety. During a society meeting held by her bedside, Keagey's memoirist observed, "Sister Keagey broke forth in ecstasies of joy, praising God aloud for his mercy and goodness. Similar feelings were kindled in kindred spirits through the congregation. The preacher in the meantime deferred his discourse till her raptures subsided saying, *this is the best of preaching.*"[49] Sally Agard's memoir explained that Agard asked the friends around her deathbed to send for a family that had denied the power of religion. After Agard emphatically exhorted the family, "Those Christian friends who were present, rejoiced from feeling a sense of the presence of God; while the unbelievers wept, and acknowledged it must be the power and work of God."[50]

The societal leeway granted and women's promotion to the role of preacher was temporary. Women who were emboldened to preach because of their impending deaths were clearly granted a limited ministerial appointment. *MM* subscribers could read these women's words, but only those who congregated around their deathbeds heard them preach. These women never delivered sermons, and the only evidence of their religious orations can be found in their memoirs. Nonetheless, in the material and discursive space of the antebellum Methodist church's first periodical, the powerful rhetorical role assumed by and ascribed to women becomes evident. Just as women primarily gain admittance to the pages of *MM* by dying, the only pulpit readily granted to early American Methodist women appears to be a deathbed. With distinctly different depictions of laymen, ministers, and women, *MM* memoirs became an important gendered space. On their deathbeds, women felt emboldened, even obligated to address groups and to speak in ways that most would not have dared prior to their deathbed confinement. Hence, this confining space became a liberating space for women.

The ministers who primarily wrote these memoirs presented women's deathbed experiences as moving appeals intended to motivate readers to shore up their faith. Some writers likely took editorial license with their renderings, but that alone does not account for this distinct women's subgenre. While no extraordinary woman emerges from these memoirs, several recurring features—women's heightened emotions, their intermediary position between heaven and earth, and their exhortations—distinguish "ordinary" women's powerful deathbed experience. Even as these women were confined to their deathbeds, their powerful rhetorical appeals could not be contained. Their appeals not only captured the attention of the audience surrounding their deathbeds, but the Methodist press as well. Recognizing the persuasive power of women's deathbed experiences, the Methodist press collected and distributed women's memoirs. In doing so, they elevated many of these women to the role of iconic ministers, granting them rhetorical license and a far-reaching pulpit that was unavailable to them during their lives.

CHAPTER THREE

Contained Inside the Ladies' Department

The good wife is one who ever mindful of the solemn contract
she hath entered into, is strictly and conscientiously virtuous,
constant, and faithful to her husband; chaste, pure, and unblem-
ished in every thought, word, and deed: she is humble and modest from reason and conviction, submissive from choice, and
obedient from inclination: what she acquires by love and tenderness she preserves by prudence and discretion: she makes it her
business to serve, and her pleasure to oblige her husband, as con-
scious that every thing which promotes his happiness must in the
end contribute to her own.

—Ladies' Department, *Christian Advocate*, 1832

In this epigraph, an excerpt from the *Christian Advocate*'s (*CA*) Ladies'
Department, the picture that emerges of a good wife is a tireless servant
devoted to the happiness and well-being of her husband. Through advice
such as this, likely written by a man and dispensed to women in its national
newspaper, the Methodist church promoted women's roles as wives and mothers as Christian endeavors. In doing so, the church helped turn the domestic
sphere into both a sacred space and a confining space. Even as the church
claimed that women were integral to the church and society, the Ladies' Department column drew tight borders around women's proper roles and proper
sphere.

Soon after the church began publishing the weekly *CA*, its popularity far
surpassed that of *Methodist Magazine* (*MM*). In fact, the *CA* quickly became
one of the most popular periodicals in antebellum America and the most powerful and far-reaching evangelical tool for the church. As such, it is another
important site for examining the rhetoricity of the religious press. Although
the *CA* contained both secular and religious news, the primary intent of the
paper was to advocate Christianity by showing God's work under way across
the new republic. The *CA* presented consistent images of individuals carrying
out Christian missions, including itinerant ministers' efforts to expand Meth-

odism across the country through new and growing Methodist societies, re-vivals, and camp meetings. The paper showed the emergence and popularity of Bible, tract, Sunday school, and benevolent societies led and managed by lo-cal laypeople. Reports on the establishment of missions among North Ameri-can Indian tribes as well as correspondence from missionaries dispatched to foreign lands were also regularly featured in the newspaper. Additionally, the *CA* targeted and delivered advice to important constituent groups, including ministers, children, and women, through a series of regular columns, includ-ing the Ladies' Department.

As opposed to *MM* memoirs, which presented women on their deathbeds, the *CA* from 1826 through 1832 shows women very much alive, assuming and being assigned to rhetorical roles as domestic evangelists, benefactors, be-nevolent organizers, and volunteers in the church's evangelical outposts. The *CA* initially consigned "women's concerns" to the back-page Ladies' Depart-ment column, and prescribed women to the roles of wife, household manager, mother, and domestic evangelist inside the domestic sphere. Later, the *CA* shows women assuming instrumental roles in their efforts to grow and expand the Methodist church and its missions. Ultimately, these changing depictions of women in the *CA* chart women's expanding boundaries in the periodical, in real life, and outside the church's control.

In the same manner that women were assigned to the domestic sphere in society, the *CA*'s Ladies' Department designated a particular space for women in its newspaper—with this latter space reinforcing the former. Both spatial consignments demonstrate what Michel Foucault identified as the funda-mental relationship between space and the exercise of power.[1] Recent work by cultural geographers has also shown how spatial assignments often operate as exclusionary processes. David Sibley highlights powerful groups' propen-sity to monopolize the most desirable spaces, relegating weaker groups to less desirable spaces. Similarly, Edward Soja warns that everyday spatial assign-ments are not always innocuous; their consequences can be significant. Gillian Rose further asserts that for feminists, "one of the most oppressive aspects of everyday spaces is the division between public space and private space" and the way this divide has been used to maintain patriarchal power.[2] Thus, the church's efforts to spatially assign women to the domestic sphere through its advice column can be seen as an attempt to limit women's access to power and ensure their subordination to men.

Antebellum America increasingly used space to both map and symbol-ize appropriate gender roles. According to the nineteenth-century ideology of separate spheres, upper- and middle-class white men operated in the broad realms of commerce, professions, and politics, while upper- and middle-class white women were appointed to the narrow realms of the domestic sphere. Whereas men's occupations increasingly took them outside of the home, women's occupations as wives, mothers, and domestic managers kept them within the home. Acknowledging the intent to maintain these separate enterprises, Alexis de Tocqueville, wrote, "In no country has such constant care been taken as in America to trace two clearly distinct lines of action for the two sexes and to make them pare with the other, but in two pathways that are always different."[3] While recent scholars have identified several fault lines in this delineation of separate spheres, the volume of print materials intended to encourage and contain women in their domestic duties cannot be denied.

By relegating the Ladies' Department to the back page of the *CA*, and by using the column's content to reinforce women's containment in the home and in the roles of wife and mother, the church used space to exert institutional power. The nineteenth-century ideology of separate spheres aligned with a recurring spatial pattern found in evangelical Methodism. Methodists often juxtaposed sacred, internal, private spaces against what they deemed threatening, external, public spaces. Repeatedly, Methodists were encouraged to focus on the internal—soul, heart, hearth—rather than the external—appearance, wealth, society, and marketplace. This pattern is also evident in Methodists' view of the church and the home as sanctuaries from a sinful world. In his examination of the domestication of American Methodism, Gregory Schneider notes how early Methodist texts reflected this view by consistently contrasting the love and warmth of the church and the home against the cold competitiveness of the world.[4] In the early nineteenth century, Methodism's spatial pattern became increasingly gendered. Men were no longer discouraged from delving into the worlds of commerce and politics as long as the home and church—two spaces dominated by women—provided purifying sanctuaries.

As a result of this gendered structure, Ladies' Department articles transformed mothers and wives into tropes in which they became both symbols and purveyors of piety. As such, women were also tasked with responsibilities previously held by ministers. Ministers and other dispensers of the domestic canon increasingly made religion women's work, assigning women the mission of spreading Christian virtue and counteracting the greed and materialism associated with men and the new market economy. From their domestic sanctuaries, women were asked to assume responsibility for the spiritual welfare of their family, community, and country. These efforts to transition sacred spaces and sacred roles from public to private demonstrate how spaces are socially constructed through discourse and the ways in which the church used its periodicals to both circumscribe and support women's rhetorical roles.

Launched on September 9, 1826, the *CA* quickly became an influential medium for the church. In a letter describing the reception of the Methodist church's new weekly newspaper, Revered Cyrus Foss wrote: "I can assure you that the Christian Advocate meets with a very cordial reception by its patrons on the Suffolk Circuit; and, indeed, who would not cordially receive a friend that every week, imparts so much useful knowledge and comes so richly laden with good news from a far country. As far as my observation extends, the happy influence of its circulation is discoverable in every neighborhood in which it is taken." According to Foss, one aged sister rejoiced that the religious news from across the country and around the world contained in the *CA* confirmed that the saving arm of the Lord would eventually prevail.[5]

The national *CA* followed on the heels of two regional Methodist newspapers, the *Zion's Herald* (Boston, 1823) and the *Wesleyan Journal* (Charleston, 1825), and reflected the vitality of evangelism and the growing popularity of newspapers in the early nineteenth century. Although the *CA* was intended as a supplement for the monthly *MM*, soon after its introduction, the *CA* usurped *MM* as the church's flagship publication.[6] The introduction of a national newspaper dramatically expanded the church's textual community. Less than ten years after its inaugural issue, the *CA* faced its stiffest competition from its own imitating offspring. Combining regional news and articles with general features from the national *CA*, several regional Methodist *CA* newspapers emerged across the country, including the *South-Western CA* (Nashville, 1832); the *Pittsburgh CA* (1833); the *Western CA* (Cincinnati, 1834); the *Southern CA* (Charleston, 1837); the *Richmond CA* (1839); the *Northern CA* (Syracuse, 1841); as well as the St. Louis, Northwestern (Chicago), and California *CAs*, which were established in the 1850s.[7] By 1860, the total circulation for all the official Methodist newspapers exceeded 400,000, which places Methodist periodicals among the most successful publications of that era.[8]

The original *CA* was the brainchild of Nathan Bangs, who was elected by the General Conference to head the Methodist Book Concern in 1820. Continuing the practice of placing ministers rather than publishing professionals in this position, Bangs had served as a missionary and preacher in Canada and New York for twenty years, including stints as "preacher in charge" of the New York City circuit and presiding elder for the New York Conference. Stressing Bangs's "indelible imprint" on Methodism, historian Nathan Hatch suggests that whereas Francis Asbury's career emblemized Methodism's triumph as a populist movement, Bangs's leadership represents Methodism's pursuit of social standing and respectability. The Methodist Book Concern was one of the primary vehicles Bangs used in this quest for social respectability. When Bangs inherited it, the Methodist Book Concern was debt-ridden and resided in rented quarters. More disconcerting was what Bangs perceived as a general apathy toward literature, which he believed was due to the Book Concern's practice of reprinting English publications rather than creating and promoting American texts. Bangs's strategic visions for the Methodist Book Concern—including the purchase of its first property, the establishment of its own bindery and press, the expansion of its publications, and the close alignment with the Methodist Sunday School Union, Tract Society, and Bible Society—ultimately set the course for the Book Concern to become the largest publishing house in the world by 1860.[9]

Bangs, with assistant book agents Thomas Mason until 1824 and John Emory until 1828, juggled his responsibilities as book agent, editor of *MM*, and editor of the *CA* until 1828, when Emory succeeded him as book agent and Bangs became full-time editor for the *CA* until 1832. The assignment of a full-time editor confirms that the newspaper quickly emerged as an important communications tool for the church. In his study of the history of the Methodist Book Concern, James Pilkington asserts that Bangs's efforts in lobbying for a general Methodist newspaper in 1826 demonstrate his keen understanding of audience and the mood in antebellum America.[10] The *CA* provided the frequent communication and distinctly American voice many people craved. While there were only 200 newspapers in the country in 1800, by 1835 more than 1,200 existed, and religious newspapers, a uniquely American invention, proved to be leaders in this burgeoning market, even in competition against secular newspapers. In 1829, the *CA* and the nondenominational *American National Preacher* attracted 20,000 and 25,000 subscribers respectively, the highest numbers then recorded by any periodical. In fact, during the same period, no secular periodical garnered a circulation higher than 4,500.[11]

The *CA*'s extensive national circulation benefited from special postal rates granted to newspapers and to the church's network of traveling and local ministers, who sold the paper as part of their ministerial duties. In return for each subscription sold, ministers received 25 cents. Rather than viewing the paper merely as a means for additional compensation, preachers were encouraged to use the *CA* as an aid in spreading the gospel. The first issue of the *CA* even characterized the paper as "a powerful preacher," whose voice extended to America's frontiers, "carrying peace to the afflicted, intelligence to the inquiring, warning to the wanderer, and news of great joy to those who delight to hear of the 'stately goings' of our God in the Churches."[12] A free copy of the first issue was sent to every Methodist preacher, and letters from ministers poured into the paper reporting the *CA*'s reception across the country. Writing from Amelia, Virginia, Reverend George C. Chesley asserted, "I have been highly gratified as I have gone around my circuit this time, in finding that the 'Christian Advocate' had been received by most of the subscribers that I obtained, and with the manifest pleasure they seemed to enjoy in perusal of it." Chesley also noted how word-of-mouth buzz about the paper had attracted additional subscribers. Two years later, another minister claimed that the *CA* had helped garner support for the Methodist movement across the Missouri District.[13]

With an annual subscription price of $2.00 in advance or $2.50 after receipt, the price of the paper was intentionally kept low to make it accessible to a wide audience. Unimaginable for a popular newspaper today, the *CA* did not carry any commercial advertisements to offset its costs. As the title indicates, the primary objective of the newspaper was to serve as an advocate for Christianity. With this goal in mind, the paper targeted a broad audience—crossing both class and denominational boundaries. The editorial in the first issue underscored this objective, asserting, "Our highest desires will be answered if our paper affords delight and instruction to all classes of men, and be found in the hands of the missionary of the cross, in the humble mansion, in the splendid drawing room, and in the lonely chamber of sickness and death."[14] Confirming the paper's reach beyond Methodist adherents and across different age groups, one reader from Berks County, Pennsylvania, wrote: "Since I received your first number I have taken pleasure in showing it to as many persons as I could, both of our own and of other Churches. . . . Several gentlemen of the Presbyterian Church, who have examined this first number, have expressed to me their pleasure; and one of them, on subscribing for it, remarked, that he was particularly desirous of leaving such publications in the way of his *children* as he found that they were often interested and profited by them in leisure moments, which might otherwise be spent in idleness, or worse."[15] Circulation numbers for antebellum periodicals, like those of today, were not an accurate representation of a publication's reach. Even though the head of the household typically subscribed to newspapers, entire families often read them. Moreover, the practice of sharing subscriptions—common among the poor and individuals in remote areas—would have certainly been a practice employed within small church congregations as well.

The editors of the *CA* included material specifically directed at women, youth, and children, and encouraged families to read the newspaper as a means of religious instruction. One *CA* article even declared, "There is hardly anything so much needed in a family as a newspaper . . . a good virtuous, well conducted newspaper, in a family, is the best economist of time and the aptest instructor of the mind."[16] The *CA*'s Children's Department, Ministers' Department, Ladies' Department, Parents' Department, and Youths' Department directed content at those particular audiences, while the rest of the newspaper featured sermons, moralistic treatises, statements of doctrine, doctrinal debates, biblical explications, and religious anecdotes as well as reports on revivals, church growth, Sunday schools, Christian mission's efforts, and memoirs.

The paper also carried secular news. During the nineteenth century, tremendous overlap existed between religious and secular newspapers; secular papers regularly featured religious news, poetry, religious columns, and short versions of religious memoirs. However, in her study of the evangelical print market in the nineteenth century, Candy Brown notes that unlike secular newspapers, which arranged content based on timeliness and coverage, religious newspapers selected and arranged content with regard to its usefulness in achieving an evangelistic purpose.[17] Hence, the *CA*'s front page typically included explications of Scripture, extracts from sermons, and doctrinal debates over topics such as predestination. The second page usually carried reports from missionaries abroad and domestic Indian missions, other general religious intelligence, and reports on revivals and camp meetings from Methodist clergy. These reports were often continued on the third page, which also featured secular news such as reports about scientific inventions, economic and political reports, medical information, domestic and international news briefs, marriage announcements, and obituaries. The fourth page comprised the paper's audience-specific departments or columns, including a Poet's Department for original and reprinted poems and a Biographical Department for short memoirs.

The content, frequency, and wide distribution of the weekly *CA* extended and strengthened the church's textual community. In his travels across antebellum America, Alexis de Tocqueville observed the power of newspapers to effectively dissolve all geographic and temporal barriers by dropping "the same thought into a thousand minds at the same moment."[18] The *CA* was particularly effective in cultivating a broader community among Methodists because its content reflected their common language, doctrine, and ideology. In his study on the origins of nationalism, Benedict Anderson suggests that a newspaper provides the technical means for representing a particular kind of imagined community through the selection of content and by interpreting or refracting information in a particular way.[19] In this way, the *CA* served as a vehicle for distributing Methodism or at least a Methodist view of religion and the world. Moreover, the *CA* literally bound the Methodist community together by serving as the primary means of communicating with book agents and customers. Each issue of the *CA* acknowledged communication and transactions by printing a list of individuals from whom letters were received and for whom book and periodical orders were filled. The paper also helped Methodists to chart the church's westward expansion and keep track of itinerant ministers by reporting the founding of new Methodist societies and ministerial reassignments.

Candy Brown argues that in addition to creating a broader religious community, the frequency of weekly religious newspapers helped to extend the Sabbath beyond Sunday services by "infusing sacred influences into everyday times and spaces."[20] The *CA* blurred boundaries between the sacred, the public, and the private as well as between the sacred and the secular. The newspaper also broadened boundaries by helping readers see their religious activities as part of a larger movement extending across the country far beyond their own communities and congregations.

While expanding the boundaries of evangelism, the *CA* also reinforced existing gender boundaries. The article titled "A Model" depicts the conception of female fulfillment characterized by most Ladies' Department pieces: "It is her happiness to be ignorant of all that the world calls pleasure; her glory is to live in the duties of a wife and mother: and she consecrates her days to the practice of social virtues. . . . Her house is the residence of religious sentiments, of filial piety, of conjugal love, of maternal tenderness, of order, peace, sweet sleep, and good health. . . . She diffuses around her a mild warmth, a pure light, which vivify and illuminate all that encircle her."[21] Heavily laden with prescriptions of women's proper sphere and pursuits, articles contained in the Ladies' Department repeatedly address three broad themes—women's roles as wives and mothers, female influence, and women's virtue.

These three subjects, which also filled popular advice columns and literature directed at women in the 1820s and 1830s, fall within the realm of what Nancy Cott labels the "canon of domesticity" and what Barbara Welter dubs the "cult of true womanhood." According to Welter, the four cardinal virtues that emerged from women's magazines and religious literature by which women were judged and were encouraged to judge themselves were piety, purity, submissiveness, and domesticity.[22] Merging the domestic sphere with the idealized true woman centered on four related ideas: (1) the clear demarcation between home and the marketplace, which supposedly paralleled the differences between men and women; (2) the designation of home as women's sole sphere of influence; (3) granting women religious and moral superiority over men; and (4) idealizing women for their sacrifices to men and children.[23] This conception made true womanhood primarily the purview of married, white, middle-class women. According to historian Susan Lindley, "The nineteenth-century image of the True Woman was both continuous and discontinuous with previous ideals or expectations. Some roles, such as subordination or domestic concerns, had a long heritage," yet the rigid insistence on gendered spheres was a radical change that was distinct to the nineteenth century.[24] While religious periodicals are frequently overlooked in discussions of separate spheres, the *CA*'s Ladies' Department should be situated within this larger domestic canon.

From the *CA*'s beginning in September 1826, the Ladies' Department column was a standard feature appearing in most issues. The paper's editors opened the November 23, 1832, column by asserting, "Ladies—We have been at some pains to promote your usefulness and happiness in the selections we have chosen for this department of our paper."[25] This statement raises two questions: Why did the editors feel compelled or take pains to promote women's usefulness and happiness? And how exactly did these male editors construe women's usefulness and happiness, or, more precisely, how did they perceive wives and mothers contributing to the newspaper's overriding objective of advocating Christianity? Articles carried in the Ladies' Department were usually unsigned, which was a common journalistic practice until the 1840s. Many of the pieces were also reprinted from other periodicals and conduct literature. Nonetheless, even if the articles were not written specifically for the *CA*, the male editors' selection of these pieces for the Ladies' Department offers insight into their conceptions about happy and useful women.

Methodism's explosive growth in America coincided with, and in many ways, helped confirm the canon of domesticity. Indeed, Methodists' embrace of the domestic canon can be viewed as part of the church's pursuit of social respectability and mainline institutionalization. Because women made up the majority of most church denominations and because women were primarily relegated to the domestic sphere, the domestic sphere became an essential religious space. Based on her study of American Methodist women, Methodist historian Jean Miller Schmidt explains, "Women in their domestic roles were to sustain traditional values and, by their selflessness, to compensate for and counteract the commercial and acquisitive values of the male world." As mothers, women were also advised "to view their children's salvation and moral character as their primary responsibility (indeed, their major contribution to society)."[26] Repeatedly, women were counseled to serve their households. Beyond their words in the pulpit and their advice to women in Methodist periodicals, Methodist ministers actively contributed to this prescriptive domestic canon. Reverend Daniel Wise wrote *Bridal Greetings* (1856), which described the duties of husband and wife, and *The Young Lady's Counselor* (1857), intended to prepare young women for the roles of wife and mother. Bishop James O. Andrew also wrote *Family Government* (1855), which stressed that the home should provide a congenial refuge for men.[27]

Beyond fortifying the home as an essential religious space, embracing the domestic canon meant preserving patriarchal order. At the same time that the church was elevating women as models of piety in the domestic sphere, it was also attempting to contain them within a patriarchal structure. Nancy Cott suggests that by containing women in the domestic sphere, evangelical ministers were pursuing what they considered proper social structure (that is, women's subordination to men).[28] By encouraging women as purveyors of piety, the *CA*'s clerical editors were strengthening the resolve and commitment of their most fervent followers. And by keeping women in subordinate positions in the kitchen, parlor, and pews, ministers also preserved their own authority.

Contributors to the Ladies' Department repeatedly claimed that men and women held comparable degrees of power, which was simply exerted in separate spheres. One of the most common article titles appearing in the *CA* was "Female Influence." Repeatedly, women read that their power came through their influence, especially in their roles as wives and mothers. One author claims, "In no relation does woman exercise so deep an influence, both immediately and prospectively as in that of mother." Another writes, "Every where throughout the circle of her intercourse her influence is to be felt like the dew of heaven, gentle, silent, and unseen, yet pervading and efficient." Upholding patriarchal order, another article explains that while a woman is "bound to 'honor and obey,' those on whom she depends for protection and support," her voice "of reason and affection may ever convince and persuade." Similarly, another article asserts, "nineteen times in twenty, while he thinks he is pursuing an independent course, and assumes all the credit of his success, the suggestions or persuasions of his companion are influencing his opinions and controlling his conduct."[29] At the same time that articles such as these acknowledge women's persuasive power, this power is generally restricted to willing subjects within the boundaries of the domestic sphere, further demonstrating the relationship between power and space. Without economic, legal, or political means, women's power was limited. Offering a characterization of republican motherhood, one article acknowledges the few roles afforded women, stating, "Though she may not teach from the portico, nor thunder from the forum, in her secret retirements she may form and send forth the sages that shall govern and renovate the world."[30] Overall, while they emphasize women's influence as mothers and wives, Ladies' Department articles affirm the belief that a woman's impact on the outside world was limited and indirect—based on her actions within the home.

Ministers repeatedly advised women to use their influence in their roles as mothers, sisters, wives, and female companions to bring men to church, convert them, or simply rein them into the realm of acceptable moral behavior. Again, these responsibilities, which had traditionally fallen under the dominion of ministers, were increasingly being transferred to women. For some women, converting male family members also became a means of exerting their own spiritual and moral views and possibly impacting their household economies as well. While women's primary motive for family evangelism was to secure the salvation of male relatives, women could also use conversion to gain some measure of influence over their own personal and economic lives, particularly because of Methodists' opposition to gambling, drinking, and slavery.

Altogether, Ladies' Department articles recognized and bolstered women's domestic evangelism. One article shares the story of a group of women in a New Hampshire town who met for the purpose of praying for their unconverted husbands.[31] In an extract from a speech delivered in Warren County, Georgia, Robert Fleming encourages women to employ their influence to discourage drinking. He instructs, "Let the young man who thinks it a small matter to indulge too freely in spirits, feel the potency of your frowns."[32] Again, while these selections acknowledge women's influence and encourage women to exert their persuasive powers, they also acknowledge that women's power was generally limited to suggestions, prayers, and disapproving frowns.

Emphasizing home and hearth as women's appointed stage, articles instructed married women to make the domestic sphere their only focus. One author counseled: "No longer let your fancy wander to scenes of pleasure or disappointment. Let home be now your empire, your world! Let home be now the sole scene of your wishes, your thoughts, your plans, your exertions. Let home be now the stage on which, in the varied character of wife, of mother, and of mistress, you strive to act and shine with splendour."[33] By encouraging women to turn their backs on the outside world, this article contributed to women's spatial containment in their homes and in their roles as wives and mothers. With its prescriptions of "good" wives and mothers, the column also attempted to dictate women's actions in their domestic roles. For instance, even before women married, the Ladies' Department carried numerous articles advising them on what type of men they *should* marry. One author cautioned, "It is no doubt a dangerous experiment for any Christian to marry an unbeliever."[34] Other articles warned women to avoid drunkards and to enter into marriage only after serious reflection. However, there was little suggestion that women would not marry. In the early nineteenth century, marriage was usually a matter of social acceptance and economic survival for women. For most, the choice was not between independence and housewifery, but between marriage or the social stigma and poverty usually associated with spinsterhood.

One contributor encouraged female readers to place all their pride, joy, and happiness in the "merited approbation" of their husbands.[35] Ladies' Department articles repeatedly presented a woman's happiness as a corollary of her husband's happiness. Consequently, women were also advised to avoid any behaviors that might displease their husbands. "A Letter to a Young Married Lady" instructed women to patiently bear their husbands' absences, suggesting, "At his return, be the first, with a heart dilating with gratitude to the *preserver of both your lives*, to welcome him to his convivial home."[36] The same article also warned ladies not to disturb their husbands while reading and not to burden them with lowly domestic concerns, suggesting, "While you enjoy the society of your husband around the social board, think him not unkind if he does not listen to every nursery tale, or inquire into some frivolous domestic concern. These may properly come under your notice, but they are beneath the dignity of a man."[37] In ways such as this, the Ladies' Department affirmed the prevailing social order. Even though its articles repeatedly asserted the importance of women's domestic duties, both women and the roles they performed were clearly ranked as subordinate to—even "beneath the dignity" of—men.

According to the Ladies' Department, women's "usefulness" required them to be both subservient and submissive in order to create a congenial home. The article "Matrimonial Paragraphs" instructed women that it was a wife's duty to concede in order to ensure reconciliation on any disagreement. The author also warned women to "never join in any jest or laugh against your husband . . . assiduously conceal his faults, and speak only of his merits."[38] Altogether, this advice suggested that women were responsible for maintaining an amiable atmosphere in the home, especially through their silence. Along these same lines, women's tempers were a particular concern addressed by contributors. One author enumerated the characteristics of a "good woman" as "mildness, complaisance, and equanimity of temper," while another article stipulated, "Sweetness of temper, affection to her husband, and attention to his interests, constitute the duties of a wife, and form the basis of matrimonial felicity."[39]

Ladies' Department articles subtly, yet repeatedly, advised women to detect their husbands' needs and attend to them. One commentary, which described a woman as "the mere dependant and ornament to man" during his happiest hours, asserted that wives must become their husband's "stay and solace" when calamity occurs—"tenderly supporting the drooping head, and binding up the broken heart."[40] In "Reflections on the State of Marriage," which was purportedly "written by a married man," readers were told, "O how dear to the memory of a man is the wife who clothes her face in smiles, who uses gentle expressions, and who makes her lap soft to receive and hush his cares to rest."[41] Advice to wives encouraged them to make their home a refuge for their husbands and focus all their efforts on making their husbands happy. Indeed, a woman's willingness to sacrifice herself for her husband and children became a source of her "special morality" and the "near sanctity" assigned to her role.[42]

The domestic canon delivered through vehicles such as the Ladies' Department, helped to convert the home into a religious sanctuary, which was intended to shield middle-class white women and their children from the cruel, competitive world and to provide husbands with a place of refuge from economic toil. Women were instructed to become part of their husband's sanctuary by assuming the roles of angels, silent ornaments, administers of comfort, and purveyors of religious salvation.

At the same time women were expected to fulfill the role of domestic manager, which encompassed all matters from ensuring order and a tranquil environment to household economy. Ladies' Department articles repeatedly emphasized that men needed to earn sufficient money to support their families, and as good domestic managers, women needed to efficiently use the money they were allocated by their husbands to manage their households. One writer claimed, "Economy is so important a part of a woman's character, so necessary to her own happiness, and so essential to her performing properly the duties of a wife and a mother, that it ought to have the precedence over all other accomplishments."[43] In referencing "other accomplishments," the writer was likely alluding to playing the piano, painting, singing, ornamental sewing, entertaining, or other parlor pursuits. Whereas girls were routinely encouraged to become accomplished in these areas in order to net a husband, wives were instructed to turn their focus from the parlor to the pocketbook and pantry. In fact, authors of advice literature often used domestic economy and women's role managing the household to substantiate home as a woman's occupation and the way in which she contributed to the well-being of society.

Most notably, Catharine Beecher attempted to elevate women's position in society by recognizing female contributions within the domestic sphere. In 1842, Beecher published *A Treatise on Domestic Economy*, which argued that women should remain in the home. Beecher asserted that women's vocation in the home was crucial to society's well-being, but the irony is evident. Even if the vocation of domesticity rhetorically placed women at the helm of the domestic sphere, women remained under the legal and economic dominion of husbands and fathers. Hence, it is not surprising that women were repeatedly instructed to manage "their" sphere with their husband's best interests in mind. One anecdote carried in the Ladies Department even describes how a woman used wise domestic economy to compensate for and conceal her husband's poor business management.[44] In that sense, domestic economy became one more way for women to take care of their husbands.

In addition to prescribing women's roles as deferential wives, Ladies' Department articles emphasized women's duties as holy mothers within the domestic sphere. Susan Lindley suggests, "The very prevalence of the stock figure of the pious mother in nineteenth-century sermons, folklore, and literature testifies to the real roots in American experience, however standardized or even caricatured that figure became."[45] Although Puritans had viewed motherhood as simply one of women's many tasks, Barbara Epstein has noted how the domestication of religion in the nineteenth century elevated motherhood to women's most important responsibility—upholding a mother-child relationship that was almost sacred in nature.[46] With the increased emphasis placed on children's early impressions, the domestic sphere was identified as a primary space where children's moral and religious beliefs were forged. Because fathers increasingly worked outside of the home, and because men were considered less religiously inclined than women, the domestic canon assigned mothers the main responsibility for molding the next generation of Christians and citizens.

Articles carried in the Ladies' Department counseled women that it was their "duty" to affectionately instruct their children and instill essential moral and religious principles. According to one author, "A pious, intelligent, and faithful mother is the greatest earthly blessing that a merciful Providence can bestow on a child. If she performs her duty, her offspring will rise up and call her blessed." Similarly stressing the consequences of ineffectual motherhood, another author cautions, "I would not be understood to insinuate that the misconduct of children is always caused by errors in domestic education . . . yet still there is reason to hope that good seed, if sown when the heart is tender and the understanding unbiased, may prevent the weeds of vice from occupying the whole soul."[47] Articles such as these employ what Gregory Schneider terms "mother rhetoric," which he defines as the "identification of mother love with God's power to constrain and transform human nature."[48] Repeatedly, Ladies' Department advice accorded women God like power over their children. The author of "Maternity" avowed, "Heaven has imprinted on the mother's face something beyond this world, something which claims kindred with the skies—the angelic smile, the tender look, the waking, watchful eye which keeps its fond vigil over her slumbering babe." Remarking on the enduring influence of mothers, this author proclaimed, "Nature has set the mother upon such a pinnacle, that our infant eyes and arms are first uplifted to it: we cling to it in manhood, we almost worship it in old age."[49] At the very least, women are upheld as emissaries of God.

The Ladies' Department omitted the type of concrete advice that one might expect to find in contemporary advice columns. Contributors did not provide "Ten Ways to Make Your Children Moral Beings" or "Helping Your Kids Get to Know God." Apparently, *CA* authors assumed that "true women" possessed some ingrained understanding of how to be effective religious and moral instructors, which underscores the common perception of women's natural predilection for religion. Sarah Robbins's study of domestic literacy narratives points to literacy instruction as one of the primary ways mothers inculcated their children with religious knowledge and principles. Because the Bible was presented as the primary text for literacy development, Robbins notes how literacy acquisition in the nineteenth century was tightly bound to religious training; at the same time that mothers taught their children to read, they also taught them to be good Christians.[50] Moreover, the domestic canon positioned religion as the "core of woman's virtue," and "the source of her strength."[51] Ladies' Department discussions consistently link religion and gender and repeatedly designate the salvation of her children as a mother's primary mission. One author even claimed that a child's conversion is prompted *more* by the piety of the mother than the piety of the father. Likewise, another author asserted, "an engine of uncomputed power is committed to her hand. If she fix her level judiciously, though she may not, like Archimedes, aspire to move the earth, she may hope to raise one of the inhabitants to heaven."[52]

Ultimately, by conflating religion and gender and emphasizing the home as the primary space for religious instruction and salvation, the Methodist church contributed to what historian Mary Ryan terms the "domestication of religion." In her foundational study of Oneida County, New York, from 1790 to 1865, Ryan identifies the "domestication of religion" as the transition of religious authority from churches and the patriarchal head of household to evangelical mothers. Increasingly, women assumed responsibility for converting their children, relying less on social authority and more on maternal affection, their own feminized form of religious influence.[53] "The important work of conversion could not be left to strangers, ministers, or even God," writes Lori Ginzberg, "it was instead the job of wives, daughters, and sisters, the women of the household."[54] By encouraging this domestication of religion, the *CA*'s Ladies' Department served as an ideological apparatus for the church. Ladies' Department advice prescribed a woman's proper sphere, assigned her to the roles of wife and mother, and stipulated the salvation of her family as her overriding purpose.

Through Ladies' Department prescriptions about dress, the body became another space around which the church attempted to draw tight borders. Moreover, attempts in Ladies' Department articles to redefine beauty and dictate proper dress offer evidence that the church considered women's attire an important rhetorical medium. During the nineteenth century, women's fashion was also linked to concerns over the import of European social structures and Catholicism.[55] Dress had long been considered an external sign of internal piety and morality. Early Methodists used plain dress both as a form of ascetic discipline and distinction. Women often shunned costly apparel or removed ruffles and lace—considered appendages of pride and vanity—to symbolize a shift in commitment from the ephemeral to the eternal. In *Appropriate[ing] Dress: Women's Rhetorical Style in Nineteenth-Century America*, Carol Mattingly identifies dress as a powerful rhetorical forum, particularly for women. According to Mattingly, a woman's dress communicated her *ethos* in terms of race, class, gender, morality, and even her religious convictions.[56] In fact, Patricia Bizzell pinpoints dress as an important element of the middle-class Methodist respectability conveyed by Phoebe Palmer and Frances Willard.[57] Through advice dispensed in the Ladies' Department, contributors encouraged women to use dress to both mold and exhibit their religious character.

According to one Ladies' Department anecdote, "A godly minister of the gospel occasionally visiting a gay person, was introduced to a room near to that wherein she dressed. After waiting some hours the lady came in, and found him in tears. She inquired the reason for his weeping. He replied, 'Madam, I weep on reflecting that you can spend so many hours before your glass, and in adorning your person, while I spend so few hours before my God in adorning my soul.' The rebuke struck her conscience. She lived and died a monument of grace."[58] This story reiterates the internal/external and private/public dichotomy frequently espoused in antebellum Methodist publications. By showing the proper internal/external balance, Ladies' Department contributors promoted dress as an important indicator of woman's virtue.

Conveying the same view, a Ladies' Department article titled "Dress Indicative of Character" blames "the sinful negligence of ministers and pious parents in not holding up the scriptural standard, and insisting that plain, simple, chaste, tasteful, modest apparel, is as much an enjoined duty as the observance of the Lord's day."[59] Suggesting that proper dress is just as important as the scriptural commandment to observe the Sabbath, the author cued readers to two scriptural injunctions against women's immodest dress: "In like manner also, that women adorn themselves in modest apparel, with shamefacedness and sobriety; not with braided hair, or gold, or pearls, or costly array," and "Whose adorning let it not be that outward adorning of plaiting the hair, and of wearing of gold, or of putting on of apparel."[60] With this prompt, the writer emphasized that modest dress was a duty dictated by Scripture, and that the Bible defined beauty as a pursuit beyond fashion and accessories. The writer concluded by noting the motive for fancy dress, warning readers that "fondness for show, ornament, brilliant appearance, and the love of distinction and applause are natural to the depraved heart."[61] The author not only elevated dress to a form of biblical obedience but also reduced dress to a binary representation of either piety or depravity.

By making modest dress a symbol of religion and virtue, the church attempted to prescribe what women should wear and also how women should allocate their time. Dress became women's public mantle of domesticity and religious virtue. Moreover, efforts by Ladies' Department contributors to dictate women's proper focus and fashion can be viewed as additional endeavors by the church to exercise control over women, particularly women's bodies. By dictating proper dress, the church further attempted to contain women in certain roles and behaviors. Contributors not only deem dress as a symbol but also a distraction. Little narratives selected for the Ladies' Department repeatedly warn readers about the dangers of frivolous amusements. The selection "The Victim of Innocent Amusements" offers a cautionary tale of Elizabeth Hazlewood, whom we are told was "brought up in the lap of luxury, and in the indulgence of every harmless pleasure," and eventually faced her death destitute of religion and any relationship with God.[62] Dying unrepentant was a dire concern for Methodists, so connecting dalliance, dress, and damnation would have had a powerful rhetorical appeal. Another Ladies' Department article carries one woman's critical observations of New York's social scene; she claims that the city's "fair daughters of luxury" are so obsessed with amusing themselves that they neglect the source of "their real dignity," which she defines as religion. Indeed, she further asserts, "I am certain that female beauty is never so attractive, as when lighted by the rays of ardent piety, and attended by those satellites, good sense and cultivated intellect."[63]

Altogether, Ladies' Department prescriptions about women's appropriate roles, influence, and dress drew both a limited conception of women's concerns and confining boundaries around women in the domestic sphere. At the same time, by acknowledging women's power to convert children and offer salvation to their husbands via their domestic sanctuaries, women can be seen moving into expanded rhetorical roles. Similar to the way in which memoirs elevated women to the role of iconic ministers, a collateral consequence of the domestication of religion proffered by the *CA*'s Ladies' Department was that women usurped many of the roles formerly under the purview of ministers. Even with their prescriptive advice, the church recognized that women's rhetorical influence extended far beyond their homes, and in that regard, it was unable and even unwilling to contain them.

Stepping Outside the Ladies' Department

> We may also learn from this short history, that there are none,
> however poor or however obscure may be their situation in life,
> but what may be the means of doing *some good* in benefiting their
> fellow creatures, and in promoting the cause of God. This poor
> woman was very poor as to this world, and yet see how exten-
> sively useful she was.
>
> —"History of Amelia Gale," *Christian Advocate*, 1828

The "History of Amelia Gale," appearing on the front page of the June 20, 1828, *Christian Advocate* (*CA*), tells the story of a poor widow living in England who spent most of her life eking out an existence by carrying a gaming board to fairs and wakes. Late in life, Amelia was awakened by a minister's preaching, and for the first time she considered life in the hereafter. Eventually, Amelia sought redemption and became a passionate believer in both word and deed. When a local missionary society was established in her church, she was moved by the sacrifices she saw fellow parishioners make in order to contribute to the church's mission efforts. Amelia, who had little to sacrifice, thought about tea, which was her only beverage and sometimes her only meal. Then she decided to forgo sugar in her tea. Depriving herself of this one luxury enabled Amelia to contribute one cent a week to the Bible and missionary fund. In a basket from which she now earned her living selling needles and cotton balls, she carried a missionary box and collected donations. Through these and other efforts, Amelia was able to increase her contribution to the missionary society to six pounds a year.[1]

Although Amelia's personal sacrifices had little financial impact, once published, read, and recited, they provided a pious model and moved others to increase their donations. Moreover, Amelia Gale's story is one of the rare instances when a story featuring a woman appeared on the *CA*'s front page, which was a space primarily reserved for male clergy and their explications of Scripture, sermon extracts, and doctrinal discussions. Conversely, the "History of Amelia Gale" presents a prototype of devotion, compassion, and generosity—a role generally ascribed to women, but typically placed on the interior or back pages of the four-page weekly paper. The persuasive power attributed to the story of Amelia Gale's life, which also became a popular tract initially distributed by London's Tract Society and produced in 1830 by the American Tract Society, likely explains why this woman's story was allowed to encroach onto traditional male territory. By collecting money for the church's mission efforts, Amelia carried her work into the public realm and became a champion for these causes. The published accounts of her efforts moved Gale into the traditionally male roles of benefactor and public spokesperson.

In ways such as this, the press both supported and circumscribed women's rhetorical roles and ultimately operated as a rhetorical agent. Whereas the content inside the regular Ladies' Department column typically contained women in the roles of wife and mother inside the domestic sphere, depictions of women as public models of piety and charity, benefactors, benevolent society organizers, Sunday school teachers, and missions' workers appearing outside of the Ladies' Department usually showed women outside the confines of the domestic sphere. By charting women's migration in the *CA*, this chapter demonstrates how religious activities enabled women to emerge from the domestic sphere and engage in social activism that contravened accepted gender norms.

Although the *CA*'s male editors managed the textual content that portrayed women in both spaces, I view women's assignment to the domestic sphere through the Ladies' Department as an intentional assignment. Conversely, women's movement onto page two and three of the paper—outside the Ladies' Department and the domestic sphere—was far more subtle and cumulative in effect. Ultimately, women's movements outside the margins of the Ladies' Department further complicated the conception of separate spheres and proved that the *CA* editors could not contain women or dictate the boundaries of their good works. The distinction I draw between women inside and women outside of the Ladies' Department confirms Roxanne Mountford's assertion that "spaces [in this case textual and material] are productive of meaning as well as endowed with meaning."[2]

The line of demarcation separating public and private has long been considered a central battle line. Political theorist Carole Pateman stresses the significance of this public/private dichotomy for women, claiming that the past two centuries of women's struggle for equality with men primarily centers on this division.[3] Of course, arguments against the rigid conception of separate spheres, which limited nineteenth-century middle-class women to a narrowly circumscribed domestic realm, are nothing new. However, the church, which is typically viewed as part of women's prescribed sphere of activity, is often assumed to operate as conservative and limiting. Yet women's efforts as church organizers and volunteers, which were initially pursued for religious reasons, often reaped unintended consequences—expanding women's public influence and altering their conceptions of themselves and their proper roles. Studies of nineteenth-century women's rhetorical history have also convincingly shown the blurring of boundaries between the private and public spheres as women pursued social activism from safe borderlands.

Churches often inhabit an ambiguous location in the public/private division of society, and the antebellum Methodist church was no exception. While it encouraged domestic evangelism and attended to individuals' private souls, it also condemned public activities such as drinking, gambling, slavery, prostitution, and the pursuit of wealth. Additionally, the church distributed Bibles and tracts; staged camp meetings and revivals; and established community Sunday schools, colleges and seminaries, orphanages, and missions among North American Indian tribes. As a result, the church blurred boundaries between the gendered separate spheres by creating middle ground shared by both men and women. David Sibley claims that these type of liminal zones, because their borders are ambiguous, mark opportunities for change.[4] Consequently, the church and church work became important sites for broadening women's rhetorical boundaries. Under the mantle of church work, white, middle-class women could step beyond the domestic sphere and still maintain their appropriate Victorian womanliness. Of course, this sanctioned space not only existed in women's benevolent organization meetings, Sunday schools, and missions' schools; it also existed in Methodist publications. In the case of the *CA*, women's movements outside the domestic sphere were authorized within the Methodist church's flagship publication—one of the most widely read periodicals in antebellum America. By printing and transmitting these movements to readers across the country, the *CA* constructed a new reality for white, middle-class women, enabling readers to imagine new spaces where women could and even should serve as Christian agents.

Women outside the Ladies' Department appear as active participants in reports of foreign and domestic mission activities, Sunday schools, and Bible and tract societies, rather than as passive recipients of prescriptive advice. In the pursuit of benevolent and evangelical missions, and in the reports of these efforts printed on page two and three of the *CA*, women entered spaces in which they were situated alongside men participating in the same spheres. Reports from women's missionary societies were dispersed amid reports from male-led missionary societies, thus blurring their prescribed gender roles. Moreover, whereas the articles printed in the Ladies' Department were often reprinted from other magazines or penned by male clergy, reports of women's charitable endeavors were submitted to the *CA* and its intermediary ministers by women themselves. Women wanted their efforts and backing to be acknowledged, and they frequently used their reports rhetorically to convince readers to take a stand or contribute to their cause. Hence, women began to shift from serving as tropes for male writers to becoming writers and speakers. Indeed, the narratives appearing in the *CA* depict the first steps most nineteenth-century white, middle-class, American women made beyond the domestic sphere.

These steps also established a path for the next generation of women. In her examination of temperance as the first mass women's movement in America, Barbara Epstein argues, "Women's piety and religious activity in the first half of the century helped to create the networks and give women the experience that made possible the flourishing of women's reform organizations in the later part of the century."[5] Temperance women and women's benevolent activities described in the *CA* also demonstrate women's eagerness to band together to address religious and social needs as well as their growing awareness of social ills, particularly with regard to fellow women. At the same time, women's benevolent activities drew them into many of the debates that were being waged in nineteenth-century America.

Surprisingly, women who had limited opportunities for earning money or were economically dependent on husbands were repeatedly depicted on the interior pages of the *CA* as model benefactors. In this sense, women were still being depicted in iconic roles. Composed and used as rhetorical models, the *CA* converted women's charity into rhetorical appeals for Christian living and benevolent giving, as is evident in the account of Amelia Gale. In another instance, under the heading "Good Examples," the *CA* printed the letter that accompanied a twenty-dollar donation from a woman in Virginia: "I have now (new year's day) by me $20, after paying all my debts. I have also a sufficiency for myself and family, and do not stand in actual need of anything; though fancy, you know, if indulged in is never satisfied. Shall I lay up this money, for fear I shall some day want it? Or shall I follow the example of many who profess the religion of the Bible, and spend it for unnecessary finery? No! I will do neither. I will enclose it to you, as a new year's gift to the missionary society."[6] For women in particular, financial and material contributions often had an emboldening effect. Nonetheless, while most of the benefactors recognized in the pages of the *CA* did not include this type of overt statement, the editors still turned their contributions into rhetorical appeals. The newspaper regularly published lists of contributors to the Methodist Missionary Society and the Methodist Publishing Fund for Bible, Tract, and Sunday School societies, with intentions not only to recognize contributors but also to encourage additional donations. At the same time, these lists provided a widely disseminated public forum in which individuals could assert their support for the church's charitable endeavors, no matter whether that support was twenty-five cents, five dollars, or one hundred dollars. This democratic forum was important to women for two reasons: women often had small discretionary funds from which to make donations, and they were rarely acknowledged in print as individuals apart from their husbands or fathers.

Examples of women's benevolence printed in the *CA* usually stress women's motivation more than their financial means. As a result, depictions of Christian generosity appearing on the newspaper's interior pages are often gendered: men gave out of their means, and women gave out of their devotion. Moreover, women's contributions often reflected a collective effort. For example, one article highlights a "female class" in which members gave a weekly one-cent offering to be divided up among the Methodist missionary, Bible, Sunday school, and tract societies. According to the article, the one-cent offering enabled fifteen to twenty women "mostly of circumscribed pecuniary abilities" to make an annual contribution of about forty-five dollars.[7] Women's efforts to pool their limited resources—money, time, and even administrative experience—are repeatedly evident in the little narratives published throughout the *CA*. Of course, with regard to money, it is important to remember that women were relegated to these limited means of contributions because of their dependent economic status.

Women who were unable to make substantial contributions during life were often recognized for their bequests after death. A letter printed in the *CA* states, "Enclosed you have $20, the amount of a bequest of the late Miss Elizabeth Butfield, of this city, deceased, and, as expressed in the will, to be applied towards feeding and clothing the Indians." Women's benevolent acts were also frequently recognized in their memoirs, which appeared alongside the Ladies' Department on the newspaper's back page. Hannah Sutton's memoir noted, "in her house the needy found assistance." Likewise, Mrs. Jerusah Crane's memoir claimed, "The poor, who freely shared in her liberality, were never forgotten. She always regarded herself as a steward of the Lord, intrusted with a portion of goods for charitable distribution." One of the most amazing female benefactors recognized in the *CA* was a former slave who left $639, the greater part of her estate, to benevolent and religious causes.[8]

Women also frequently made material donations. One article describing a revival at Washington Female Academy in Washington, Mississippi, acknowledged the academy's benefactor, Mrs. Elizabeth Greenfield, who gave the academy its edifice and one hundred acres of land. In recognition, the Mississippi Conference renamed the school the Elizabeth Female Academy.[9] An account of the rise of Methodism in Rhinebeck, New York, also noted a Mrs. Montgomery's gift of land for a church. Jewelry was another material possession that women frequently donated. Earrings given by Eliza Foster were noted as a $1 contribution, Mrs. Redfield's gold chain was recorded as a $2.75 contribution, and a report from the New Hampshire Conference Missionary Society listed among its donations "a string of gold beads from an aged mother and her daughter from Berlin, VT." Notably, the donation of jewelry by women carried a dual message. Jewelry was usually one of the few possessions women owned that had a substantial monetary value; thus, donating it was a personal sacrifice. Jewelry was also a vanity in the sense that it accentuated one's appearance, so applying it toward the conversion of lost souls aligned with the evangelical theme of reprioritizing the eternal over the external.[10]

Apparel was another material item women donated—usually for Sunday schools or domestic missions. In a report from the Wyandotte Indian Mission House in Upper Sandusky, Ohio, Thomas Thompson recognized the bequest of a box of clothing donated by Sister Larkin. Another report recognized a box of apparel valued at $88.25, "prepared by the praiseworthy exertions of the Female Missionary Society of Potsdam."[11] Because of the public recognition these gifts received in the *CA*, women's gifts carried moral credence. Moreover, women's collective contributions, which were usually critical to the survival of fledgling religious organizations, provided a way for women to exercise influence and power in institutions that precluded them from voting or serving as trustees.

The *CA*'s pages are also filled with little narratives of women who moved outside the role of domestic dependents to raise money for the church. Sewing enabled women to maintain their respectability while providing an independent means for raising money. For instance, in a report sent to the *CA*, the Dorcas Society of John Street Church in New York noted their contribution of one hundred dollars to the Indian missions in the Canada Conference. The Dorcas Society also specified that the sum was the result of membership subscriptions and money earned from sewing done between the hours of two in the afternoon and nine in the evenings during monthly meetings. By detailing how they raised their contribution, the society subtly encouraged other women's groups to exert their own financial agency. In another example, a foreign news brief acknowledged that the Church Missionary Society had recently received nearly $1,800 from the public sale of ladies' works.[12] A letter

printed in the paper also explains the efforts of Choctaw women at the Mayhew Mission School to raise money for the Female Bible Society in Ceylon:
"We thought we would endeavor to assist you in some way in your benevolent
exertions of distributing Bibles to your poor countrymen who are in the road
to hell; and for that purpose we formed ourselves into a society, which we call
the Female Bible Society of Mayhew School, and have sewed Saturday after-
noons from about 2 o'clock until five, and have earned twelve dollars, which
we sent to the American Board [of the Missionary Society]."[13] In this instance,
women who had been the recipients of the church's missions were now applying their newly acquired skills to contribute to foreign missions. The religious
community would have considered these contributions evidence of the mission school's effectiveness.

Collections such as those raised by Amelia Gale offer another example of
women's labor to support the church's charitable endeavors. The lists of contributions printed in the *CA* often include money collected by women. Mrs.
Ann Thompson was recognized for collecting $7.25, Miss Mary White col-
lected $3.25 from persons on the Caroline circuit; Miss Charlotte Demmem
of Newark, New Jersey, collected $12 for the education of an Indian boy; a
woman simply acknowledged as "a lady in Lynn, Mass.," collected $3 in her
contribution box, and a report from the secretary of the Female Missionary
Society in New York acknowledges that the society's female managers raised
$20 for the Missionary Society through their own collections.[14] Embedded in
these collections are women's agency, advocacy, and activism. In order to collect money from family, friends, fellow congregants, and people in the community, women had to become vocal proponents for the church's missionary
efforts. Stepping beyond their prescribed domestic roles, women often felt
empowered by the call to spread the gospel. Through depictions of their devotion, labor, and their fortitude to raise collections, women emerged as model
benefactors in the pages of the *CA*. More than the sums they contributed,
women's willingness to give whatever they could, as well as the public, vocal
advocacy inherent in many of their collected contributions made their donations noteworthy and powerful examples for emulation.

Women's desire to give to the church and its good works, even from their
impoverished means, is further conveyed through a mimetic narrative of the
New Testament widow's mite story, which appears repeatedly on the interior
pages of the *CA*. Through this narrative, poverty is converted into a trope for
piety as the two become intermingled in depictions of women as models of
unwavering faith amid dire circumstances. With antebellum coverture laws
and few "respectable" avenues for earning an income, the ideology of separate spheres made women dependents by precluding them from all but the

most meager realms of economic activity. This reality was depicted in numerous stories of destitute mothers and widows, who were relegated to the lowest rung of society when they lost their male bread winner.

According to Paul Lewis, "most discussions of poverty in the antebellum period proceeded from the assumption that being poor, while not necessarily a result of moral failure, was often a sign of it."[15] Dating back to the eighteenth century, British and American charitable organizations tried to separate the "deserving" poor from the "undeserving" poor. One key distinction was gender. Indigent widows; deserted wives with young children; educated females, who had been reduced from their comfortable circumstances; or females impoverished by the death or misfortune of their families or husbands were usually deemed deserving. However, the continual influx of laboring classes and immigrants into American cities during the nineteenth century intensified the problem of poverty, and the sympathy that was once extended to indigent women and widows was replaced with growing hostility and scorn.[16]

The *CA*'s depictions of poor women, particularly its mimetic widow's mite narrative, offered an alternate representation. According to this New Testament story, Jesus watched a crowd put their offerings into the temple treasury. While many rich people contributed large sums, Jesus was particularly struck by a poor widow's offering of two copper coins—worth only a fraction of a cent. Jesus called this widow's contribution to the attention of his disciples, noting that while the others had given from their abundance, she gave all she had.[17] Stories in the *CA* mirrored this theme of women. For instance, an article titled "The Widow's Mite" reported the donation of a Bible by a "poor, pious widow" to the missionary society of Connecticut. According to the widow, the Bible represented "all her living," and she hoped that it would be given to someone destitute of God's word because the Bible had provided comfort in her poverty and ultimately "an inheritance among the saints." Concluding this article, the newspaper's editors assert, although "poor in this world, [the widow] was rich in faith."[18]

Another article also titled "The Widow's Mite," tells the story of a missionary for the American Home Missionary Society who, after preaching at the local church, went door-to-door taking up collections. Coming to the house of a poor widow, the missionary suggests to the woman answering the door, "your domestic burdens are so great, that, perhaps, you ought not aid our object, except with your prayers." To which the woman replied, "I was so afraid you had passed me by." The woman and all her children proceed to hand the man small contributions, mostly change, as she explains how her family received the gospel from missionaries, whom she credits for the hope she feels in Jesus and her prospect for heaven. She then instructs the missionary to take her family's small contribution so that it "may carry to some weary sinner in the wilderness, the consolation which I have found."[19]

The women in these stories are constructed as rhetorical models in both their faith and their desire to support the church's work. Also evident in these and other *CA* stories is the depiction of faith as poor women's sole ballast against despair. For instance, one article tells the tale of a pious elderly woman who lived alone in a remote thatched cottage. A young man passing by the cottage found her sick and close to death "lying in the corner of the room on a little straw, with a tattered garment wrapped around her as her covering to screen her from the chilling blast." When the man suggested that the woman was suffering with no one to relieve her distress, the woman claimed she had all she needed with Jesus and a crust of bread.[20]

Another story similarly reports a preacher's visit to a poor blind woman. When the preacher inquired about her temporal circumstances, she admitted her family had not had a morsel of food in the house in three days, but had survived on milk from their cow and whortleberries picked up in the woods by her grandchildren. The widow then added, "And we have God too." The story concluded, "Often since then, when the preacher has been at tables where there was an abundance, he has asked himself this question—have those people got God too?—if not, the poor blind widow is abundantly the richest."[21]

Oddly missing from these accounts is any sense of outrage or urgency about the conditions in which the visitors find these women. Part of the reason may be that these accounts follow the common conventions of poor-visit narratives popular in nineteenth-century nonfiction and fiction. Home visits to the poor, which had long existed as an individual practice, were used by religious reform groups in the early nineteenth century to evangelize, distribute Bibles and tracts, and evaluate potential recipients of charitable aid. Accounts of poor visits typically downplay or purposefully use dire material conditions as a device to accentuate an individual's Christian piety.[22] This reversal is evident in the *CA*; instead of depicting women who need to be saved from dismal living conditions, the newspaper stressed that these women were saved by their faith. Moreover, the one who is frequently helped is the visitor who draws spiritual sustenance from the unwavering faith of the poor individual.

By publishing these stories, *CA* editors hoped readers would vicariously participate in these visits. This subtle encouragement is particularly evident in a story titled "Poor Mary, an Aged Female, and the Rich Professor." This little narrative shares the story of a poor woman, who, on her way home, encounters a rich woman who is a "professed" Christian. The rich woman relates several sorrows and apprehensions to poor Mary, who listens with the "kindness of Christian sympathy" and encourages the woman to abide by her faith, reminding her that God has promised never to forsake his followers. When the two women arrive at Mary's home, Mary invites the rich woman into her humble dwelling and proceeds to show her that every closet in her house is empty. Nonetheless, Mary insists, "Why should I be unhappy? I have Christ in my heart and heaven in my eye."[23]

Through these depictions of poor women resolute in their faith, the *CA* redefines poverty and the image of these poor women by lauding the superiority of a faith-filled soul over external riches. Counter to aid societies that defined poor women as frail, passive, and weak victims, the *CA* depicted them as strong and steadfast. Even though they were rendered poor through socially-determined circumstances, they were shown exerting agency and influence— persuading others through their personal faith. Even so, celebrating poverty as an unimpeded path to heavenly riches downplays or even negates concern for these women's impoverished circumstances and the social, economic, and legal systems that contribute to them. By pitting piety against riches, *CA* articles also romanticize poverty. Certainly, this is the case with an article titled "Poverty a Blessing," which asserts, "The rich are seldom very pious, nor are they very benevolent generally speaking . . . the poor have their evil things in this life . . . nevertheless, they are (the pious part of them) happy in the abodes of poverty and wretchedness; and in the world to come they will be comforted, while many of the rich will be tormented." The author concludes the article with the example of a lonely widow with small children—noting that even amid an uncharitable world, the woman says she is happy, because even "in these afflictions [she] feel[s] Christ within."[24] In addition to romanticizing poverty, these stories can also be interpreted as a way of instructing women to accept their lot in life, which contemporary readers might view as a disservice to women. But that argument denies the evangelical context and culture in which these women lived and in which these articles were written. It also ignores the question, what realistic recourse did these poor women have in an economic and social system that offered women few, if any, options to earn a living?

While noting all the problematic aspects of these stories, I believe that a fascinating narrative of women's agency emerges out of this redefinition of poverty and riches. Amid stereotypes of poor women as helpless victims or unworthy rabble, the *CA* holds up many poor women as strong and steadfast models for inspiration and emulation. Granted, the text exploits these women. But at the same time, these women are shown asserting their independence outside of a patriarchal economy and social strata. In the little narratives published by the *CA*, readers saw women who took control of their destiny by recognizing a source of power beyond social and economic measures and ultimately attained contentment by turning their attention beyond the physical world.

The women depicted outside the Ladies' Department are often linked to either indigence or benevolence. In addition to the representation of widows as pious models amid abject poverty, women repeatedly appear in the *CA* organizing support for benevolent and evangelical causes. Reports from women's benevolent organizations that regularly appeared on pages two and three of the *CA* confirm women's support of charitable efforts. This support not only required them to move beyond the domestic sphere but also encouraged them to assume new rhetorical roles as fundraisers, organizers, and spokespersons.

An ideology that conflated femininity and morality underpinned women's benevolent activities in the early nineteenth century. Lori Ginzberg suggests that whereas benevolence in the late nineteenth century was increasingly associated with controlling poor and vagrant populations, benevolence during the antebellum period was viewed as a "mission of moral regeneration."[25] Indeed, secular-social concerns often overlapped with religious endeavors because of the belief that social change required moral transformation. Women's benevolent organizations, which were either tied to specific churches or ecumenical in nature, enabled women to safely exercise their intellectual and physical powers in the liminal space between the private and public spheres. Women's exclusion from formal leadership and administrative roles in churches also became a springboard for female benevolent associations. In fact, women's benevolent activities, which often addressed pressing social issues, provided women with a circuitous route to public reform and influence and in many instances served as precursors for public welfare systems.[26]

Although charitable societies initially included both male and female members, in the early nineteenth century, these societies emerged as a vehicle for women to band together and operate autonomously. Reports of new benevolent societies printed in the *CA* confirm a trend toward women establishing and running their own societies: two Female Missionary Societies were established in Clinton, Upper Canada; a Female Assistance Society was formed in Mississippi; a Female Methodist Tract Society in Homer, New York, attracted forty members; a Female Missionary Society with sixty members was organized on the Kent Circuit in the Philadelphia Conference; a new Dorcas Society was established by the women of Morristown, New Jersey; a newly established Female Missionary Society in Lynchburg, Virginia, attracted fifty members and contributions totaling one hundred dollars; and the new Roscoe Circuit in the Ohio Conference reported a new Female Missionary and Tract Society.[27]

Anne Firor Scott claims organizing as an essential strategy for women:

"In retrospect it is clear that such women, constrained by law and custom, and denied access to most of the major institutions by which the society governed itself and created its culture, used voluntary associations to evade some of the constraints to redefine 'woman's place' by giving the concept a public dimension."[28] This pattern is evident in antebellum benevolence endeavors. While women had always performed charitable acts, in the nineteenth century, women's charitable endeavors became more formally organized. Whereas men often had more authority to pursue charitable endeavors individually, women increasingly acted collectively. Women, who constituted the majority of most church congregations, also considered charity a Christian responsibility; Dorcas and Mite societies even drew their names from examples of women's charity in the Bible. Other societies appearing in the *CA* included cent societies, widows' and children's aid societies, Bible and tract societies, Sunday School unions, and missionary societies. Most of these local societies were auxiliary members of larger organizations overseen by the Methodist church or other religious institutions.

Until 1835, almost all women's associations were allied with churches, and denominational organizing continued as the most common form of women's grassroots organization throughout the nineteenth century.[29] This fact underscores how the church served as a primary site and sponsor for women's rhetorical development during the nineteenth century. While general oversight usually rested in the hands of clergy or prominent laymen, women overwhelmingly provided the labor. Articles and reports published in the *CA* often depicted women as the primary foot soldiers in charitable endeavors, including distributing moral reading material.[30] An article titled "Utility of Tracts," composed of extracts from the annual report of the American Tract Society, offered several anecdotes of women as participants. A report from the Brooklyn Female Tract Society noted its members had distributed eight thousand tracts the previous year.[31] Additionally, a treasurer's report from the New York Missionary, Tract, Bible and Sunday School Society provides a list of debits and credits with the accompanying explanation for the group's credits, "The above sums were collected principally by females, who visit every house in the place for that purpose."[32]

Collecting donations door-to-door, making poor visits, and distributing tracts—often in taverns, at seaports, or in poor neighborhoods—allowed women to traverse between private/public and class boundaries in order to observe social problems firsthand. For instance, the annual report submitted by the New York Female Assistance Society for the Relief and Religious Instruction of Sick Poor Women and Children noted that the society's female managers had made 716 visits, during which "disease of every name has met their eye." A report from the Female Benevolent Society also described its mission to reclaim prostitutes in New York.[33] Working in these types of disreputable and depressed areas required women to become persuasive spokespersons and tenacious religious advocates.

Women's passionate embrace of missions and other "good works" perpetuated a growing belief that charity was women's work in much the same way that women's overwhelming majority in the church had given rise to the perception of religion as a more "naturally" feminine quality.[34] This view is evident in a letter to the editor titled "Our Finances in England and America," in which the author compared England's and America's commitment to missions. Arguing that Americans needed to increase their missions' efforts, the author pointed to females as the primary group that should pursue this work. "It seems to have entered the minds of but few, that the main business of the preachers as to these matters is to set our members to work, especially our female members. O! what a commanding influence have these women over society, if they could but be brought to exert it here as they do in England."[35]

Benevolent endeavors, which were initially undertaken by both men and women, were increasingly placed under women's purview. The feminization of benevolent efforts ultimately reduced the status of the work. This trend mirrors what Barbara Reskin and Patricia Roos have termed the "feminization of occupations" occurring in the late nineteenth and early twentieth centuries. As women increasingly dominated jobs such as clerical workers, telegraph and telephone operators, food-service waiting staff, public school teachers, and bank tellers, both the prestige and pay for these positions decreased.[36] Women themselves often contributed to this reduced status by characterizing their benevolent endeavors as merely an extension of women's domestic maternal, moral, and religious roles rather than a means of activism and advocacy. For instance, in her *Treatise on Domestic Economy*, Catharine Beecher, retraced the public/private boundary, claiming, "In civil and political affairs, American women take no interest or concern, except so far as they sympathize with their family or personal friends." Conversely, she asserted, "In matters pertaining to the education of their children, in the selection and support of a clergyman, in all benevolent enterprises, and in all questions relating to morals or manners, they have superior influence."[37] Hence, Beecher located women's benevolent endeavors in the domestic sphere.

Through their efforts to help indigent women, distribute tracts, and collect money for missions, Beecher argued that women were merely acting in their appointed roles as mothers and moral guardians for society. Minimizing the boldness of these efforts can also be viewed as a strategy used by women to ensure that their actions remained socially acceptable. Nan Johnson has examined rhetorical tactics used by female reformers in the latter half of the nineteenth century, and labeled this "the eloquent mother trope." Johnson writes, "By capitalizing on rather than resisting cultural norms about women's roles, [Frances] Willard, [Elizabeth Cady] Stanton, and others shaped a subtle refutation to the cultural arguments that public rhetorical activity by women contradicted their natures as wives and mothers."[38] Such rhetorical tactics highlight an important distinction between image and reality. As women stepped beyond their prescribed roles, they needed to maintain an acceptable image—even if that image did not necessarily mesh with reality. Indeed, the roles women assumed outside the domestic sphere had little resemblance to the motherly roles prescribed to them in the Ladies' Department and the rest of the domestic canon. Managing benevolent organizations offered women a respectable means for gaining business skills such as neighborhood canvassing, grassroots organization, compiling minutes, submitting reports, fundraising, expenditure, and keeping financial accounts. Although the women who worked in benevolent organizations often acquired and exercised many of the same skills that men used in the marketplace, the embedded and pervasive nature of separate spheres caused the business side of women's benevolence to be often ignored.[39]

Many of these business skills can be extrapolated from reports printed in the *CA*. For instance, the annual report submitted by Mary Wharton, the corresponding secretary of the Union Female Missionary Society in Philadelphia, outlined the addition of 119 members and receipts of $447.61, "of which sum $200 have been paid to the treasurer of the parent society, $10 for printing the report, and $1.95 for incidental expenses—leaving a balance in the treasury of $235.66."[40] The skills required to organize and run benevolent societies were new to women, so women often educated each other, which is apparent in the first annual report submitted by the Allen Street Methodist Church Dorcas Society in New York City: "At our first formation, although kindly aided by a committee from the John Street [Methodist church] Dorcas Society, for whose counsel and assistance we are under great obligations, yet by reason of our own inexperience, we are slow in becoming acquainted with our duties, and a great portion of the year was employed before we became fully organized."[41]

Similarly concealed was the acceptable channel benevolent societies provided for women to learn and begin exercising untapped leadership and rhetorical skills.[42] The Methodist church appears to have perceived some benefit in forming separate male and female missions' societies. In a report to the corresponding secretary of the Tract Society of the Methodist Episcopal Church, Elias Crawford admitted that when "numbers are not sufficient in one place to form male and female societies separately, we connect both together, by electing our managers from both sexes," which suggests that separate societies were preferable.[43] Women likely felt more comfortable actively participating in separate societies; this gendered space enabled women to act freely while maintaining social propriety.[44] In societies with both male and female members, even when equal numbers of male and female managers were appointed, the offices of president, vice president, secretary, and treasurer were almost always occupied by male members. Conversely, in female societies, women were in charge and they began to assume leadership and managerial roles that were rarely accorded to women in public society. A report from the New York Female Assistance Society submitted by their treasurer, Maria Harper, listed the group's transactions for the year as well as the names of female officers and managers. Similarly, the report on the annual meeting of the Asbury Female Mite Society listed its female officers and reported that $230 was collected the previous year.[45] In the early nineteenth century, seeing women recognized as organizational officers was a relatively new experience for male and female *CA* readers.

In addition to acquiring financial, organizational, and leadership skills, women also began to exercise rhetorical skills nationally by submitting reports for publication in the widely circulated *CA*. In her study of nineteenth-century temperance women, Carol Mattingly notes that despite women's lack of rhetorical training, they exhibited a keen sense of their language use, cultural context, purpose, and audience.[46] This type of rhetorical *facilitas* is evident in the reports submitted to the *CA* by women's benevolent organizations. Organizations strategically used their reports to reveal social issues, encourage support, and even condemn apathy among church members. Evident in these appeals is women's careful consideration of purpose, audience, and context, as well as the way they grounded their words in Scripture to establish *ethos* and religious authority. A letter to the Baltimore Conference from Mary Hewitt on behalf of the Female Preacher's Aid Society discussed the plight of preachers who were no longer able to work. Hewitt wrote, "the Methodists love their preachers too well to see them suffer, if they are only made acquainted with their situation."[47] Hewitt's appeal, which employed the *pathos* of both sympathy and shame, recognized the *CA*'s Christian and overwhelmingly Methodist audience.

A report submitted to the *CA* by the Female Assistance Society similarly exhibited a keen sense of the *CA*'s audience. After presenting the details of several visits in which society members provided relief, comfort, and religious instruction, the society posed the rhetorical question, "Ye remember the words of the Lord Jesus. 'I was sick, and ye visited me, —inasmuch as ye have done it unto one of the least of these, ye have done it unto me.'" The society then asserted, "It may not be in the power of every one to visit the abodes of sickness and poverty, yet many are ready to say, 'send me.'"[48] Through its use of Scripture, the Female Assistance Society established its *ethos* and the propriety of its work by defining it as a Christian duty. The report seemingly intends to embolden readers, particularly women, to carry their spirituality into poor neighborhoods. The Female Benevolent Society in New York similarly used the *CA* to draw attention and donations to their efforts to save prostitutes. In announcing the formation of the Female Benevolent Society in New York, which helped establish an asylum to reclaim prostitutes, the six women on the executive committee penned and submitted the following urgent plea to the editors of the *CA*: "for the want of pecuniary means we have been obliged to refuse the benefits of the institution to more than twenty applicants within a few weeks, and must abandon the work unless sustained by the prayers and contributions of the pious and benevolent. . . . Let us rescue these cast-off daughters, and send joy and gladness through all circles of domestic misery created by this extensive evil. It is the command of our Lord that 'the Gospel should be preached to every creature,' and in their abodes of wretchedness they are entirely precluded from all means of grace."[49] These women subtly claimed their cause as one that "pious and benevolent" persons should support, again appealing to readers' Christian duty. This is especially amplified by the description of having to turn away sinners in search of redemption and their argument that every creature is worthy of grace. By aligning their efforts with Scripture and Christian duty, reports from women's benevolent organizations repeatedly justified their movement into areas and issues that might otherwise be deemed inappropriate for them.

The Society for the Relief of Poor Widows with Small Children is another example of women's savvy use of print to promote their cause. For instance, one of their reports emphasized the economic plight that women faced in the city, asserting:

> It has been alleged against societies of this nature, that they do but increase the number of the poor; and that if people are honest and industrious, they may always make a decent living in this happy land. There may be some truth in this assertion as it respects the other sex, for they are well paid for their labour: but what can a bereaved widow do with five or six little children, destitute of every means of support but what her own hand can furnish (which in a general way does not amount to more than 25 cents a day)? What can she do without some aid? Her children to provide for and keep decent, house rent to be paid, fuel, food and raiment to be procured.[50]

Rhetorically, this society's printed statements and actions condemned the inferior economic status to which women were relegated. Given visibility on the second page of the *CA*, alongside articles written by men, this female author attempted to dispel the assumption that the poor included only men who were unwilling to work. Exhibiting a measure of frustration, the author emphasized women's economic dependence with a series of rhetorical questions that stressed women's limited options for earning money and the paltry wages awarded for women's work. While some scholars have tried to draw distinctions between women's benevolent organizations and reform organizations, I do not believe such divisions are helpful.[51] These reports show the overlap between women's efforts to relieve suffering and women's efforts to change political and social systems. Other than poetry, benevolent society reports are the *CA* pieces most commonly written by women, which underscores the church's role as a rhetorical sponsor and the new rhetorical space and stature opened to women through their participation in benevolent societies and the publication and promotion of their efforts in the *CA*.

Benevolent organizations helped women redefine what Jacqueline Jones Royster terms their "notions about self-in-society" by adding new responsibilities and expanding their spheres of influence.[52] Participation in benevolent societies enabled women to earn and allocate money and to establish identities apart from their husbands outside of the domestic sphere. To men, good works were simply part of their larger careers, but for women, charitable endeavors offered occupations beyond their domestic duties. Indeed, many women cobbled together full-time benevolent careers, juggling their work as Sunday school teachers, church visitors, and members of multiple benevolent societies.

In submitting the articles of constitution for the newly formed Female Missionary Society in Paris Hill, New York, Lucy Richards, who was responsible for establishing the society and was elected president by its members, wrote, "I have often felt a desire that something should be done, but who should set about the work? I thought surely it did not belong to me, for neither my health nor abilities were sufficient. However, as the former gradually restoring, I was presented with a missionary report for the year 1827, upon the reading of which I felt my heart stirred within me to use what little influence I could."[53] This example demonstrates the way in which written texts could motivate female readers to action. Moving from her role as president of her local missionary society, Richards eventually became a missionary assistant, teaching Native American children at a mission school. She also traveled to local missionary societies to raise funds—often speaking before crowds of both men and women. In fact, excerpts from her speeches and from correspondence between Richards and local missionary societies appear in later issues of the *CA*.[54] Richards is just one example of how women's involvement in local benevolent organizations often served as a springboard into broader evangelical and social reform activities and expanded rhetorical responsibilities.

The formation of local missionary societies in the Methodist church reflects a broader trend. By 1828 there were 592 local women's auxiliary societies to the American Board of Commissioners for Foreign Missions.[55] So it is not surprising that missionaries as well as church leaders recognized women as an essential constituency in missions' efforts in foreign countries and among Native Americans. In fact, women's societies often maintained direct correspondence with missionaries in the field. The *CA* reprinted a letter from Mr. Bardwell, one of the missionaries of the American Board, to a Female Missionary Society in Middletown, Connecticut, in which he described a revival among the Choctaw people. Bardwell wrote: "All the former amusements have ceased; the Sabbath is almost universally regarded—people throng in multitudes to hear the word of God—and the domestic altar has been erected in most of the houses around us. The yell of the savage which used to salute our ears from every quarter, has given place to the songs of Zion. Indeed the change is so wonderful, so apparent, that we feel almost surrounded by a new race of beings."[56] In a sense, Bardwell's letter reports the "return on investment" to an important group of stakeholders. It also shows that through their contributions women moved into the problematic space of religious and cultural imperialism. Female missionary societies were complicit in the conflict, disruption, and decimation of Native American culture that resulted from government policies and religious missions' efforts. In his analysis of the Methodists' outreach to Native Americans, David Forbes stresses how religious missions generally spread the gospel and white American culture hand-in-hand. Thus, Christian conversion often entailed eliminating anything white Americans deemed "savage" such as tribal dress, language, and rituals.[57]

Through their support of foreign missions' efforts, women also expanded their worldviews but again became active participants in cultural imperialism. Frequently, women were rallied to foreign missionary causes with descriptions of women's treatment in non-Christian or "heathen" countries.[58] For instance, a report from the Oneida Conference Missionary Society made the following appeal to women, "After taking a view of the debased and servile state of females in heathen and savage countries, and after considering that you owe your elevation in society to the blessed influence of the gospel of Christ, can you withhold a helping hand in the promulgation of the gospel?" An article reprinted from the *Christian Register* titled "Heathen Cruelty" carried a similar message: "Let me remind females how much they owe in society to the diffusion of gospel light, and let me thereby attempt to stimulate them to employ their influence in diffusing its healing beams. Could you behold the cruel slavery and degradation of your sex in heathen nations, I should scarcely need any other argument with you."[59] The article later lists examples of mothers forced to destroy female infants in South America and widows in the East Indies being burned to ashes alongside their husbands' graves. As these appeals demonstrate, through their missions' efforts, women believed they were helping improve conditions for other women. Indeed, this type of religious feminism became a predominant appeal in the women's foreign mission movement. However, as Joan Jacobs Brumberg suggests in her study of missionary Ann Judson, this appeal became an impediment domestically. By celebrating all the religious, social, and educational freedoms that American women enjoyed, this message ultimately undercut American women's pursuit of equal rights.[60]

Nonetheless, the local women's missionary societies that flourished during the antebellum period also established a legacy of gendered mission work. Methodist women formed the Woman's Foreign Missionary Society in 1869 and the Woman's Home Missionary Society in 1880; both were autonomous organizations operating outside of the Methodist church's General Missionary Society, which gave women greater control. The Woman's Foreign Missionary Society eventually became the largest organization in the broader woman's foreign mission movement. By 1915, more than three million American women contributed membership dues to forty different denominational missionary societies—making the women's foreign mission movement by far the largest mass women's movement in the nineteenth and early twentieth centuries.[61]

This rich legacy of women's missions work can also be seen in the many roles women eagerly assumed in the antebellum Methodist church's key evangelical outposts—Sunday schools, rural and frontier churches, and domestic and international missions. During the first half of the nineteenth century, Methodist churches established thousands of Sunday schools in communities across the country. Methodists also dispatched itinerant ministers and their wives to rural and frontier regions of the country and established Christian missions and mission schools for Native Americans. The *CA* also reported the efforts of foreign missionaries and their wives stationed around the world. In many instances, women in these evangelical outposts were clearly stepping into public roles, yet because they were working under a religious mantle, they would have been perceived as operating in an acceptable and appropriate space. Hence, church work created an ever-widening liminal space that allowed women to assume roles far beyond the domestic sphere. However, just as women's roles as benefactors and benevolent organizers are often omitted or downplayed in discussions of women's rhetorical development and women's initial movement beyond the domestic sphere, so too are the various roles women assumed in antebellum church's evangelical outposts. These omissions are especially unfortunate considering the seriousness with which women pursued these occupations and the emphasis that antebellum churches placed on these evangelistic pursuits. Nevertheless, women's contributions to the Methodist church's evangelical outreach are revealed in the little narratives that appear in the pages of its national newspaper.

Working as Sunday school teachers to instill religious precepts into the tender minds of their community's children is a role that is frequently portrayed on the interior pages of the *CA*. An article titled "The Teacher in the Sabbath School"[62] depicts the common Sunday school practice of assigning students Bible verses to memorize. The student described recited a verse, "Remember now thy Creator in the days of thy youth . . . ,"[63] but was unable to explain its meaning. The teacher used this as a teaching moment. She provided her interpretation of the verse and then stressed the importance of understanding and applying these assigned Bible verses, rather than simply memorizing them. Reassuring her students while affirming the importance of their Sunday school lessons, the teacher explained: "If you endeavour to faithfully remember and practice the lessons we set before you, this little school may be to each of you, the door to heaven. Having 'remembered your Creator in the days of your youth,' he will never forget you. In this world he will be your support and your refuge, and when you stand, as we all shall, before the judgment seat of Christ, he will welcome you to his glorious home in the heavens." Later in the article, the author shared a conversation in which the teacher described her pedagogy: "My method necessarily takes time . . . ," she explained, "But I find reason every Sabbath to persevere in my plan, for I see it must be by 'line upon line, precept upon precept,' that these young minds can be enlightened." She stressed, "I am not anxious that *much* should be either read or acquired. I am anxious only that they should comprehend what I teach."[64] By stressing to her students that these Bible verses were far more than a rote exercise in memorization and by encouraging them to critically engage with Scripture, this teacher believed that she was not merely instructing her students but endeavoring to save their souls.

This was a common motive among Sunday school teachers. Based on her study of the American Sunday school movement, Anne Boylan confirms that single women were particularly drawn to the role of Sunday school teacher out of their desire for increased responsibility and spiritual commitment and individual identities apart from their families.[65] Teaching Sunday school was one of the first Christian programs and occupations receptive to women's services, and for some, teaching Sunday school served as preparation for their religious careers as writers, ministers' wives, or missionary teachers. In addition to enacting their evangelical beliefs, Sunday school teachers also helped execute an important church-building strategy. Antebellum churches considered Sunday schools a vital evangelical enterprise—making them nurseries of piety and morality for the benefit of church congregations and local communities. In the following article, submitted on behalf of the Methodist Episcopal Sunday School Association, J. W. Harper emphasized Sunday schools' role in the moral and religious welfare of antebellum America. He asserts:

> It is estimated that there are in the United States 300,000 children. To these it is reasonable to look to the future actors in the affairs of our country. When arrived to manhood they will be expected to take their stations in active life as the servants of the nation. But it must be recollected that a great number of these children are the offspring of poor, and in many cases profligate parents. The question arises by what means are they to be prevented from pursuing the course presented by their ungodly parents, and qualified to answer the demands and expectations of their country. It is the benevolent object of Sabbath schools to effect these ends by instilling into their young and tender minds the salutary precepts and sentiments of the gospel. In the majority of cases, it is doubtful whether the attendants in Sabbath schools would receive this instruction at home; but here they enjoy the most favourable opportunities for receiving it. Instead of spending their Sabbaths roaming the streets and engaging in crime and wickedness, they are led to the church by the hand and there instructed in those things that tend to their present and eternal happiness.[66]

As this article indicates, Sunday schools were not merely an evangelical enterprise, but also a republican one, which is interesting considering that Sunday schools were an English import.

In his study of the Sunday school movement in England from 1780 to 1980, Philip Cliff notes that Sunday schools had numerous forerunners, including catechism classes, charity schools, and individual efforts across England. However, he dates the movement's beginning at 1780, claiming that the expansive Sunday school movement was driven by two factors: the shift in population from rural areas to industrial centers and the loss of traditional means of religious socialization. One of the most visible results of these two factors was hordes of children left to roam and play in city streets on Sundays. In late eighteenth-century England, laboring class children helped support their families by working in factories, mines, and other industries six days a week. On Sundays, these children were often left on their own. Hence,

Sunday schools were initially advocated as a means of combating idleness, immorality, and ignorance among the poor laboring classes. From a religious viewpoint, these schools also enforced observance of the Sabbath.[67]

At Sunday schools, social control and literacy instruction were bound up in Christianity; children learned reading, writing,[68] and catechism, which included the Lord's Prayer, the Ten Commandments, and other tenets of faith. Because these schools combined basic education with spiritual, moral, and civic training, and because they did not interfere with the six-day workweek, British Sunday schools were endorsed and financially supported by city leaders, churches, and factory managers.

While Sunday schools were not a Methodist invention, Methodists in Britain and America quickly embraced them. Methodists had always encouraged the religious instruction of children. The Doctrines and Disciplines[69] adopted in 1785 by the newly formed American Methodist Episcopal Church instructed ministers to preach on education, pay special notice to children, pray for them, and, wherever possible, gather children together to teach them. That same year, Methodist layman William Elliot established one of the first American Sunday schools in his home in Bradford's Neck, Virginia, and later transferred the school to the local church.[70]

As free, local public schools increasingly became available in America between 1810 and 1830, Sunday schools shifted their focus primarily to religious instruction. Consequently, Sunday schools, which in some cases operated like para-churches, became an important vehicle for spreading evangelical Protestantism. In 1824, the Philadelphia Sunday and Adult School Union transformed itself into a national organization, the American Sunday School Union in order to formalize the process for establishing Sunday schools across the country and to supply Sunday school materials. Up to this point, local Sunday schools had been the impetus of individuals, churches, or communities, with local Sunday schools often serving entire communities regardless of denominational affiliation. However, with the shift in focus to religious instruction, Methodists began to view Sunday schools as an important part of the church's evangelical mission, and in 1827, the Methodists established their own centralized denominational Sunday school union. In part, the rationale for a denominational union was concern over Calvinist and other conflicting doctrines seeping into Sunday school classrooms through the publications produced by the American Sunday School Union. While the American Sunday School Union was established as an ecumenical organization, it was primarily managed by Presbyterians and Episcopalians.[71] Another likely motivation was the church's desire to produce its own Sunday school publications. Not only would this allow the church to control the doctrine contained in these publications, but also to expand its publishing domain. It is probably not a coincidence that Nathan Bangs, who oversaw the new Methodist Sunday School Union, also oversaw the Methodist Book Concern and edited the *CA*. In fact, with the establishment of the church's own Sunday school union, Bangs added a regular Sunday school column to the *CA*.

The goal of the Methodist Sunday School Union was to encourage local church congregations to form Sunday schools "to aid in the instruction of the rising generation, particularly in the knowledge of the Holy Scriptures, and in the service and worship of God."[72] Churches were careful to position Sunday schools as an extension of, not a replacement for, family religious instruction. While churches considered mothers in the home the primary religious instructor for their children, Sunday schools reached beyond church members to those children whose parents neglected their responsibility for religious instruction. In describing the benefits of Sunday schools, one *CA* article acknowledged, "These benefits, however, are not confined exclusively to the offspring of the poor and profligate. There are many parents who are qualified to instruct their children, but are not willing to become their teachers on the Sabbath."[73]

Ultimately, Sunday schools had an underlying missionary impulse that reflected changing views about childhood and adolescence. Boylan asserts, "No longer were they [children] considered capable merely of receiving religious information; they were candidates for evangelization, perhaps even conversion."[74] Additionally, the Methodist church's push to establish Sunday schools underscores what Gregory Schneider describes as a gradual shift from the religious socialization of adults to children.[75] Beyond Sunday schools, the strategic emphasis on indoctrinating children rather than adults is also evident in the expansion of mission schools for Native American children.

In the nineteenth century, churches began to believe that it was easier to mold the malleable minds and souls of children than to persuade willful adults. An unattributed Sunday school address reprinted in the *CA* espoused this view, claiming: "The astonishing pertinacity of young minds in retaining first impressions is a reason why the morality of the gospel should be first implanted there, that it may take deep root, and check the evil propensities of the heart, which are ever ready to spring up, and to prevent those evil habits which are perpetually forming and gaining strength when they are not counteracted by divine truth and instruction in righteousness."[76] At the same time that Methodist churches eagerly established Sunday schools, the church's traditional adult class meetings were falling by the wayside. In many places, class meeting attendance was no longer a requirement for church membership, and class meetings had ceased to operate as forums in which adult church members held each other accountable for religious practices such as prayer, fasting, Scripture reading, and family devotions.[77] Consequently, as Sunday school teachers, women became essential agents redirecting the church's evangelical and educational focus from adults to children. Whereas few women had been allowed to serve as class leaders for adults, women were enthusiastically welcomed as Sunday school teachers for children.

A Sunday school teacher's primary responsibility was imparting biblical literacy, which included learning the names of the books in the Bible, the order in which those books are arranged, foundational Bible stories, and acquiring a corpus of Bible verses. Along with Bible lessons, students were assigned verses to memorize. Both the lessons and memorization were intended to instill basic biblical knowledge and "biblical truths" and ultimately convert children.[78] The method appears to have worked; Sunday schools reported a striking number of conversions among their pupils, and stories of Sunday school conversions frequently appeared in the *CA*. For instance, a report from the Sabbath schools in Newark, New Jersey, lauded the religious zeal of its teachers and proudly noted "that several of the scholars give evidence of a change of heart." Similarly, the Gloucester, Massachusetts, Methodist Sunday School Society reported, "some of the children were awakened to a sense of sin" and "one has given evidence of conversion."[79]

Even though Sunday schools primarily pursued evangelical objectives, they manifested broader social effects as well. Because the Bible was a seminal text in both nineteenth-century sectarian and secular society, Sunday school teachers contributed to students' cultural literacy and transmitted social values such as self-discipline, orderliness, cleanliness, and benevolence, as well as honoring the biblical commandment to keep the Sabbath holy. In this sense, teaching Sunday school extended women's role beyond the private religious and moral inculcation of their own children to the public indoctrination of the children in their classes. Again, this shift is often characterized as merely an extension of women's maternal domestic roles. However, this characterization not only overlooks the spatial shift from private to public, but also the fact that Sunday school teachers were not always women and that teaching Sunday school required women to acquire and enact new rhetorical and pedagogical skills and, in some instances, supervisory responsibilities.

While depictions of Sunday school teachers almost always portray women, the *CA* tells a different story—depicting a fairly even split between male and female teachers. Reports from Sunday school unions across the country, which filled the *CA*, typically included the number of students, teachers, and even the cumulative number of Bible verses that students had memorized. For instance, a report from the McKendrean Female Sabbath School

Society of Baltimore announced that the society had five schools managed by thirteen superintendents, serving 531 students, who were taught by 90 teachers. It also proudly reported that in the past year, its scholars had recited 113,679 verses of Scripture, catechism, and divine songs.[80] Frequently, reports also provided a breakdown of the number of male and female teachers. For instance, a report from the large New York Sunday School Union reported that their combined schools had 10,116 pupils and 1,551 instructors, of which 794 were male and 757 were female.[81] Reports from seventeen smaller Sunday school unions published in the *CA*, which also provided a breakdown of male and female teachers, showed a cumulative total of 162 male teachers and 193 female teachers. These numbers illustrate that while teaching Sunday school was a role open to females, it was not solely considered women's work. Moreover, the equivalent numbers of male and female teachers negate the view that teaching Sunday school was merely an extension of women's domestic-sphere duties.

Whereas advice dispensed in the *CA*'s Ladies' Department presumed that religious instruction was an ingrained ability, teaching Sunday school required women to learn new rhetorical skills, such as preparing lessons, leading classes, and mentoring students in their spiritual growth. A *Sunday-School Teacher's Guide* published by the church in 1848 included an abridged teacher's manual, which in 130 pages copiously addressed subjects such as maintaining order, weekly assignments, planning, ascertaining students' character, gaining students' affections, promoting students' spiritual improvement, and visiting students' parents.[82]

Sunday school teachers even precipitated a pedagogical shift away from the random memorization of Bible verses. Heeding Sunday school teachers' advice, the Methodist church developed lesson schemes that provided selected verses for students to memorize and questions for teachers to ask. Interestingly, while the new lesson schemes provided the Bible verses and the questions, they did not provide the answers. Hence, these lessons required teachers and students to draw their answers from the memorized verse. Intended to motivate religious conversion, these verses and questions repeatedly emphasized the doctrines of sin, repentance, and regeneration. Consequently, teachers and students were not grappling with light matters in their Sunday school lessons, but serious spiritual matters and Methodist beliefs.[83]

Women's contributions to Sunday schools went beyond teaching. A report on the Trinity Church Sunday School noted that the school was organized and established by a group of women in 1825. These women, who felt "a deep interest in the welfare of the rising generation," decided to gather children in the surrounding area to offer them religious instruction. These women's efforts were supported by the Female Bible Society of Poughkeepsie, which donated six Bibles and several testaments to the new school.[84] In many cases, Sunday schools represented an extension of women's benevolent and organizational work. Moreover, Sunday schools often expanded the church's efforts to distribute Bibles and tracts by putting these materials in the hands of children who might otherwise not receive them. Additionally, the *CA* was filled with moving accounts of Sunday school pupils who became conduits for their parents' religious education and conversion. An article titled "A Monster of Wickedness Reclaimed" shares the story of a mother who initially sent her younger children to Sunday school simply to rid herself of them on the Sabbath, yet the Sunday school eventually drew both her and her husband to church.[85]

Through Sunday schools, women also assumed leadership roles as managers, directors, and superintendents. In reporting the opening of the Peekskill Sabbath School, Reverend L. Clark acknowledged: "I am greatly indebted to our sister Taylor, for the lively interest she has taken in the prosperity of the school. She is the superintendent of the girls, and indeed has the principal management of the affairs of the school. Some of the poorer children would not attend for the want of decent apparel; and she has kindly removed their objections by furnishing them with the clothing they need."[86] The report reflects the common practice of segregating Sunday schools by sex, then assigning female teachers to teach girls and female superintendents to manage female teachers. While women had opportunities to manage other women in Sunday schools, they were customarily placed in subordinate positions to men. Female teachers, even female superintendents, were usually subordinate to male teachers and male superintendents. Only when women ran their own Sunday schools, such as the McKendrean Female Sabbath School, did they garner full decision-making power.[87]

By 1844, 2,000 Sunday schools existed in the Methodist church, serving over 100,000 students, and the rapid expansion of Sunday schools ceased only when the church entered schism.[88] However, as the initial excitement of each new Sunday school abated, local Sunday school unions often faced an ongoing challenge of recruiting teachers. Increasingly, Sunday schools turned to single women and young male and female students in their own upper-level courses for new recruits. As a result, Sunday school teaching was increasingly viewed as a female occupation, even though this was not the case throughout much of the antebellum period.

Undoubtedly contributing to this view was the fact that teaching Sunday school, like other benevolent endeavors, was an occupation that women eagerly assumed. This is evident in a memoir honoring Mary Mitchell and Mary Ann Day, two teachers at the McKendrean Female Sabbath School. In describing Mitchell's devotion to teaching, the memoirist wrote, "in this work of faith and labour of love did our beloved sister enter, and with untiring patience continue, until she closed her eyes in death." Similarly, Day was memorialized as a "faithful Sabbath school teacher," whose "whole soul seemed to be interested in the spiritual improvement of the precious immortals committed to her care."[89] These teachers were hallowed for their contributions during their lives as well as the manner in which they died. In that sense, they resemble the laymen's memoirs in *Methodist Magazine*, which recognized men for occupations as class leaders and church trustees. Moreover, while teaching Sunday school was not solely a female pursuit, it had different implications for women. Sunday school teaching became liberating and ennobling work that enabled women to establish clearly defined social identities. As Sunday school teachers, women received recognition from their churches and communities for their religious and moral instruction as well as their leadership and organization. As a result of this movement outside of the domestic sphere, women shifted from private to public agents in their efforts to shape the next generation of Christians.

Working alongside their husbands to gain converts and expand Methodism's reach into rural and frontier regions, itinerant ministers' wives assumed roles in another of the church's strategic evangelical outposts. In the early nineteenth century, becoming the wife of an itinerant minister was viewed as a career choice for women. Assuming responsibilities beyond the commonly prescribed domestic duties, the wives of ministers often became assistants, helpmates, and partners in their husband's profession. For instance, Shuah Virgin's memoir depicted her as "a woman of great courage." The wife of Reverend Charles Virgin, Shuah was described as "an amiable and agreeable companion; such a one as her husband needed through the varied scenes of sacrifice and sufferings he was called to pass." Her memoir also recognized that "she was strongly attached to a missionary life, and would never listen to any thing about locating."[90] Indeed, Shuah Virgin was praised for her dedication to spreading the gospel alongside her husband. Unlike the wives lauded in the *CA*'s Ladies' Department, who were defined solely by their duties within the domestic sphere, descriptions of ministers' wives depicted women publicly ministering to believers beside their husbands in rural and frontier regions of America.

In *The Minister's Wife*, Leonard Sweet outlines four overlapping roles that ministers' wives typically assumed: Companion, a subservient wife who encouraged her husband; Sacrificer, a martyr figure who enabled her husband to pursue his calling by requiring little financial or emotional support and by assuming sole responsibility for their home and raising the family; Assistant, a wife who worked alongside her husband, assisting in his ministry; and Partner, a wife who developed and pursued her own ministry parallel to that of her husband's endeavors.[91] In memoirs printed in the *CA*, ministers' wives are repeatedly elegized for their roles as assistants and partners, which indicates that their roles were expanding in the early nineteenth century.

Because marriage and families were considered a distraction from a minister's higher calling, the first generation of Methodist itinerants in America usually remained single. Marriage was also impractical for these early itinerants because they could not support a family on their meager salaries or attend to a family while constantly traveling. Consequently, most itinerant ministers left the profession if they did marry. In the 1810s and 1820s, as Methodist congregations grew and prospered, views about marriage changed, and more itinerant ministers began to marry. Noting this shift in the perception of marriage, John Wigger suggests that unlike the pioneering first generation of itinerants, nineteenth-century Methodist ministers' attitudes toward families began to reflect those of average Americans.[92] Increasingly, clerical wives were perceived as an asset for ministers because of the preponderance of women in churches and the presumption that women were more spiritually inclined and attuned to the heartfelt religion espoused by Methodists.[93] For women committed to spreading the gospel, the dual role of wife/minister's assistant emerged as a coveted vocation, and choosing a mate became an important career decision for ministers and prospective wives. Reverend Herrick Eaton's *The Itinerant's Wife: Her Qualifications, Duties, Trials, and Rewards* (1851) as well as Mary Orne Tucker's *Itinerant Preaching in the Early Days of Methodism by a Pioneer Preacher's Wife* (1872) represent two attempts to outline the qualifications of an ideal minister's wife and dispel any romantic illusions held by prospective wives. These texts also cast the role of clerical wife as a demanding career that moved women into the public sphere.

Alongside their husbands, itinerant preachers' wives often endured tremendous hardship as a result of traveling, continually relocating, and living in remote areas. Similar to the epideictic memoirs written to honor itinerant ministers, the memoirs of ministers' wives printed in the *CA*'s back-page "Biographical Department" often recognized women for their sacrifices and devotion as well as their own efforts to spread the gospel. In their occupations in the church's evangelical outposts, women were recognized as instruments for the church and, like early itinerant ministers, many were celebrated as martyrs for their faith. According to her memoirist, Elizabeth Larkin, who lived with her husband Reverend Benjamin Larkin on the Ohio and Kentucky frontiers, shared both her husband's religious commitment and the toils, suffering, and privations he endured on the frontier. Her memoirist wrote that she "seems to have possessed a large share of the missionary spirit, and to have felt an ardent love for souls and an earnest desire for their salvation. She was diligent and persevering both in the public and private means of grace, in which she took great delight." Sarah's memoir also suggested that the fatigue and exposure she suffered while traveling with her husband likely laid the foundation for her early death. Similarly, accompanying her husband on his assignment to the northern New York district had a dire effect on Mary Ann Pier's health. Even though she was predisposed to consumption, her husband claimed, "She remonstrated against soliciting any alternation of my appointment on her account." Likely as a result, Mary Ann died seven years into their marriage at age twenty-seven. Laura Gary's memoir also noted "a willingness to endure many privations and sufferings to encourage and help her husband [Reverend Gray] in the great work in which he was engaged."[94]

Itinerant ministers' wives were repeatedly celebrated for their willingness to endure these difficult conditions and dissuade their husbands from permanently locating. For instance, Sarah Starr's memoirist claimed, "Instead of fettering him [Reverend William H. Starr] in the work, as some of her sex have done, she always held up his hand, and urged him forward."[95] The poem "The Methodist Minister's Wife to Her Husband," which appeared as a poetry selection on the *CA*'s back page, similarly praised the sacrifices of women married to itinerant clergy.

> The one dear thought that I am thine, can more than compensate
> For all I have resign'd for thee, ease, pleasure, friends, estate,
> And surely I have gain'd in rank, the chosen wife of one
> Commission'd from on high to preach redemption thro' the Son!
>
> True, I have left my father's smile, and O! all else above,
> The looks which beam'd on me will all a mother's sacred love
> A sister's depth of tenderness, a brother's fond regard.—
> And still I feel, to soothe thy lot, no sacrifice too hard![96]

As the poem indicates, ministers' wives were lauded for the sacrifices they willingly made. Also evident is the belief that being a minister's wife was a position—a *gain in rank*. Similar to the wives depicted in the Ladies' Department, ministers' wives were recognized for their efforts to sustain and encourage their husbands; in addition to that supportive role, they were recognized as an active part of the church's ministry, which extended their reach and influence. For example, in addition to acknowledging Sarah Starr's support, her memoirist also described her as "a valuable assistant in the ministry." Her memoirist noted her participation in class meetings and her work in Sunday schools. Moreover, she was said to be "profitable in prayer meetings; an active assistant in the altar, at camp meetings, and useful among mourners in Zion elsewhere."[97] Likewise, Sarah Henry was described as not only useful "in holding up her partner's hands, but in assisting in female prayer meetings; in labouring with mourners; in persuading persons who she saw affected, to go forward to the altar." Her memoirist asserted, "Never, it is thought, did a preacher's wife on that circuit secure to a greater extent, the confidence and affections of the people."[98]

In her study of itinerant ministers' wives on the trans-Mississippi frontier, Julie Roy Jeffrey also describes how ministers' wives struggled to balance their domestic and ministerial duties. Clerical wives were primarily responsible for establishing homes for their husbands and children, and with each new appointment, those homes moved. Hence, women had to maintain their roles as wives, mothers, and domestic managers along with their ministerial duties, which often included accompanying their husbands on pastoral visits, leading women's prayer and Bible groups, caring for sick and dying parishioners, assisting with camp meeting conversions, teaching in Sunday schools, and even fundraising.[99] Ultimately, ministers' wives offer insight into women's changing relationship with the domestic sphere. Instead of defining women, domestic duties became part of a tenuous balance that women continually negotiated as they assumed vocations beyond the domestic sphere. Unlike nineteenth-century men, who typically exchanged their responsibilities when they moved from the private to the public sphere, women assumed additional responsibilities. Enacting these expanded roles, ministers' wives were recognized as both wives and partners in ministry.

In recent years, scholars have begun to recover the powerful influence that many nineteenth-century women exerted in foreign and domestic missions. Missionary reports printed in the *CA* offer scant glimpses of women's contributions in missions abroad. For instance, three reports on American missionaries Adoniram and Ann Judson in Burma appeared in the *CA*. The first of these reports rejoiced in the receipt of communications from the couple after an anxious two-year silence. The next year, the newspaper included excerpts from "Mrs. Judson's Narrative of the sufferings and deliverance of the Missionaries in Ava." Initially printed in the *London Missionary Register,* the narrative outlined some of the trials the Judsons endured during the Burmese War. These trials included Adoniram's imprisonment as a suspected spy and Ann's efforts to gain his release. Of these and other efforts, the *Register*'s editor asserted the, "heroic fortitude evinced by Mrs. Judson at every new peril which threatened either her husband or herself, will give her name an immortality of the brightest luster." Stressing the importance of *their* mission, Mrs. Judson concluded the narrative by claiming, "Burmah will yet be given to Jesus for this inheritance! We shall have as many schools as we can support at Mergui or Tavoy, to which places the Burmese population are flocking in crowds." The final mention of Ann Judson appeared later that same year in the *CA*, announcing Mrs. Judson's death in late October 1826.[100] Even from these brief glimpses, Ann Judson's courage and evangelical commitment would be evident to *CA* readers. Moreover, in 1829, using personal journals and letters, James Knowles wrote the *Memoir of Mrs. Ann H. Judson*, which became a classic missionary biography and established Ann Judson as an inspirational model for future generations of female missionaries.

Drawing from Judson's memoir and letters Knowles's book shows how Judson established her own vision of the missionary wife vocation. Ann Judson was one of the first American females to pursue missionary work, traveling with her husband to Burma in 1813. Alongside her husband, she worked as a teacher, translator, and publicist. Susan Hill Lindley notes, "While Adoniram worked on a mammoth project of Bible translation and corresponded with the mission boards on official business, Ann fulfilled a direct missionary calling by writing short tracts and catechisms and teaching the women. She also wrote letters home to be published in missionary journals, which had enormous influence."[101] Joan Jacobs Brumberg suggests that it was Ann who captured readers' imagination. Whereas her husband's correspondence addressed methodological questions and other logistic concerns, Ann's letters were more emotional, describing their personal struggles as well as describing the Burmese people and their culture. In this sense, Judson pioneered women missionaries' use of print to garner support at home, which would become an essential component of the women's foreign mission movement.[102]

American churches began dispatching missionaries to foreign lands in 1813 when the American Board for Foreign Missions was founded by the Congregationalist, Presbyterian, and Dutch Reformed Churches. The American Board for Foreign Missions recruited missionaries and supported their efforts through finances, supplies, and regular communications. In 1819, the Methodists established the Missionary and Bible Society of the Methodist Episcopal Church in America. The primary objective of that society was to supply Bibles and to better coordinate churches' missionary efforts throughout the United States.[103] Methodists maintained a domestic focus up until the mid-nineteenth century, claiming that the North American continent—particularly new territories, Canada, and Native American peoples—remained the church's primary missionary concerns. In essence, the church continued to view its own itinerant preachers as missionaries within America's expanding borders. The church also supported missions to slaves going back as far as 1808, and as the influx of immigrants increased, the church began to establish foreign language missions as well.[104]

In the second half of the nineteenth century, Methodists dramatically expanded their missions' efforts overseas. Contributing to this rapid growth was the Woman's Foreign Missionary Society of the Methodist Episcopal Church. By the end of the century, the Women's Foreign Missionary Society supported more than 150 foreign missionaries; 750 assistants, teachers, and Bible readers; 390 day schools; 50 boarding schools; 11 orphanages; 10 training schools; and 13 hospitals and dispensaries.[105] In the first half of the nineteenth century, women were seldom recognized as missionaries in their own right. Yet women married to missionaries frequently pursued missions (alongside or independent of their husbands) that were repeatedly sanctioned and publicized in print. For instance, a report from the Sandwich Island Mission reprinted from the *Missionary Herald* described the scope and effect of a female prayer meeting initiated by the women at the mission. The meeting eventually grew so large that it was organized into thirty classes led by thirty native leaders under the direction of three missionary wives, Mrs. Bingham, Mrs. Clark, and Mrs. Chamberlain.[106] Women also appeared in missionary reports as housekeepers, teachers, and leaders of women's Bible studies, but these women were seldom recognized as missionaries. Highlighting this reluctance, a report on the missions' efforts of the United Brethren noted that at the close of 1825 the church had thirty-eight stations staffed by "one hundred and eighty-seven missionaries, including females."[107] The language used in the report seems to indicate that these women are missionaries, yet the need to clarify women's inclusion in that total number suggests that missionaries were assumed to be male. Conversely, an 1830 report from the American Board of Foreign Missions clearly designated women as missionary assistants. Of its 44 mission stations, including missions among North American Indians, the board reported having 46 ordained missionaries, 5 licensed preachers, 3 catechists, 171 missionary assistants (47 men and 124 women), 41 native assistants, and 600 native teachers.[108] As these categorizations indicate, some of the confusion may be due to the fact that missionaries were often ordained or licensed ministers—two positions that were not open to most antebellum women. Also, this report shows that the role of missionary assistant was predominately filled by women. Because single women who pursued mission work usually did so under the auspices of a male missionary, they were considered missionary assistants, although many performed the same work as their male counterparts.

The narrative of Eliza Barnes, gleaned from reports of the Methodist church's expanding mission efforts among native peoples in Upper Canada, provides insight into the variety of roles women performed in the church's North American missions. One article reprinted from the *Zion's Herald* depicted Barnes as a teacher. According to the article, two schools for native children in Upper Canada were established, one headed by Barnes and another by a Miss Hubbard. The author reported, "Both [women] are in health and are delighted with their task of training their increasing charge in the ways of piety and industry." Almost two years later, Barnes appeared again. An update from the Upper Canada Indian Mission reported, "Our sisters E. Barnes and Phebe Edmunds arrived . . . Miss Barnes brought with her many things for the convenience of the house and families in these new missions in this wilderness, which are much wanted, and will be of great use. I pray God the donor may not lose their reward." In this instance, Barnes appears to have assumed the role of managing the care and provisions for new mission houses. This role was also suggested in a letter from William Case (the superintendent of the Upper Canada Indian Missions) to Barnes, in which he reported on the state of the mission house and school at the Snake's Island Mission. Case wrote, "At Snakes Island we found the mission house and school house in good order. Every thing was neat and clean. Sister Crane, daughter of brother Snake, keeps the house nicely."[109]

Other articles suggest that Barnes was dispatched to the United States to raise funds and material donations for the Upper Canada Mission. In one letter, Case updated Barnes on the mission work and then made a request: "Wherever you can obtain cash turn your attention to that subject. Boxes are liable to delay. Besides, they are expensive and difficult to get to the stations. You will however, not refuse the offers of clothing. You will not forward any more old books. We don't need these, as we have many now on hand, and we don't wish to pay out money for the freight of articles which we don't at present need. Maps, books, and pictures for the infant schools will be highly acceptable." An earlier report from Case warned that without additional funds, the Upper Canada Mission would be unable to maintain its sixteen schools, which served four hundred students. A report from the anniversary meeting of the John Street Dorcas Society also noted a presentation by Barnes, who was described as a "teacher of the Canada mission schools." According to the article, Barnes discussed several mission stations in Upper Canada with which she was connected, noting the progress at Grape Island, Rice Lake, Lake Simcoe, Yellow Head's Island, and Snake Island. In describing Barnes's presentation, the author of the article claimed, "there was so much simplicity and artlessness, so much fervency and feeling derived from the relation of circumstances occurring under her own observation, and withal so much touching incident that the congregation paid to the tribute of many tears, which flowed from eyes unused to weeping." Barnes collected $167 and several gold rings, and received an additional $100 donation from the women's society. The group's secretary wrote, "this is but a small portion of our heart's desire toward them, yet we understand from our beloved sister Barnes that it will be thankfully received."[110]

It is evident that Barnes was well-versed in the progress of the Upper Canada Mission and that she was a confident and persuasive public speaker. She had previously preached in both America and Canada, although she was best known for her missionary work in Upper Canada and eventually became a missionary wife when she married William Case. From these different glimpses, it is apparent that Eliza Barnes, and certainly other women who entered public missions work, juggled many different responsibilities, including teacher, property manager, public speaker, and fundraiser—all of which expanded their rhetorical influence. Indeed, according to record books, journals, and newspaper accounts, Eliza Barnes was one of twenty-five women who in the 1820s and 1830s held leadership positions in the Methodist Indian Missions in Upper Canada.[111] Moreover, Barnes offers insight into the limited avenue available for antebellum women to channel their religious zeal and rhetorical talents. Catherine Brekus asserts that while it is impossible to ascertain exactly why Eliza Barnes gave up preaching to pursue missionary work, the desire to "appear more respectable" was a likely motive. Even though she continued to preach informally as a missionary teacher, missionary assistant, and missionary wife, in those roles she was widely accepted and praised rather than rejected or ridiculed.[112]

The Methodist church and its national newspaper served as important rhetorical spaces for antebellum women because they provided safe borderlands where women could step beyond the domestic sphere and begin blurring private and public boundaries. At the same time that the *CA* continued the practice of depicting women as pious models, it also showed women actively raising money for benevolent causes, forming charitable organizations, volunteering as Sunday school teachers, working alongside their minister and missionary husbands, or entering mission fieldwork as missionary teachers and assistants. These are all roles that women assumed outside of the margins prescribed by the *CA*'s Ladies' Department, and as such, chart women's initial steps outside of the domestic sphere. These little narratives also depict women's expanding rhetorical boundaries and the broader roles for women that were sanctioned and communicated to the newspaper's national audience. While women's participation in these benevolent and evangelical endeavors did not transform them into ardent feminists, historian Patricia Hill suggests that these activities "served as a bridge between the domestic sphere and the male-dominated arena of public life." Moreover, she argues, that although women initially pursued occupations that aligned with their notions of women's talents, "crossing that bridge eventually changed women's estimation of themselves and their capabilities."[113]

That said, the wide and varying assortment of women's rhetorical roles in the antebellum Methodist church suggests that we should resist the temptation to cast women's expanding rhetorical roles as a direct evolutionary march. These little narratives, which reveal women's rhetorical development and influence in the antebellum Methodist church, are more accurately read as disparate leaps. This may explain why the church is often overlooked as an essential rhetorical site for women in antebellum America. Additionally, because many of the social, benevolent, and educational roles women assumed were later relegated to "women's work," they are often dismissed or ignored in contemporary mappings of American women's rhetorical history. By contemporary measurements, the steps women took—carrying collection boxes door-to-door, establishing local benevolent organizations, teaching Sunday school, assisting their minister husbands, and working in domestic or foreign missions—may appear small if not insignificant, yet they laid the groundwork for the next generation of female social reformers, temperance workers, and foreign missionaries. Women's endeavors beyond the domestic sphere also demonstrate women's eagerness to band together; their desire to actively address religious and social needs; and their growing awareness of economic, social, and cultural issues. In many instances, this work enhanced women's rhetorical talents and began to alter their conceptions of themselves and their roles in society. Ultimately, if remapping women's rhetorical history is critical to constructing a more accurate legacy, then it is important to examine the ways in which women's expanding roles caused private and public borders to blur, and to recognize the church's role both containing and enabling, and ultimately publicizing women's movement between those spheres.

CHAPTER FIVE

A Magazine of Their Own

How few parents feel the same degree of solicitude for their
daughters to be deeply learned that they cherish for their sons.
—Mrs. Dumont, *Ladies' Repository*, 1845

In her essay titled "Female Training," initially read before a college for
teachers and later reprinted in the Methodist church's *Ladies' Repository* (*LR*), Mrs. Dumont acknowledged the persistent bias against female
education. She asserted that while the "day of woman's proscriptive seclu-
sion from the advantages of intellectual culture has but recently gone by . . .
the prejudices existing against female erudition—I should rather say against
a learned female—no longer an *opinion* indeed, but a *feeling*, is yet floating
among us."[1] Dumont argued against the pervasive sentiment that education
detracts from women's graces, instead claiming that women, like men, are err-
ing mortals in need of the strength of reason, purpose, direction, and discipline derived from intellectual application. Ultimately, she insisted that public
views about women's education and educated women must change. In doing
so, she indicted several influences she believed were propagating this preju-
dice. Included among this list was women's periodical literature, which is a
little surprising considering that this list, and Dumont's essay for that matter,
appeared in a women's periodical. Then again, the inclusion of Dumont's article in the *LR* highlights the magazine's distinct nature.

The early nineteenth century marked an unprecedented flourish of texts
directed at women. Hundreds of women's magazines were launched, and popular fiction, especially romances and melodramatic novels, were aggressively

marketed to women. Debates ensued over what constituted proper reading for ladies, since texts were imputed with the power to both convert and corrupt. Indeed, throughout the nineteenth century, evangelicals worried about the consumption of "pernicious" reading. Moreover, the question of "what should women read?" was tied to women's appropriate roles and the education women needed to adequately perform those roles.

With its introduction in 1841, *The Ladies' Repository and Gatherings of the West* entered the fray over women's intellectual development. Based on her examination of early American women's magazines and their audiences, Amy Beth Aronson claims, "By the 1820s, women's magazines appeared in virtually every city or town large enough to have a printing press," making them a staple in the industry long before they became a conduit for advertising.[2] Women's magazines confirmed and nurtured a distinct female audience and often provided an outlet for female editors and writers. Consequently, Mary Ellen Zuckerman identifies women's magazines as important cultural artifacts that tell us about the construction of gender in American society. Based on her study of women's magazines from the late eighteenth century to the late twentieth century, Zuckerman claims, "Topics discussed, images displayed, activities presented all affected women's perceptions of themselves, their possibilities and the world."[3]

Produced by the Methodist Western Book Concern, the *LR* emerged amid Methodism's rapid growth and westward expansion. Located in Cincinnati on the banks of the Ohio River, initially, the Western Book Concern simply acted as a depository for Methodist publications produced in New York. But Cincinnati quickly became a center for trade and midwestern states sought their own media outlets. The *LR* was a professionally published monthly that continued for thirty-five years. With paid subscriptions reaching a peak of more than forty thousand by the eve of the Civil War, the *LR* became the second-largest Methodist publication, one of the most widely circulated midwestern magazines, and one of the most popular women's periodicals in the country.[4] According to Frederick Norwood, "It expressed the democratic spirit of the West, which encouraged women to play a more active role" in church and society.[5]

Printed on large octavo pages, the *LR* was initially thirty-two pages, but increased to sixty-four pages during its heyday in the 1850s and, by the time of its demise, had expanded to ninety-six pages. Quality steel engravings were a special feature of the magazine. These usually illustrated landscapes or portraits of individuals such as eminent Methodist preachers. A series of portraits featuring literary women appeared in the 1850s. These included Sarah Hale, Alice Cary, Harriet Beecher Stowe, and Lydia Sigourney, whose engraving was considered scandalous for showing the poet wearing short sleeves. Responding to these comments, the exasperated *LR* editor wrote: "We were just about doing as we promised [providing a true likeness] when a severely Puritanical friend inquired of us, 'Why did you not have Mrs. Sigourney taken with long sleeves?' We answered, 'Simply for the reason that she did not have long sleeves on when she was taken.' We sought not a Quaker, not a Presbyterian, nor a Methodist portrait; but a portrait just such as would give a fair and truthful representation of the original."[6] This exchange is emblematic of the magazine's approach toward women. While acknowledging traditional views, *LR* editors often lobbied for society—and women themselves—to move beyond their traditional "long-sleeved" prescriptions.

Affirming the need for Methodist women to have a magazine of their own, Reverend J. S. Tomlinson of Augusta College asserted, "I have long felt that the amount of reading matter included in the 'Ladies' Departments' of our [Methodist] periodicals, was altogether inadequate to the just and reasonable wants of that interesting class of our readers."[7] Ranging in price from $2 to $3.50 during its circulation, the magazine was targeted primarily to white, middle-class readers. Frank Mott's *A History of American Magazines*, notes that the *LR* was well-written and contained nearly all original material, although most of its contributors were not well known.[8] Methodist ministers as well as the presidents and professors of western colleges contributed numerous articles. Female contributors included western writers Alice and Phoebe Cary, Julia Dumont, and Frances Gage. New Englander Lydia Sigourney also contributed to the *LR* as well as Frances Willard, who in the 1870s was also briefly considered as a possible candidate for the magazine's editorship. In fact, she was the only woman ever considered for the post. Like the editors of *Methodist Magazine* (*MM*) and the *Christian Advocate* (*CA*), editorship of the *LR* was considered an important position, one reserved for Methodist ministers. Indeed, four of the magazine's eight editors were later appointed as Methodist bishops.

The *LR* was intended to be the Methodist church's version of *Godey's Lady's Book*, which was the most popular women's magazine of the era. Early American women's magazines, such as *Godey's*, generally included etiquette, conduct advice, sentimental fiction, and fashion, most notably the *Godey's* fashion plates.[9] Consequently, by creating its own competing women's magazine, the church recognized women readers as a valuable audience and offered them an alternative to popular secular magazines full of fashion and sentimental tales. In their extensive reference of nineteenth- and twentieth-century women's periodicals in the United States, Kathleen Endres and Therese Lueck assert, "While competing in eye appeal with *Godey's* the magazine had different editorial intentions. Instead of teaching women to dance, sing, and flirt, the *Repository* contained earnest essays of a moral nature, poetry, articles on historical and scientific affairs, and book reviews." In fact, for many years the *LR* editors did not accept fiction.[10]

In the first issue of the *LR*, editor Reverend L. L. Hamline outlined the magazine's purpose, "to promote the healthful cultivation of the female mind, and draw it from trifles into its appropriate sphere of privilege." According to Hamline, this "sphere of privilege" would focus women's minds on more serious matters of virtue and morality. While this seems to echo the general domestic canon advice dispensed twenty years earlier in the *CA*'s Ladies' Department column, closer inspection shows Hamline encouraging women to move beyond reading for amusement and domestic advice. He warned women in the habit of reading these "lighter works of taste" that unless they are "willing to resign the luxury of being 'beguiled,'" they will not be able to read the *LR* with "pleasure" or "patience." The more substantive nature of the content is evident in the magazine's introductory issue, which included articles titled: "Reading," "Physical Science," "Female Education," and "Self-Cultivation." Eighteen pages of this first thirty-two-page issue were broadly devoted to women's intellectual development. Consequently, these contents, which envision an intellectual sphere for women, vary distinctly from the subjects addressed in the *CA*'s Ladies' Department.[11]

In his own introductory article titled "Reading," Hamline implored women to "cultivate a taste for books." Railing against novels, the editor challenged his female readers to turn their attention to loftier matters than sentiment and romance. Subtly arguing for a shift in female priorities, he remarked that "the cost of a silk dress or a fashionable bonnet will purchase a decent library," which he suggested should include collections of poetry, biographies, works on science, and sermons. Furthermore, Hamline asked, "Whose husband will not buy his wife a book, when she furnishes the proper evidence that she wants a good book . . . she who can say, '*mine will not*,' has made a poor choice of matrimony." Situating this advice in a church periodical, the editor drew on both institutional and ministerial ethoses to cede agency to women and deliver guidance to men.[12]

Hamline's article also addressed the connection between education and piety. In a reiteration of republican motherhood, he suggested that women should equip their minds for Christian duty—particularly preparing the next generation of Christians. In essence, the *LR* professed that an educated woman would be a more pious woman. Yet the magazine suggested that piety did not simply come from reading religious works. In both its editorial comments and selected contents, the *LR* promoted a more rigorous edification for women and directed their attention to spheres beyond the home, the parlor, and even the church. Indeed, the article immediately following Hamline's discussion of reading introduced an instructive series on the branches of physical science written by Professor Merrick of the University of Ohio. By broadening women's reading selections and base of knowledge, the male ministers and academics contributing to the *LR* believed they were building character. Moreover, they believed an educated woman was less likely to be corrupted, and they considered the world of intellect much closer to God than the world of fashion and frivolity.

The *LR*'s editorial comments and the magazine's content, especially during its early years of publication (1841–1850), helps forge a path for its female readers by acting as an agent, albeit an inadvertent one, in the nineteenth-century transition from the "true woman," who was relegated to the domestic sphere, to the "new woman," who began defining her own spheres of influence.[13] By advocating equal education for women and engaging them in discussions of science, philosophy, theology, and various intellectual debates of the era, the *LR* helped to redefine women's roles, even as it attempted to bolster traditional roles. In *Nineteenth-Century Women Learn to Write*, Catherine Hobbs claims that even education intended to prepare women for their separate sphere sometimes had unintended consequences; the changing patterns of literacy for nineteenth-century women offered more of those women the "prospect of wielding greater control over their lives by the century's end."[14]

The *LR* empowered and sponsored women's rhetorical development by encouraging them to develop their intellect and directing their attention toward broader concerns. By doing so, the *LR* marked a significant progression in the roles assumed by and ascribed to women in antebellum Methodist periodicals. With the 1841 introduction of the *LR*, women, whose roles were often hidden or obscured on the pages of Methodist periodicals, finally arrived on the title page. In *MM*, the church's first periodical initiated twenty-three years earlier, memoirs were the primary spaces women occupied. The *CA* created a column just for women; however, its Ladies' Department relegated women's concerns to the back page, and through its prescriptive advice contained women in the roles of subservient wives and dutiful mothers. Reports published in the *CA* also acknowledged women's roles as charitable benefactors, benevolent organizers, and instructors in the church's strategic Sunday school and missions movements. With the *LR*, the church undertook the task of preparing women for these public roles. By promoting an equal and more substantial education for women and by conceiving concerns appropriate to women far more broadly than other women's magazines of the era, the *LR* began opening more roles to women, which would further expand their rhetorical influence. Moreover, with its publication of the *LR*, the Methodist church recognized women as a valuable audience for which it was willing to compete. Methodists, who had long connected reading and salvation, were proponents of education and instrumental in establishing numerous seminaries and colleges. While women's education was a popular topic of discussion in ladies' periodicals, Caleb Atwater's tone and treatment of the topic in the first issue of *LR* is distinctive. Drawn from his *Essay on Education*, in the article titled, "Female Education," Atwater, an author and former government envoy, poses the biting rhetorical question, "Are our females to be mere kitchen maids, without a particle of information?" In the same stinging tone, he attacks the fashionable female education espoused by most women's academies and seminaries, inquiring: "If they are taught any thing more, shall it be only how to play the harp, the guitar, and the piano forte; to draw figures on paper or cloth with a painter's brush or a needle? To dance a waltz; walk gracefully on their toes; make a handsome curtsey; keep an album; sing a fashionable song; wear corsets, false curls and artificial flowers; hold a silly conversation on nothing; leer and look languishing; and—net the fool?" Atwater contends that a proper education for women would include the traditional subjects of reading, writing, English, grammar, and arithmetic, as well as geography, chemistry, botany, astronomy, algebra, rhetoric, philosophy, civil and ecclesiastical history, and the "lives of great, good and distinguished women." In this article, he also refutes common arguments against women's education, which include: education for women takes too much time and costs too much money; education makes women disagreeable companions; and education prevents women from attending to their domestic duties. Moreover, Atwater scolds male opponents, asserting, "pompous men, who fear women as their rivals in knowledge, prefer ignorant women, yet men of liberal minds and true politeness, enthusiastically prefer a learned woman as their wife, companion and friend, and for the mother of their children." The *LR* was not challenging society's conception of women's proper place. "Domestic life is her proper sphere," affirms Atwater, "it is there that she is most happy and useful." Yet, he promotes an intellectual education as better preparation for these traditional roles. Additionally, he claims that an educated woman will be more pious and less likely to be misled.[15]

Education was also a recurring topic of discussion in the *LR*'s rival, *Godey's Lady's Book*. Responding to a reader who complained about "harping on that same theme," Sarah Hale, the longtime editor of the magazine, outlined her belief that "the moral improvement of the world depends almost entirely on the kind of education which women receive and the way in which they use the influence it gives them." While *Godey's* also published articles written by men advocating women's education, Hale's own editorials in the 1841 issues of *Godey's* situate education as subordinate to domestic duties. At the same time that the *LR* purports education as the proper training for the domestic sphere, Hale focuses primarily on women's role within that sphere. It is a minor distinction, yet an important one. For example, in Hale's December 1841 editorial, she contends, "It is not the possession of erudite knowledge which women need to make her influence felt, and her character respected. It is the sincere love of truth, the taste for quiet and refined social enjoyments, and the power and disposition to promote the pure happiness of home." Hale considers the effective execution of a woman's role as wife and mother to be her source of influence and, thus, where she should devote her time. This is in stark contrast to the *LR*'s male editors and male and female contributors, who consider reading and intellectual development as essential avocations for women. In her May 1841 editorial, Hale condemns the pursuit of "outward adornments" as substitutes for intelligence and virtue, but her definition of a woman's cultivation is solely dependent upon a woman's domestic function. Hale writes, "The kind smile, the welcome greeting, the thoughtful care that has provided for the comfort of the beloved one, these are beauties of domestic cultivation, which make home and family paradise."[16] In fact, this mirrors the advice repeatedly delivered in the domestic canon and the *CA*'s Ladies' Department.

Hale also promotes a more utilitarian approach to education. Barbara Welter highlights *Godey's* emphasis on practical domestic education: "*Godey's* went so far as to suggest coyly, in 'Learning vs. Housewifery' that the two were complementary, not opposed: chemistry could be utilized in cooking, geometry in dividing cloth, and phrenology in discovering talent in children."[17] Indeed, Amy Beth Aronson suggests that during her forty-year stint at the helm of *Godey's*, "Hale became identified with the discourse of domesticity," which Aronson describes as "a set of beliefs about women that guaranteed great benefits to men."[18] Ultimately, by limiting education to domestic practicality, Hale seems to preclude the possibility of any role outside the domestic sphere, which is ironic, considering Hale's position as the magazine's paid editor. The *LR*'s editors, who were men and ministers, and *Godey's* own male contributors may have felt more confident advocating women's education than Hale. Whatever the case, by connecting piety and intellect as well as promoting reading and education as appropriate pursuits for women, the *LR* began to open the door to broader roles for women.

In numerous articles, the *LR* strongly advocated that girls should receive the same education as boys—whether that education was administered at home or in a private or public institution. Using the magazine as a bully pulpit, one *LR* editor declared, "we maintain that the intellect of woman is equal to that of man, and that the means of developing one are suitable to the evolution of the other." This view was fervently supported in earlier articles by ministers. Reverend J. Adams, for instance, began his article this way: "How great is the absurdity, and how pernicious the tendency of a belief in the intellectual inferiority of females." Similarly, Reverend S. Comfort strongly opposed those who would "wish to see the mind of *man* cultivated, expanded, and disciplined, and the mind of *woman* neglected, stinted, and undeveloped," asserting, "let both be improved with equal solicitude, and with equal pains." These ministers dismiss and even chastise what they deem as outdated notions of women's intellectual inferiority.[19]

Countless articles noted that women were fully capable of pursuing the same course of study as men but were denied that opportunity. In his report on "Female Education," Reverend Joseph McDowell Matthews, principal of the Oakland Female Seminary, avowed, "Let girls be sent to school under the same impression that they are expected to learn whatever their brothers learn." Matthews listed several examples of women who excelled in classics, languages, astronomy, and mathematics to demonstrate women's intellectual capability. Further bolstering his argument with religious support, Matthews claimed, "the possession of capacity is proof that it should be cultivated; for the great Author of being bestows no gift without an object and an aim."[20] The intent of these arguments was likely twofold: to embolden female readers in self-cultivation and to make them proponents of equal education for their daughters. Fathers and husbands may have been an intended secondary audience.

Education was also advocated as a means of disciplining the mind. One contributor argued that women should learn Greek instead of French because "the female mind will be better disciplined, and she prepared to be more eminently useful to the world." Likewise, the article "Hints of Education," by an unnamed physician, asserted, "Parents sometimes leave the minds of their daughters untutored and unstrengthened, and then wonder that they take pleasure only in novels, parties, dress. . . . Having no resources in themselves, they must seek amusement in the world."[21] This link drawn between education and discipline is closely aligned with another key argument for women's education promoted in the *LR*—the belief that intellect could strengthen a woman's religious conviction. Incorporating the popular nineteenth-century conception that women should serve as moral and religious arbiters for their families, *LR* contributors argued that a rigorous education, equivalent to the education men received, better prepared women for this role. For instance, in 1846, the *LR* editor declared, "Far be it from every man to let her angelic moral qualities lie buried in neglect. Let her soul be fully fed, her high capacities expanded. Let all influences of education be spent upon her faculties."[22] The insinuation that a woman has angelic moral qualities was not new; however, the advice that an exhaustive education would hone those qualities moves beyond the conception of women as mere angels and ornaments inside the domestic sphere. In an address presented to the students at the Oakland Female Seminary in Hillsborough, Ohio, which was reprinted on the first six pages of the *LR*, Samuel Galloway likewise claimed, "Another consideration in favor of a more rigorous female education was, *the influence which educated females may exert in creating and sustaining a purified public sentiment.*"[23] He further upheld that female influence "may and must, by education become the strongest palladium of the morals and institutions of our country." Again, these proponents of equal education for women were not advocating new or broader roles for women; they simply viewed education as a way to fortify women's moral and religious influence in their roles as wives, mothers, and parishioners. That said, when women began to receive the same education as men, many developed their own ideas about where and how they wanted to exert their influence.

The *LR* also encouraged women's education through its promotion and evaluation of female seminaries. Although schools for girls existed in colonial America, most of these were finishing schools. Female academies with curriculum comparable to men's colleges did not appear until the early nineteenth century, and these were rare. The first was the Troy Female Seminary, which Emma Willard opened in 1821. Two of Willard's protégés, Catharine Beecher and Mary Lyon, became advocates for women's education and established their own seminaries, the Harford Female Seminary in 1823 and Mount Holyoke in 1838. These three seminaries and others like them played an important role in promoting education for women and establishing teaching as a female profession. In her book *The Education of Women in the United States*, Averil Evans McClelland asserts, "More than the seminaries that taught 'frivolous' subjects, these schools advanced the idea that women were not intellectually inferior to men . . . that they could, and should, make significant contributions to the life of the community and society."[24] In 1841, the year that the first issue of the *LR* was published, three women graduated from Oberlin College, representing its first co-ed class. Yet fifteen years later, only 6 of the 250 colleges and universities in the United States admitted women.[25] Thus, throughout the antebellum period, female academies, seminaries, and private tutors remained women's main sources for advanced education.

Most women's seminaries also stressed religion and moral principles. Indeed, the majority of female seminaries were started and supported by churches.[26] In the nineteenth century, Methodist conferences, churches, ministers, and congregants established hundreds of female academies and seminaries across the country. Many of these were short-lived due to lack of funding or the expansion of public education. Others merged with men's colleges or became public institutions. Notably, the oldest college for women in the world is a Methodist college. Wesleyan College in Macon, Georgia, was established in 1836 as Georgia Female College and acquired by the Methodists in 1839. Through the efforts of local citizens and the Georgia Conference of the Methodist church, the college was created to provide women with a collegiate liberal arts education, and it continues that mission today.

In his extensive examination of women's education in the United States, Thomas Woody notes the growing interest in female education in the first half of the nineteenth century. He provides a long list of female seminaries established between 1830 and 1850 in Ohio, the home state of the *LR*.[27] Similarly, content inside the *LR* reflected this growing interest in female education. In an 1846 issue, the editor remarked, "There is no subject in which we take a livelier interest than that of female education . . . the Repository ought to be the first and most faithful patron of female education in this country." The editor invited schools to send catalogs and notices, so that the paper could help promote their institutions. The magazine's concern about female seminaries was also evident in an earlier issue when the editor bemoaned the lack of financial support provided to the Methodist Female Collegiate Institute in Cincinnati. The editor complained that the institute did not "attract much attention from the Churches which have called it into existence." His frustration was evident in his long series of rhetorical questions: "Do we originate schools merely to let them perish? . . . Do we expect that all that is needed to endow a seminary of learning is, to put a label upon a wall, and appoint a principal? . . . Do we intend to abandon our children to the Catholics?" In the last question, the editor alluded to a growing number of Catholic schools established in the West. In closing, he claimed, "our female seminaries are of at least as much importance as our institutions for the other sex."[28]

In addition to printing information about the instructors and curriculums of seminaries, particularly those in Ohio and Kentucky, the *LR* editor occasionally attended and reported on the oral examinations at these institutions. One such report described the final exercises administered at Oakland Female Seminary in Hillsborough, Ohio, in 1846. The editor noted the size of the audience present for the exams, remarking that the exercises "retained for three days the largest audience ever beheld at a similar festival." He went on to describe the way in which these public examinations were administered:

The classes were called out by the Principal to take their position, stand-ing on an elevation at one extremity of the house, and the teacher stood a little in the rear of the middle of the room. The teacher's voice was thus distinctly heard in every part, and the replies, so enunciated as to make the teacher hear them, were equally audible to every individual in the house . . . [the questions] exhausted every topic undertaken to be dis-cussed. When the teacher dismissed the class, it was evident that they had not only been over, but through the work. Thoroughness seemed to be the order of the day.[29]

These public examinations not only highlight one way that private seminar-ies were held accountable, but also one way that schools and female students could promote women's education. During these examinations, women were lauded for their learning and intellect. By attending and publishing favorable reports of these examinations, the *LR* assisted in sanctioning and promoting these seminaries and women's education overall.

The *LR*'s advice for women's education is particularly intriguing when placed within the context of American women's education in 1841. The de-bate over women's education continued throughout the nineteenth century, and a primary issue was not whether education was beneficial for women but how women's education would impact men. Even women's suffrage periodi-cals, the first of which began in 1849, initially presented a diversity of opinions on the purpose of female education, including traditional republican mother-hood, the cultivation of suitable companions for men, and self-fulfillment.[30] While the *LR* was by no means the first voice to promote women's intellectual development, it was situated in the early phase of this debate, particularly with regard to its push for women to receive an education equal to that of men.

The *LR* also encouraged women to enhance their understanding on a wide array of subjects through reading. In her article titled "Books Indispens-able," Caroline Burrough emphasized how reading can broaden an individu-al's worldviews. Aligning this benefit with Christian principles, she declared, "Reading enlarges our charity by showing us how other minds, other com-munities, other nations, have all and each some claim to our toleration; and that however different they be, there yet exists some sympathy, some common bond of humanity, which we should respect by that charity which 'believeth all things,' and 'hopeth all things.'"[31] Embedded in Burrough's comments are the ideas that women should have opinions about people and nations around the world, and that these should be formed through their own reading.

The magazine's contributors rarely promoted reading for pleasure. Instead, reading was almost always described as a "study," a means of "personal improvement," and even a "duty." For instance, in the November 1849 issue, the editor encouraged readers to acquire a "good store of books" for the long winter. He recommended an assortment of religious books, history, and "polite literature," noting that "all belles-lettres productions, if pure and moral, exert a peculiarly refining influence upon the soul." *LR* contributors repeatedly counseled readers on book selections. In a series of articles, Reverend A. Stevens encouraged readers to establish domestic libraries—offering guidance on location, contents, arrangement, and use.[32] Inherent throughout the *LR*'s ongoing discussion of reading is the power of written words and the desire to make women discriminating readers. Aronson identifies this as a common characteristic in many women's magazines. "The 'good woman' reader constructed by the early women's magazines was made to understand intimately where a text was taking her . . . she was charged with the responsibility *not* to be duped or led astray by anything she read."[33] The *LR* attempted to guide its female readers by including brief reviews along with notices of new books and periodicals. For example, in the *LR*'s book notice for a *Narrative of an Expedition to the Polar Sea*, the editor suggested that a "reader's geographical knowledge will be much improved by its perusal." Similarly, the *LR* recommended expository works such as the *Western Lancet*, a periodical on medical and surgical science, and *The Practical Manual of Elocution*. The *LR* also regularly promoted works by female authors, including *The Complete Works of Hannah More* and Phoebe Palmer's *Way to Holiness*. In fact, of Palmer, the editor stated, "she is among few who may safely be permitted to write and speak on the important and delicate subject which she has chosen." The editor was alluding to Palmer's discussion of sanctification, which was the sort of doctrinal subject customarily reserved for ministers' explications.[34]

Included alongside their recommendations, *LR* editors also issued stinging rebukes, such as the comments accompanying Eliza Farnham's *Life in the Prairie Land*: "What, now, could have induced a *lady* to write such a book . . . which no one of good taste can read without pain and disgust." Similarly, the *LR* suggested that *Captain O'Sullivan* and *Livonian Tales* were not intended for "a Christian people" and that *The Wandering Jew* "may just wander along, till he can find quarters."[35] All three of these books were published by Harper and Brothers, which enjoyed a close affiliation with the Methodists. In fact, the brothers who established the business in 1818 were devout Methodists and had initially conceived of their publishing as "a priestly calling to sanctify the world of print."[36] So, the editors' strong criticisms were likely directed at the publisher as well as the magazine's readers.

At the same time that the *LR* steered its readers to "appropriate" texts, the magazine espoused proper reading material through its own contents. While a thirty-two-page issue typically included numerous poetry selections, meditations, travel narratives, and editorials, the magazine also regularly featured a wide range of expository writing; excerpts from speeches; and theological, philosophical, historical, scientific, and political discussions. The April 1842 issue, for example, contained a theological discussion on prophecy, part of a continuing series on Greek history and classical writers, and a scientific discussion of metallurgy and its effects on civilization. Additionally, the magazine's editors used the "Editor's Table" column at the back of each issue to voice opinions on current events, address readers' letters, discuss submissions, announce changes to the magazine, and preview upcoming issues of the *LR*. The *LR*'s content often reflected the political and ideological views of the editors. Edward Thompson (1844–1846) and David Clark (1853–1863) were vocal antislavery advocates who often used the magazine as a bully pulpit. In an 1861 issue, Clark declared, "The Union ought to be preserved at any and every hazard. Peaceful secession is not possible." Further, he argued: "We have a right to demand that the African slave-trade—that most fiendish of all forms of piracy—shall not be reopened under the sanction of the stars and stripes. We have the right to demand that peaceful citizens shall be protected in the Territories. We have the right to demand that the United States Government shall be the friend of freedom and not the propagandist of slavery."[37] Editorial comments addressing political issues such as the slave trade, the status of territories, and secession—common in secular and even religious newspapers—were rare in popular women's magazines. Turning to *Godey's Lady's Book* during the Civil War years, Sarah Hale's Editor's Table seldom even acknowledged that a war was being waged by Americans on American soil.

Editorial comments such as those included in the *LR* implied that women should be politically aware and politically active. These were not comments they were reading in their fathers' or husbands' newspapers; these ardent political views were directed at them. *LR* editors clearly believed it was important to include their readers in political debates. They also attempted to keep their female readers up-to-date on current events through a series of different columns they initiated. In 1846, they began a column simply titled "Ladies' Repository," with the intent "to give our readers a general idea of the intellectual activity and various movements of the age in which they are living."[38] In 1849, the editors began a regular column called "The World in Miniature," which provided readers with a synopsis of the political situations in countries around the world. Similarly, in 1850, they initiated a column composed of domestic news briefs drawn from newspapers across the country. The *LR* envisioned broader social and political concerns for its female readers and attempted to intellectually equip them for those spheres.

The *LR* also provided a forum for its female readers to participate in current social and political discussions, thus increasing their voice in the public realm. The June 1845 issue of the *LR*, for instance, includes an essay written by a seventeen-year-old Cherokee girl, A. A. Ross, describing the government's despicable treatment of the Cherokee people. The essay, which was read as part of the examination exercises for Ross's school in New Jersey, argues against the conception of the Cherokee as savages. Ross wrote, "It was not perhaps, generally known in the United States to what extent the arts of civilization had been introduced among the Cherokees, or surely they would not thus have been hunted down like wild beasts." In her moving account of what would later come to be known as the Trail of Tears, Ross lamented: "No one but those who accompanied them can have a just conception of their sufferings, during their journey to the far-off region where they now wander unsheltered. The inclemency of the weather, and a prevailing epidemic, caused them to be much longer on the road than had been expected. Scarcely a day or night passed without the occurrence of one or more deaths."[39] In addition to the *LR*'s indictment of the perception and treatment of the Cherokee, by printing this essay, the magazine provided a public venue for a Cherokee voice. This same issue of the *LR* contained a letter titled "Woman's Rights," in which the female writer renounced women's exclusion from inheritance laws. Her caustic letter, which is ironically signed "Honey," protested, "It seems to me, notwithstanding the chivalry of the age, that it does not yet understand woman's rights. The men make all the laws and hence those of inheritance are partial."[40] The editors followed Honey's remarks by affirming, "Our correspondent is right," and declared that women are more than capable of managing complicated estates.

Increasingly, the *LR*'s Letters to the Editor section became an important forum for the magazine's readers. Joanna Bowen Gillespie's study of women's letters to the editor published in the *LR* confirms that the magazine opened an important avenue for ordinary women to comment on theological and intellectual debates and other areas typically considered male topics of discourse.[41] In one such letter, Ann M'Laughlin inquired about the etymology of the word "baptism," noting that some groups point to the Greek root of *baptism* as support for their argument that immersion is the only true form of baptism. In their two-page reply, the editors noted a variety of ways in which ancient Greeks, including Homer, used the words *baptizo* and *bapto*. Debates on immersion versus sprinkling as the proper means of baptism were frequently waged, especially between Methodists and Baptists—so the editors were clearly equipping their readers for denominational warfare.[42] Overall, this type of sanctioned and widely dispersed public forum that encouraged women's comments on these issues was rare for antebellum women.

The *LR* also gave voice to female writers. Women often made anonymous contributions or simply signed their first names, which was a common practice at the time. Consequently, it is impossible to track the number of female contributors. However, those pieces attributed to women primarily consisted of poetry, travel writing, and meditations or musings, although men regularly contributed poetry and religious meditations as well. The *LR* published work by writers such as Alice Cary and Lydia Sigourney, whose names are still recognizable today. It also published works by unknown writers as well as writers who would have been familiar to the magazine's readers. For instance, Miss De Forest, who had twenty-six poems and meditations published in the 1841–1846 issues, and Mrs. Gardiner, who had twenty-seven works published in the 1847–1850 issues, are two examples of prolific *LR* contributors.

Poetry had long been a genre accessible to women, and spurred by newspapers and magazines that published poetry and a reading public who voraciously consumed it, the number of women writing and publishing poetry in the nineteenth century grew dramatically. Most of these women poets have been forgotten and the poetry published in this era has been maligned or stigmatized by the terms "sentimental" or "female poetry." Indeed, Paula Bennett asserts, "No group of writers in United States literary history has been subject to more consistent denigration than nineteenth-century women, especially the poets."[43] In recent years, Bennett, Cheryl Walker, Janet Gray, and other scholars have focused on recovering nineteenth-century women's poetry.[44] While only a few women poets from this era are anthologized, studied, or taught today, Bennett encourages readers to examine nineteenth-century women's poetry collectively to appreciate the craft and creative expression that can be found even in the verses of unknown poets.[45] In recognizing poetry as one of the most popular genres written by female *LR* contributors, my intent is not to venture into literary criticism or aesthetic judgments. I am primarily interested in the ways the *LR*'s women contributors used poetry.

Excluded from the pulpit and church seminaries, women were deterred from writing sermons, treatises, and other theological genres. Consequently, women usually turned to socially acceptable genres for their theological expression. These included Sunday school materials, novels, and the emerging periodical press, which welcomed meditations, devotionals, and poetry. In the *LR*, women frequently used poetry as an experiential means of personal and religious exploration as well as a means of expressing their religious convictions. Kristina Groover notes that while "constructing spirituality" through poems and prose was not unique to women, these genres were especially important outlets for women. Groover claims that women have used poetry to engage in the process of "'doing theology' . . . exploring the nature of the sacred and the relationship of humans, especially women, to the sacred."[46] This type of contemplation is evident in the original poem "The Tempest's Lesson," in which the author, Mrs. Howe, reflected on the power of religious faith amid tragedy. Howe's poetic lines impart the voice of someone whose faith has sustained her through the anguish of disappointment and loss.

> The tempest had pass'd in its fury and wrath,
> And scatter'd destruction along in its path;
> The stars had come out from their homes of bright blue—
> Eternity's watchers—the pure and the true!
> As I wander'd abroad 'neath the beautiful moon
> That lit up the skies of our radiant June,
> There lay the proud oak that had sheltered the vine
> Thro' winter's dark tempests and summer's warm shine.
> It lay in the pomp of its towering pride,
> The vine's gentle tendrils all crush'd to its side,
> The vine flowers scatter'd, still bright in their bloom,
> And yielding in dying their richest perfume!
> As I gazed on the ruin the tempest had wrought—
> The blossoms of spring with such promises fraught,
> I saw by my side in the cleft of a rock,
> A flower unscathed by the hurricane's shock,
> Still blooming so sweetly, its delicate form
> Defying the wrath of the pitiless storm!
> I look'd at the flower, and I turn'd to the sky,
> And though of the "Rock that is higher than I,"[47]
> And humbly I ask'd when the tempest might lower,
> When sorrows are loosen'd to have their brief hour,
> That I e'en might dwell in the cleft of the rock
> Unscath'd by the might of the hurricane's shock;
> Afflictions like tempests oft visit life's way,
> And threaten with danger, and promise decay.
> But as storms are refiners to earth's atmosphere,
> So sorrows but strengthen us in our career;
> We are apt to forget when it thunders so loud

That the sun is but hidden behind the dark cloud—
That the cloud will dissolve, and his light will appear
With meridian splendor our pathway to cheer.[48]

Howe's poem prompts readers to reflect on their own tragedies and the sustaining power of faith. The poem contrasts the weak and temporal nature of earthly objects, even those that appear sturdy and strong, with the stability and unwavering shelter provided by the divine. Ultimately, the tempest's lesson is one of hope.

In addition to contemplating human and sacred relationships, women's poems often operated as a form of rhetorical evangelism. In "Mourn Not for Christians," Mrs. Gardiner constructed an argument that contrasts mortal life with the eternal life God promises Christians. Issuing a similar call in "Be Ye Also Ready," Miss De Forest employed a sense of urgency, inquiring in the first stanza:

> Art thou ready, careless sinner,
> Should the summons come to-day
> Thrilling through the vaulted heavens,
> That dread mandate to obey?
> Could'st thou meet the king Messiah,
> With thy guilt upon thy brow!
> Or, "not ready, not yet ready,"
> Would'st thou murmur then as now![49]

With an ample supply of dated, rhyming, flowery prose and religious rhetoric, it is easy to dismiss much of the poetry contained in the *LR*, but to do so overlooks the ways in which women used their poetry to express and explore theological issues.

In the November 1849 Editor's Table, the editor sought critics encouraging the magazine's readers to submit more critical pieces, explaining that of the many contributions in their drawers, "the poetical outnumber the prose articles." "We get but few critical pieces," the editor implored, "though it cannot be supposed that we have among our correspondents, no good critics. Give us, friends, some spirited reviews of the good and great one's of earth." In an attempt to stem a tide of crudely written verse, one editor encouraged readers to develop their writing, "Write prose at least five years before you attempt poetry." In response to one woman's inquiry about writing a magazine article, another editor advised, "the best method to be pursued in the preparation of an article, is, to read and reflect upon an interesting subject, and then write precisely what you think. This course, guided by good taste, will generally succeed." Editors also warned writers away from common topics such as "Female Influence"—one of the most common article titles found in the *CA*'s Ladies' Department—which further conveys the *LR*'s change in purpose. With its advice to women, the *LR* attempted to cultivate discriminating female writers as well as discriminating readers. By encouraging women to expand their reading selections and their modes of writing, the periodical acted as a sponsor of literacy.[50]

Caroline Burrough, who had thirty-five pieces published in the first seven volumes of *LR*, was one of the magazine's most prolific contributors. She often penned editorials and advice columns, including a four-page article titled "Girls and Their Training," in which she argued that while girls have the same capacity and aptitude for study as boys, they usually do not have the same opportunity. She explained, "The young lady of seventeen or eighteen years is already married, or engaged in its engrossing preliminaries; whilst the male youth of the same age is perhaps advancing from his Sophomore to his Junior class, in college, with yet two years of study prescribed." While suggesting that this "loss or lapse of education" for girls should be addressed, Burrough proposed as an interim solution to have women pursue a different course of study that would concentrate their efforts in a few subjects. In other words, given women's limited time in school, she prescribed depth rather than breadth of study.[51] This article and Burrough's numerous other contributions highlight the argumentative forum the *LR* made available to women.

The *LR* also provided women with the opportunity to venture into scriptural exegesis. In churches, there had long been anxiety about who gets to act as an intermediary for God. Predominantly, these were roles reserved for male ministers. Marion Ann Taylor and Heather Weir assert that women in the nineteenth century did write biblical interpretation, but most of this writing has been lost or forgotten. Taylor and Weir argue that recovering this gendered exegesis can offer insight into these writers' social, religious, and cultural contexts as well as their gender identity. In fact, they note that women's scriptural interpretation usually "looked for connections between their lives and experiences and the biblical characters' lives."[52] By doing so, they often judged biblical women based on the nineteenth century's conception of true womanhood.

One prominent example of exegesis in the *LR* is the series "Scriptural Portraitures of Women," by Mrs. Lyttleton F. Morgan. From 1843 through 1847, Morgan examined thirteen women in the Bible: Eve, Sarah, Rebekah, Jochebed, Miriam, Rahab, Deborah, Jael, Jephthah's daughter, Samson's mother, Samson's first wife, Delilah, and Rebekah's nurse. Susan Rigby Dallam Morgan was raised a Methodist and married itinerant Methodist minister Lyttleton Morgan. In fact, her husband initially became enamored with his future wife from reading her writing in church periodicals. Mrs. Morgan wrote prose and poetry and frequently published her work in periodicals. However, if Morgan is studied at all today, it may only be in regard to the disparaging review Edgar Allan Poe wrote in the 1836 issue of the *Southern Messenger* about Morgan's novel the *Swiss Heiress*.[53]

In many of her scriptural portraits, Morgan used the license afforded to her in a women's magazine to posit alternate interpretations. For instance, in her description of Abraham's wife, Sarah, she wrote:

> It is generally supposed by commentators on the subject that Sarah was not informed of the purposed sacrifice of Isaac until after the transaction on the mount, as the anguish of the mother might have triumphed over the submission of the patriarch to the Divine command. The surmise is plausible, for the whole history of Abraham evinces his regard for her feelings; yet I have sometimes imagined her acquainted with the mandate of God to her husband, and his intended fulfillment of it, and pictured her during the sorrowful six days of his mysterious journey, supplicating Heaven for a repeal of the apparently harsh behest. How often must she have wandered beyond the precincts of her tented home, with her straining eyes turned toward the distant summit of Moriah, sometimes shuddering lest the curling smoke which rose from the funeral pile of her only child should meet her agonized gaze; and then, encouraged by a scarcely defined hope of his safe return, almost believing that she distinguished his beloved form in the misty perspective.[54]

Morgan's readings often seem derived from her female insight as well as her desire to depict scriptural women as living and breathing individuals full of emotion. Some of the Old Testament women she described, like Sarah, are well-known figures, while others are more obscure, requiring Morgan to piece together their portraits from fragments of text. In these instances, Morgan appears to employ a strategy of imagination similar to the one described by Jacqueline Jones Royster in *Traces of a Stream*. Royster suggests that when only fragments exist, critical imagination demonstrates a scholar's "commitment to making connections and seeing possibility."[55] Morgan's use of this type of imagination in her exegetical portraits is especially evident in her depiction of Rebekah's nurse.[56] Drawing from Genesis that Rebekah's nurse was her lone companion when she traveled far from her home to become Isaac's wife, and the acknowledgment of the nurse's death during Jacob's return to Bethel—a critical moment in the Jacob story, Morgan interpreted the nurse as an important figure.[57] She imagined a maternal relationship between Rebekah and her nurse, and in her portrait, suggested:

> The young girl's situation ceases to wear so lonely and isolated an aspect. Something of past affection and companionship go with her. The humble guardian of her infant years—the being to whom, next to her mother, the developing love of the child most early and most fondly clings, accompanies her. Thoroughly acquainted with her girlish inclinations, prepared to understand and sympathize with the prejudices of early habit and education, her nurse had a hold upon her heart no other attendant could ever win. It was almost maternal in its character. With her Rebecca could talk of the past—of her father's house—of her mother. With her, trust and freedom might exist, without lessening her dignity, or degenerating into improper familiarity.

Morgan inserted emotion as she imagined the relationships and sentiments existing between the women she describes. Drawing on another scriptural fragment, Morgan also suggested that it may have been the nurse who warned Rebekah of Esau's intent to harm his brother Jacob: "It is said that the words of the elder brother were reported to the mother. Who so likely to have ventured the disclosure as the aged and trusted nurse of, probably both mother and children?" Morgan also interpreted the mention of the nurse's death as an indication of her influence and impact on the lives of both Rebekah and Jacob: "The name bestowed upon the tree which marked her resting place, is the record of the affectionate regret with which they laid her there." Finally Morgan advanced a moral to the story with her claim, "The true dignity of position consists in the propriety with which its duties are discharged."[58]

Morgan also infused emotion into her depiction of Jochebed, Moses's mother. In describing the difficult decision Jochebed faced when she placed Moses in a basket in the Nile, Morgan wrote, "as if she could not endure to be the direct instrument of his destruction, she manufactures a frail cradle, and places him in it among the willowy flags. . . . Apprehending that her yearning heart might betray its weakness if she continued near him and watched the rising of waters as they floated toward his resting place, or that her tenderness might be overcome by his cries, she left him to his fate, stationing his sister 'afar off' to observe 'what should be done unto him.'"[59]

Morgan's writings are shaped by the nineteenth century's feminization of

Christian piety and perhaps by her own experiences. In her introduction to
the series, Morgan stressed the "common features" readers would recognize
in these biblical women. She repeatedly highlighted the characters' unwavering faith as well as the way that they influenced the men around them. Her
depiction of the prophet Deborah from the book of Judges contrasted Deborah's steadfast belief with the wavering faith of Barak, who ignored God's call
to deliver his country out of tyranny. In this case, Morgan identifies Deborah's use of "true feminine tact" noting how she both rebuked and bolstered
Barak. Morgan then uses this example to deliver the following prescriptive
advice: "The records of woman present numerous examples of heroism and
self-sacrifice in the pursuit of great objects; but the considerate gentleness and
delicate propriety, which seek to shun the expression of all that could inflict
uneasiness, even when the retort is challenged as well as merited, are by no
means common qualities, and the deportment of Deborah toward Barak is
worthy of earnest emulation."[60] Morgan chose certain women for emulation
while she presented others, such as Miriam and Delilah,[61] as cautionary tales.
Her identification of certain obscure women and her concentration and conceptions of these women's emotions and influence on men suggest a different
exegetical treatment than one would likely find in scriptural interpretations
by men. Hence, the *LR* provided its readers with scriptural exegesis probably
unavailable elsewhere.

The women who read the *LR* in 1876 differed vastly from their mothers
and grandmothers who read it in 1841. By the time of the magazine's demise in
1876, Joanna Bowen Gillespie suggests that its female readership had simply
outgrown it. "Increasingly self-confident Methodist women were no longer
enthralled with male prescriptive religious journalism; women were writing it
themselves as well as moving into other intellectual fields" and areas of Christian activism.[62] In that sense, the magazine's mission was accomplished. It had
helped usher in a new generation of club women, college women, teachers, and
missionaries, as well as activist temperance women and advocates for women's
rights. At the same time that the *LR* reinforced the traditional female values of
home and motherhood, it was an early advocate and sponsor for women's intellectual development and public voice—supporting women's education and
self-cultivation and encouraging women writers. By constructing this odd co-
existence on its pages, the *LR* ultimately promoted new and expanded roles
for women. Published under the Methodist masthead, the magazine's affiliation with the church, and its editors' positions as ministers, gave the *LR*
greater editorial license and authority. Unlike popular women's magazines
that had to be mindful of their dual audience—the father or husband, whose

wages likely purchased the magazine, and the daughter or wife who read it—the *LR* had the church's financial backing and moral sanctioning. As a result, the *LR* actively contributed to women's transition in the nineteenth century from the "true woman," who was relegated to the domestic sphere, to the "new woman," who began defining her own spheres of influence.

Ambiguous and Liminal Spaces

When the Nineteenth Amendment granting women the right to vote passed in the House of Representatives in 1918, the women standing in the gallery celebrated by singing the Doxology, a refrain ritually sung in many Protestant churches.[1] This image of ardent first-wave feminists praising God seems peculiar today because feminist activism and religion are seldom cast as complementary belief systems. However, the line of demarcation dividing feminism and religion is a modern construction that can obscure and obstruct our work as rhetorical scholars and teachers. The neat borders that often exist in theory rarely exist in reality. A close examination of nineteenth-century women's rhetorical activities reveals blurred and messy margins between private and public spheres and between religion and the pursuit of women's rights and numerous social reforms. A view of our past—one that encompasses the everyday women that many of us find in our own lineage in addition to those exceptional figures we have begun to include in the rhetorical canon—can guide us in the present. Their stories warn us about the dangers of constructing rigid borders in our thoughts, our scholarship, and our classrooms.

Susan Hill Lindley acknowledges the complex relationship that existed between religion and women's political and social reform efforts even in the nineteenth century. She claims that religion: "provided the motives, means, and locus for much early reform, yet 'religion' in the form of clergy, biblical injunctions, and institutional churches sometimes opposed or restricted women's reform work. As a result, some women backed away from a given cause. Other women moved away from 'religion,' at least in its orthodox and institutional forms. Still others redefined the content of their faith and its implications for action, reinterpreting the Bible as they did so."[2] Lindley highlights the many ways in which women negotiated their religious beliefs and the reforms they pursued. For women, religion has offered both empowerment and oppression; however, an emphasis on oppression has often overshadowed religion as an emancipatory force. According to Phyllis Mack, this emphasis "leads us to ignore the indisputably significant historical fact that in the history of Western culture, it was devout Christian women who demonstrated the greatest degree of agency, particularly that element of agency that involves activity in the public sphere."[3]

The first American women to speak before large male and female audiences were female preachers and evangelists, bolstered by their devout faith and prophetic calls. Early public speeches by women such as Maria Stewart and Angelina Grimké, who dared to broach social and political issues before mixed audiences, are also replete with scriptural references augmenting their arguments and their right to speak. Indeed, women's religious upbringings and their beliefs often emboldened their activism. In the nineteenth century, many early female abolitionists and suffragists were Quakers, fortified by Quaker doctrine, which granted women equal authority under God. In fact, three Quaker women, Lucretia Mott, Martha Coffin Wright, and Mary Ann McClintock, collaborated with Elizabeth Cady Stanton to write the "Declaration of Sentiments" and organize the Seneca Falls Convention, which was held in a Methodist church. Indeed, churches have repeatedly served as sites for grassroots organization and activism. Modern examples include the civil rights movement and recent rallies for immigration reform.

Other nineteenth-century, women such as Susan B. Anthony and Alice Paul were also influenced by their Quaker roots. Paul organized the nonviolent Silent Sentinels, who waged protests for women's rights in front of the White House from 1917 to 1919. Phoebe Palmer, leader of the Holiness Movement, and Frances Willard, president of the Women's Christian Temperance Union, were two of the most celebrated female speakers in the nineteenth century. Both were members of the Methodist church, and for a brief period, Willard even traveled as an evangelist with the famous revivalist D. L. Moody. Sojourner Truth also traveled the country speaking as an itinerant minister and a women's rights activist. Nancy Hardesty also links Stanton, Willard, Palmer, Lucy Stone, Antoinette Brown, Matilda Joslyn Gage, and Paulina Wright Davis to Charles Grandison Finney, the popular revivalist, who later became the president of Oberlin College. Finney's revivals throughout the northeast in the 1820s and 1830s urged crowds, predominantly filled with young, middle-class women, to save their sin-ridden communities. These calls to Christian activism during the Second Great Awakening inspired women's pursuit of numerous social reforms including abolition, temperance, and moral reform. These movements' most passionate proponents were driven by their religious beliefs. They identified prostitution, drunkenness, and slavery as sins against God and neighbor that impeded America's path to becoming a moral and Christian society. For many women, combating these sins became a God-authorized Christian duty.[4]

The evangelical revivalism that emerged out of the Second Great Awakening emphasized free will, experience, and activity. These evangelical religious tenets not only motivated women's participation in antebellum reform efforts, but also influenced their theology and their rhetoric. Many women became increasingly uncomfortable with traditional biblical interpretations, yet rather than turning away from the Bible, some began performing their own exegesis. Women reformers often drew rhetorical proofs from their own scriptural interpretations. Especially important to them was the belief that they were moral agents accountable to God's word rather than man's interpretation of it. Indeed, women reformers began highlighting the inconsistencies between Scripture and men's interpretations and actions. The American Female Moral Reform Society (AFMRS),[5] the first national women's reform organization, especially stressed these inconsistencies. In its rhetoric, the AFMRS encouraged women to enact their faith by forcefully fighting the double moral standard that severely penalized women for immoral sexual conduct but seemingly excused men. Female moral reformers directly linked their efforts to upholding the seventh commandment, "Thou shalt not commit adultery," and stressed that God drew no distinction between man and woman in this commandment. The first edition of *The Advocate of Moral Reform*, the bimonthly periodical of the AFMRS, posed the rhetorical question, "Are those Christians and ministers, who advocate the doctrine of 'doing and *not* saying,' aware that their doctrine finds a hearty believer in every libertine in the land?"[6] This condemnation of other Christians and ministers, which cast them as accessories to immoral behavior, demonstrates how women began to publicly exert moral authority outside the church. Even as women used religious tenets to justify their actions, many were beginning to wrest authority away from the church and its clergy.

The Grimké sisters' arguments for women's right to speak in public also emphasized that women and men were moral equals created by and under the dominion of God. In 1838, Sarah Grimké wrote in her *Letters on the Equality of the Sexes, and the Condition of Woman*, "God created us equal;—he created us free agents;—he is our Lawgiver, our King and our Judge, and to him alone is woman bound to be in subjection, and to him alone is she accountable for the use of those talents which her Heavenly Father has entrusted her." Angelina Grimké likewise claimed in her *Letters to Catherine E. Beecher*, "Human beings have rights, because they are moral beings; . . . whatever it is morally right for man to do, it is morally right for woman to do."[7]

The Bible provided a powerful source of evidence for women to defend their voices and actions and was also a common and comfortable language. Nineteenth-century women were generally much better versed in the Bible than men and many believed in the authority of Scripture even if they did not agree with institutional and patriarchal interpretations of it.[8] Women repeatedly used three scriptural defenses to endorse their public activism. They cataloged women who played prominent religious and political roles in the Bible—including Deborah, Miriam, Huldah, Jael, Anna, Priscilla, and Phoebe—and held these women up as models to show that God has acted through both men and women. Female reformers also offered their own scriptural interpretations, particularly alternate readings of passages used by men to justify women's subordination and public silence. These included the creation story as well as Apostle Paul's oft-quoted decrees against women speaking in church.[9] Finally, women emphasized scriptural passages that they believed demonstrated equality in God's eyes. These include Galatians 3:28, "There is neither Jew nor Greek, there is neither bond nor free, there is neither male nor female: for ye are all one in Christ Jesus" and Matthew 7:12, "Therefore all things whatsoever ye would that men should do to you, do ye even so to them," which is commonly referred to as the Golden Rule.

The religious beliefs, motivations, and scripturally based arguments of many women's reformers in the nineteenth century are an important but frequently overlooked facet of women's rhetorical history. Even though these early women activists resented deeply rooted religious patriarchies, they were also emboldened by their religious beliefs and their own biblical interpretations. Nonetheless, contemporary scholars are often uncomfortable addressing the religious influences of women rhetors. As a result, the religious backgrounds and beliefs of these women are frequently cropped from their portraits. Noting the way in which feminist discussions of women's agency often exclude religion, Phyllis Mack muses whether secular scholars are "tone-deaf to religious sensibilities" or simply unable or unwilling to describe the "religious person's complex experience of agency."[10]

Religious institutions are essential sites for studying early nineteenth-century American women's rhetoric; however, the church and other religious institutions are frequently ignored or overlooked. There are numerous reasons for this omission. Institutional records are lacking, and the academic fields of rhetoric and composition, speech communications, history, religion, and women's studies are still knee-deep in efforts to recover women rhetoricians and redefine activities by women and other marginalized groups that were not previously considered rhetorical. That said, I am certain that a general reluctance to study churches and other religious institutions is also a contributing factor. In their own studies of women's rhetoric, both Carol Mattingly and Roxanne Mountford have acknowledged how feminist scholars often steer clear of religious institutions.

This reluctance is disconcerting, but I also find it ironic. Throughout the nineteenth century, many of the women who were active in religious movements were wary of associating with ardent women's rights activists. While nineteenth-century churchwomen often sought and assumed broader rhetorical roles, they tended to view women's rights activists as radicals. Susan Hill Lindley notes that the women's missionary movement supported many single women in missions around the world and grew into the largest national women's movement by the turn of the century. At the same time, she claims that women active in the missionary movement often perceived demands by women activists as "radical and unwomanly." According to Lindley, "A widespread image of the women's rights movement, however unfair, was of women, loud and strident in their public posture, selfishly concerned with their own advancement to the detriment of husband, children, and less fortunate neighbors."[11] In other words, feminists' judgments about churchwomen and churchwomen's judgments about feminists prevented them from recognizing some of their common goals and mutually beneficial achievements. In another ironic twist, rhetorical scholars have reclaimed this relatively small group of "loud" women's rights activists and too often forgotten the throngs of women who made up the women's missionary movement and Women's Christian Temperance Union or who participated in Sunday schools and an array of religious and benevolent organizations. These are just a few historical examples that illustrate the complex relationship that often exists between religion and feminist activism and the precarious nature of attempts to separate them. These examples can also serve as a caution to those who hold fast to the view that religion and feminism are counterproductive.

Charting the spatial and discursive locations in which women appear in *Methodist Magazine* and the *Christian Advocate* reveals an array of rhetorical roles assumed by and ascribed to women. Methodists repeatedly used representations of women and women's own words to persuade readers. In doing so, the church's periodicals recognized women's religious authority and widely disseminated their voices and actions. The little narratives by and about women in these popular periodicals also attest to women's empowerment in benevolent organizations and the church's wide-ranging evangelical outposts. Antebellum Methodist women enacted their faith through their actions. They exhorted and evangelized fellow Christians, converted nonbelievers, and taught and trained the next generation of Christians. They labored as missionaries in foreign lands, among Native American tribes, and along America's frontiers.[12] Reporting women's social and religious outreach, the church broadcast women's movement beyond their homes and encouraged its female readers to likewise enact their religious convictions. Through their depictions in Methodist publications, women became spiritual models, exemplars, and heroines for a rapidly expanding Methodist community. Altogether, these little narratives show essential roles that women played in expanding the Methodist church; they also show how the church operated as an integral site for women's rhetorical development in antebellum America. And by offering alternatives to the "true woman," who was relegated solely to the roles of wife and mother in the domestic sphere, the church's periodicals began to acknowledge the "new woman" and her right to define her own rhetorical spheres of influence.

Ann Braude explains, the story of religion in America is a story that women controlled through their presence: "Where women are present, religion flourishes, where they are absent, it does not."[13] That fact in itself seems to acknowledge that women were far more than a passive audience occupying church pews. Women were essential participants in the Second Great Awakening that swept across the country and they were a crucial part of the Methodist church's rapid ascent to the largest denomination in nineteenth-century America. Today, women continue to represent the overwhelming majority in most churches, and many still bring their spouses, partners, and children along with them. Although churches' influence on American society has decreased, women's influence within churches has increased—impacting doctrine as well as churches' social agendas. Consequently, proponents of feminist theology have continued to exercise influence from within and outside of religious institutions. Women's ordination, women's struggles to obtain senior clerical posts, women's efforts to promote the use of neutral language including God-language,[14] and women's reproductive rights offer a few highly publicized examples that link feminist activism and religion. Other examples include numerous social services that are often provided through churches; these include childcare, afterschool programs, adult daycare, emergency shelters, English as a Second Language programs, and Meals on Wheels. Many of these services especially benefit single mothers and working women.

Ultimately, history shows us that the church both circumscribed and supported women's rhetoric. Did the Methodist ministers who authored and edited women's memoirs *use* these women or simply attempt to harness the power of their faith for the benefit of others? It is impossible to know. Nonetheless, they transformed their female subjects into spiritual heroines and models of piety and even elevated them to the post of preachers exhorting from deathbed pulpits. At the same time, through the prescriptive Ladies' Department advice that it dispensed in its weekly national newspaper, the church tried to contain women in the domestic sphere. However, a collateral effect of this didacticism was assigning women religious duties previously under the purview of ministers. The church also recognized and lauded women's efforts beyond the domestic sphere. And through its publications, it sanctioned and disseminated women's voices and actions to audiences far beyond their homes, congregations, and communities. The antebellum Methodist church was thus both an oppressive and emboldening force in women's lives.

Charting the Methodist church's influence on women's rhetorical development is a messy and muddled story. In some places it is blank or blurry, and even in the places where the story becomes clearer, there are no neat lines. It is a story full of ambiguous and liminal spaces in which women are both empowered and contained. Additionally, it is a story in which women are constructed as pious models and also celebrated as active foot soldiers. While it shows how churches served as essential developmental sites for American women's rhetorical practice, it also shows the difficulty women have always encountered in negotiating social mores and operating within male-dominated institutions. Rather than reducing the story's impact, I believe this messiness represents an important part of its contribution.

Notes

Introduction: Looking Beyond the Pulpit

1. Collins's later publications appear under the name Vicki Tolar Burton.

2. Although the church was officially established in the United States as the Methodist Episcopal Church in 1784, members of the church were customarily referred to as Methodists. I use the more common references "Methodists" and the "Methodist church."

3. Catherine A. Brekus, *Strangers and Pilgrims: Female Preaching in America, 1740–1845* (Chapel Hill: University of North Carolina Press, 1998), 343–46.

4. For more on Julia Foote, see Laceye Warner, *Saving Women: Retrieving Evangelistic Theology and Practice* (Waco, TX: Baylor University Press, 2007). For more on Jarena Lee, see Marilyn Westerkamp, *Women and Religion in Early America, 1600–1850* (London: Routledge, 1999); and Jean Miller Schmidt, *Grace Sufficient: A History of Women in American Methodism 1760–1939* (Nashville: Abingdon, 1999). For more on Fanny Newell and Hannah Pearce Reeves, see Schmidt, *Grace Sufficient*. For more information on Phoebe Palmer, see Patricia Bizzell and Bruce Herzberg, eds., *The Rhetorical Tradition*, 2nd ed. (Boston: Bedford, 2001).

5. Roxanne Mountford, *The Gendered Pulpit: Preaching in American Protestant Spaces* (Carbondale: Southern Illinois University Press, 2003), 15.

6. See Sean Latham and Robert Scholes, "The Rise of Periodical Studies," *PMLA* 121, no. 2 (2006): 517–31.

7. See Nathan O. Hatch, "The Puzzle of American Methodism," in *Methodism and the Shaping of American Culture*, ed. Nathan O. Hatch and John H. Wigger (Nashville: Kingswood, 2001), 27–28. See also Dee E. Andrews, *The Methodists and Revolutionary America, 1760–1800: The Shaping of an Evangelical Culture* (Princeton: Princeton University Press, 2000), 4.

8. Heck's words are quoted in Frank Baker, *From Wesley to Asbury: Studies in Early American Methodism* (Durham, NC: Duke University Press, 1976), 43. For more on Heck, see also Schmidt, *Grace Sufficient*, 55–56.

9. Hatch, "Puzzle," 27, 37.

10. John H. Wigger, *Taking Heaven by Storm: Methodism and the Rise of Popular Christianity in America* (New York: Oxford University Press, 1998), 57.

11. Nancy A. Hardesty, *Women Called to Witness: Evangelical Feminism in the Nineteenth Century*, 2nd ed. (Knoxville: University of Tennessee Press, 1999), 3.

12. Hatch, "Puzzle," 10.

13. Ann Braude, "Women's History *Is* American Religious History," in *Retelling U.S. Religious History*, ed. Thomas A. Tweed (Berkeley: University of California Press, 1997), 91.

14. Evelyn Brooks Higginbotham, *Righteous Discontent: The Women's Movement in Black Baptist Church, 1880–1920* (Cambridge: Harvard University Press, 1993), 2.

15. Joy Ritchie and Kate Ronald, "Introduction: A Gathering of Rhetorics," in *Available Means: An Anthology of Women's Rhetoric(s)*, ed. Joy Ritchie and Kate Ronald (Pittsburgh: University of Pittsburgh Press, 2001), xix; Barbara Biesecker, "Coming to Terms with Recent Attempts to Write Women into the History of Rhetoric," *Philosophy and Rhetoric* 25, no. 2 (1992): 140–61.

16. Roxanne Mountford provides a sample of dates when mainline Protestant denominations began ordaining women: Congregationalist, 1853; American Unitarian Association, 1871; Disciples of Christ, 1888; Assemblies of God, 1935; Methodist Church, 1956; United Presbyterian Church, North America, 1958; Southern Baptist Convention, 1964 (revoked, 2001); Christian Methodist Episcopal Church, 1966; Lutheran Church in America, 1970; Mennonite Church, 1973; Episcopal Church, 1976; Reformed Church in America, 1979. *Gendered Pulpit*, 162.

17. Wigger, *Taking Heaven by Storm*, 151.

18. Quoted in Cynthia Lynn Lyerly, *Methodism and the Southern Mind, 1770–1810* (New York: Oxford University Press, 1998), 100.

19. See Westerkamp, *Women and Religion*, 176; and Susan Juster, *Disorderly Women: Sexual Politics and Evangelicalism in Revolutionary New England* (Ithaca: Cornell University Press, 1994), 216.

20. Nathan O. Hatch and John H. Wigger, "Introduction," in *Methodism and the Shaping of American Culture*, ed. Nathan O. Hatch and John H. Wigger (Nashville: Kingswood, 2001), 19.

21. Delineating exact timelines is difficult because situations vary between the more established Methodist congregations in the Northeast and cities and those newly formed congregations in rural and frontier regions.

22. Catherine A. Brekus, "Female Evangelism in the Early Methodist Movement, 1784–1845," in *Methodism and the Shaping of American Culture*, ed. Nathan O. Hatch and John H. Wigger (Nashville: Kingswood, 2001), 143, 172.

23. Wigger, *Taking Heaven by Storm*, 156–57.

24. Andrews, *Methodists and Revolutionary America*, 118, 122.

25. Andrea A. Lunsford, "On Reclaiming Rhetorica," in *Reclaiming Rhetorica: Women in the Rhetorical Tradition*, ed. Andrea A. Lunsford (Pittsburgh: University of Pittsburgh Press, 1995), 3.

26. Beth A. Daniell, *A Communion of Friendship: Literacy, Spiritual Practice, and Women in Recovery* (Carbondale: Southern Illinois University Press, 2003), 3–7.

27. Deborah Brandt, *Literacy in American Lives* (Cambridge: Cambridge University Press, 2001), 19.

28. For an in-depth discussion of Wesley's dynamic use of literate practices in early Methodism, see Vicki Tolar Burton, *Spiritual Literacy in John Wesley's Methodism: Reading, Writing, and Speaking to Believe* (Waco, TX: Baylor University Press, 2008).

29. First convened in 1792, the General Conference meets every four years and is the highest legislative and representative body in the Methodist church. The General Conference determines the church's future direction and is the only body with the authority to alter doctrinal standards.

30. *Journals of the General Conference of the Methodist Episcopal Church*, vol. 1, *1796–1836* (New York: Carlton and Phillips, 1855), 17.

31. Nathan O. Hatch, *The Democratization of American Christianity* (New Haven, CT: Yale University Press, 1989), 142.

32. See Candy Gunther Brown, *The Word in the World: Evangelical Writing, Publishing, and Reading in America, 1789–1880* (Chapel Hill: University of North Carolina Press, 2004), 93.

33. Hatch, *Democratization*, 125–26.

34. For a discussion of the role of mass-produced publications in creating unity, see Benedict Anderson, *Imagined Communities: Reflections on the Origin and Spread of Nationalism* (London: Verso, 1991), 35.

35. In 1829, the *Christian Advocate* and the nondenominational *American National Preacher* attracted 20,000 and 25,000 subscribers respectively, the highest numbers then recorded by any periodical. Gaylord P. Albaugh, *History and Annotated Bibliography of American Religious Periodicals and Newspapers Established from 1730 through 1830* (Worcester: American Antiquarian Society, 1994), xiii.

36. Candy Gunther Brown discusses the role texts play in establishing new sacred places. *Word in the World*, 109, 144–45.

37. *Christian Advocate*, 1832: 54. *Christian Advocate* (New York), 1826–1832 from American Periodical Series II, reels 1749–1750. Microfilm (Ann Arbor, MI: University Microfilm). For future references to the *Christian Advocate*, I will use the abbreviation *CA* and provide the year followed by the page number. The four-page weekly newspaper used continuous pagination for each yearly volume.

38. *CA*, 1832: 54.

39. This term comes from Gérard Genette, *Paratexts: Thresholds of Interpretation*, trans. Jane E. Lewin (Cambridge: Cambridge University Press, 1997).

40. Vicki Tolar Collins, "The Speaker Respoken: Material Rhetoric as Feminist Methodology," *College English* 61, no. 5 (1999): 545–73, 555.

41. Gillian Rose, *Feminism and Geography: The Limits of Geographical Knowledge* (Minneapolis: University of Minnesota Press, 1993), 17.

42. Brekus, *Strangers and Pilgrims*, 13.

43. David Sibley, *Geographies of Exclusion: Society and Difference in the West* (London: Routledge, 1995), 33.

44. Sarah Robbins, "Woman's Work for Woman: Gendered Print Culture in American Mission Movement Narratives," in *Print Culture of American Women from the Nineteenth and Twentieth Centuries*, ed. James P. Danky and Wayne A. Wiegand (Madison: University of Wisconsin Press, 2006), 252–80.

45. *CA*, 1831: 155.

46. Jennifer Sinor, *The Extraordinary Work of Ordinary Writing: Annie Ray's Diary* (Iowa City: University of Iowa Press, 2002), 4.

47. Brekus, "Female Evangelism," 151.

48. Mountford, *Gendered Pulpit*, 12; and Carol Mattingly, *Well-Tempered Women: Nineteenth-Century Temperance Rhetoric* (Carbondale: Southern Illinois University Press, 1998), 8.

49. See Susan Hill Lindley, *"You Have Stept Out of Your Place": A History of Women and Religion in America* (Louisville: Westminster, 1996), 60–61.

50. Gerda Lerner, *Why History Matters: Life and Thought* (New York: Oxford University Press, 1997), 52.

51. Robert Connors, "Dreams and Play: Historical Method and Methodology," in *Methods and Methodology in Composition Research*, ed. Gesa Kirsch and Patricia Sullivan (Carbondale: Southern Illinois University Press, 1992), 17.

Chapter One. Dying Well

1. *Methodist Magazine*, 1822: 409–10. *Methodist Magazine*, (New York) 1818–1828 from American Periodical Series Online (Ann Arbor, MI: ProQuest, 2000). When referencing articles from *Methodist Magazine*, I will use the abbreviation *MM* and provide the year followed by the page number. The forty-page monthly magazine used continuous pagination for each yearly volume.

2. *MM*, 1822: 407.

3. See Scott E. Casper, *Constructing American Lives: Biography and Culture in Nineteenth Century America* (Chapel Hill: University of North Carolina Press, 1999), 33.

4. Quoted in Earl Kent Brown, *Women of Mr. Wesley's Methodism* (New York: Edwin Mellen, 1983), 112.

5. See Burton, *Spiritual Literacy*, 259.

6. Elizabeth Prentiss, *Stepping Heavenward: One Woman's Journey to Godliness* (1869; repr., Ulhrichsville, OH: Barbour, 1998), 20.

7. See Brown, *Word in the World*, 89.

8. See Joanna Bowen Gillespie, "'The Clear Leadings of Providence': Pious Memoirs and the Problems of Self-Realization for Women in the Early Nineteenth Century," *Journal of the Early Republic* 5, no. 2 (1985): 199–200.

9. See Jane P. Tompkins, *Sensational Designs: The Cultural Work of American Fiction, 1790–1860* (New York: Oxford University Press, 1985), 165.

10. See James Penn Pilkington, *The Methodist Publishing House: A History*, vol. 1 (Nashville: Abingdon, 1968), 85, 110.

11. *Journals*, 17.

12. Francis Asbury was one of the first ministers dispatched to America by Wesley in 1771 and one of the first American Methodist Bishops. During his forty-five years in America, Asbury solidified the Methodist movement and laid the plans for its populist success.

13. For information about John and Betsy Dickins, see Pilkington, *Methodist Publishing House*, 59–61.

14. *Journals*, 171–72.

15. George G. Smith, *The Life and Letters of James Osgood Andrew* (Nashville: Southern Methodist Publishing House, 1882), 98.

16. Anderson, *Imagined Communities*, 133.

17. Russell E. Richey, *Early American Methodism* (Bloomington: Indiana University Press, 1991), 83–89.

18. Pilkington, *Methodist Publishing House*, 161.

19. These calculations include those memoirs extracted from British periodicals as well as memoirs discussing the lives of well-known individuals such as Calvinist John Elliot. Going forward, I have limited my examination to memoirs written by and about American Methodists with the exception of two Canadians. In the Northeast, some Methodist ministers' circuits crossed the border into Canada.

20. *MM*, 1818: 3–4.

21. Quoted in Burton, *Spiritual Literacy*, 23.

22. Brown, *Word in the World*, 89.

23. James W. Carey, *Communication as Culture: Essays on Media and Society* (Boston: Unwin Hyman, 1988), 14–18.

24. For an explanation of interpretive communities, see Jane P. Tompkins, "An Introduction to Reader-Response Criticism," in *Reader-Response Criticism: From Formalism to Post-Structuralism*, ed. Jane P. Tompkins (Baltimore: John Hopkins University Press, 1980), xxi.

25. *MM*, 1822: 239.

26. Brown, *Word in the World*, 93.

27. See Gérard Genette, *Narrative Discourse: An Essay in Method*, trans. Jane E. Lewin (Ithaca: Cornell University Press, 1980).

28. *MM*, 1819: 257.

29. *MM*, 1821: 367.

30. *MM*, 1822: 222.

31. *MM*, 1820: 330.

32. Jerald C. Brauer, "Conversion: From Puritanism to Revivalism," *Journal of Religion* 58, no. 3 (1978): 227–43, 227.

33. A. Gregory Schneider, *The Way of the Cross Leads Home: The Domestication of American Methodism* (Bloomington: Indiana University Press, 1993), 113.

34. See Virginia Lieson Brereton, *From Sin to Salvation: Stories of Women's Conversions, 1800 to the Present* (Bloomington: Indiana University Press, 1991), 3–4.

35. For a detailed discussion of the stages of conversion, see Schneider, *Way of the Cross*, 43–44.

36. *MM*, 1819: 14.

37. See Sharon Crowley and Debra Hawhee, *Ancient Rhetorics for Contemporary Students*, 2nd ed. (Boston: Allyn and Bacon, 1999), 31.

38. Christine Leigh Heyrman, *Southern Cross: The Beginnings of the Bible Belt* (New York: Knopf, 1997), 41.

39. *MM*, 1821: 206; 1819: 422.

40. *MM*, 1819: 18.

41. *MM*, 1822: 79.

42. Michael Haines, "Fertility and Mortality in the United States," *EH.Net Encyclopedia*, ed. Robert Whaples, June 26, 2005, http://eh.net/encyclopedia.

43. *MM*, 1820: 20; 1819: 261.

44. *MM*, 1822: 102.

45. *MM*, 1818: 20.

46. *MM*, 1820: 139.

47. Douglas N. Walton, *On Defining Death: An Analytic Study of the Concept of Death in Philosophy and Medical Ethics* (Montreal: McGill-Queen's University Press, 1979), 41.

48. *MM*, 1821: 329.

49. *MM*, 1819: 327; 1820: 408; 1822: 453; 1821: 335.

50. *MM*, 1822: 449; 1819: 423.

51. See Schneider, *Way of the Cross*, 46–47.

52. *MM*, 1818: 24.

53. *MM*, 1822: 102; 1819: 217.

54. *MM*, 1823: 291.

55. *MM*, 1819: 67–71. This comes from Zechariah 3:2: "Is not this a brand plucked out of the fire?" John Wesley also frequently referenced this Scripture especially in regard to an affecting childhood experience when a neighbor climbed on another's shoulders and pulled John out of a window to rescue him from his family's burning house.

56. *MM*, 1824: 105–6.

57. *MM*, 1824: 199.

58. *MM*, 1819: 146.

59. *MM*, 1819: 338; 1821: 462–63.

60. *MM*, 1822: 62.

61. *MM*, 1822: 295.

62. *MM*, 1819: 375.

63. *MM*, 1818: 343.

64. *MM*, 1818: 400; 1821: 336.

65. *MM*, 1822: 309.

66. See *MM*, 1823: 400.

67. See *MM*, 1820: 440; 1823: 295.

68. See *MM*, 1820: 406.

Chapter Two. Women's Deathbed Pulpits

1. *MM*, 1818: 150.

2. *MM*, 1818: 23–25.

3. Gregory Schneider also uses the terms *iconic* and *instrumental*. He describes how Methodists constructed a dialectic of social religion with both iconic and instrumental moments. Broadly, Schneider distinguishes iconic moments as moments of inner holiness and instrumental moments as those instances when this inner holiness operates as a transformative power for virtue and morality. *Way of the Cross*, 151.

4. See Collins, "Speaker Respoken," 546.

5. Mountford, *Gendered Pulpit*, 1–15, 24.

6. *MM*, 1818: 22.

7. Barbara Welter, "The Feminization of American Religion: 1800–1860," in *Religion in American History: A Reader*, ed. Jon Butler and Harry S. Stout (New York: Oxford University Press, 1998), 161.

8. Tompkins, *Sensational Designs*, 127–28.

9. Schmidt, *Grace Sufficient*, 43.

10. *The Account of Hester Ann Rogers*, published after her death, was a popular religious memoir throughout the nineteenth century—issued in over forty editions. See Collins, "Speaker Respoken," 545–46; and Schmidt, *Grace Sufficient*, 17–19.

11. Increasingly, the class leader position was viewed as a training position for potential ministers. See Andrews, *Methodists in Revolutionary America*, 118–19.

12. Lyerly, *Methodism and the Southern Mind*, 109.

13. *MM*, 1823: 38.

14. *MM*, 1824: 144–46; 1822: 224.

15. Laymen and women's memoirs appear to depict different generations. The average age at death for the laymen elegized in *MM* is fifty-three, while the average age at death for women is thirty-three. These average ages are based on those memoirs that provide ages.

16. The posts of class leader, licensed exhorter, and local preacher comprised the lay ministry in local Methodist societies and often served as a training ground for future traveling ministers. Class leaders were responsible for holding regular class meetings and visiting class members, as well as advising, reproving, and exhorting them along their spiritual journeys. The class leader role represented the lowest rung of the lay ministerial hierarchy. Licensed exhorters, the next step on the lay ministerial hierarchy, were responsible for assisting preachers with prayer and exhortation during meetings, and local preachers, the highest post on the lay ministerial hierarchy, sometimes assisted itinerants and also ministered to individuals in their neighborhoods. Unlike itinerant ministers, local preachers were stationed in one location. Typically, local preachers were not paid, so they pursued secular employment in ad-

dition to preaching. For some, local preaching provided a stepping stone into itinerancy; for others, it offered an alternative to those preachers unable to travel because of family, health, or financial reasons. Yet, in the Methodist hierarchy, local preachers were clearly a notch below traveling ministers. When individuals left the itinerancy to be stationed as local preachers, they were precluded from certain activities and sacraments and could not vote at the church's annual conference. All lay ministers were supervised by the itinerant minister over the circuit, but because itinerant ministers constantly traveled throughout their circuits, lay ministers provided the backbone of many Methodist societies. See William Warren Sweet, *Religion on the American Frontier 1783–1840*, vol. 4, *The Methodists* (Chicago: University of Chicago Press, 1946), 573.

17. *MM*, 1823: 87–88.

18. *MM*, 1819: 174–76.

19. Wigger, *Taking Heaven by Storm*, 56.

20. Hatch, *Democratization*, 88.

21. See Schneider, *Way of the Cross*, 173.

22. Diane H. Lobody, "'That Language Might Be Give Me': Women's Experience in Early Methodism," in *Perspectives on American Methodism: Interpretive Essays*, ed. Russell E. Richey, Kenneth E. Rowe, and Jean Miller Schmidt (New York: Abingdon, 1993), 142.

23. Burton, *Spiritual Literacy*, 74.

24. Schmidt, *Grace Sufficient*, 35–36.

25. Vicki Tolar Burton distinguishes spiritual letters as "correspondence in which the writer addresses religious or spiritual beliefs, often in a personal way, raises or answers spiritual questions, and offers testimony based on experience, usually with the goal of persuading the reader in matters of faith and fostering the spiritual growth of both writer and reader." *Spiritual Literacy*, 175–76.

26. *MM*, 1824: 165, 177.

27. *MM*, 1819: 17.

28. *MM*, 1821: 329.

29. *MM*, 1821: 335.

30. *MM*, 1822: 376.

31. *MM*, 1822: 309–10.

32. *MM*, 1818: 182.

33. Brekus, "Female Evangelism," 143–44.

34. Brekus, *Strangers and Pilgrims*.

35. Wigger, *Taking Heaven by Storm*, 157–58.

36. For discussions of exhortation, see Brekus, "Female Evangelism," 136; *Strangers and Pilgrims*, 48; and Heyrman, *Southern Cross*, 167.

37. See Burton, *Spiritual Literacy*, 114.

38. Wigger, *Taking Heaven by Storm*, 152.

39. Robert Connors, *Composition-Rhetoric: Backgrounds, Theory, and Pedagogy* (Pittsburgh: University of Pittsburgh Press, 1997), 50.

40. *MM*, 1820: 416.

41. *MM*, 1823: 258.

42. *MM*, 1822: 101.

43. *MM*, 1818: 307–8.

44. See Lindal Buchanan, *Regendering Delivery: The Fifth Canon and Antebellum Women Rhetors* (Carbondale: Southern Illinois University Press, 2005); Nan Johnson, *Gender and Rhetorical Space in American Life, 1866–1910* (Carbondale: Southern Illinois University Press, 2002).

45. Lobody, "'That Language Might Be Give Me,'" 135.

46. *MM*, 1823: 382.

47. *MM*, 1820: 19–20.

48. *MM*, 1823: 302.

49. *MM*, 1823: 259.

50. *MM*, 1821: 337–36.

Chapter 3. Contained Inside the Ladies' Department

1. Michel Foucault, "Space, Knowledge, and Power," in *The Foucault Reader*, ed. Paul Rabinow (New York: Pantheon, 1984), 252.

2. Sibley, *Geographies of Exclusion*, ix; Rose, *Feminism and Geography*, 17; and Edward W. Soja, *Postmodern Geographies: The Reassertion of Space in Critical Social Theory* (London: Verso, 1989), 6.

3. Alexis de Tocqueville, *Democracy in America*, trans. Henry Reeve, rev. Francis Bowen (1835, 1840; repr., Ware, Hertfordshire: Wordsworth, 1998), 297.

4. Schneider, *Way of the Cross*, 167.

5. *CA*, 1827: 98.

6. For a discussion of the regional newspapers that preceded the *CA*, see Pilkington, *Methodist Publishing House*, 179, 199. Pilkington also notes that in an effort to revive *Methodist Magazine* in 1830, the editors changed it to a quarterly publication under the title *Methodist Magazine and Quarterly Review*, 215–16.

7. Frederick A. Norwood, *The Story of American Methodism* (Nashville: Abingdon, 1974), 214.

8. Brown, *Word in the World*, 156.

9. See Hatch, *Democratization*, 201–4; and Pilkington, *Methodist Publishing House*, 176–210.

10. Pilkington, *Methodist Publishing House*, 199.

11. For discussions of religious newspapers, see James D. Hart, *The Popular Book: A History of America's Literary Taste* (New York: Oxford, University Press, 1950), 67; and Frank Luther Mott, *American Journalism: A History of Newspapers in the United States through 260 Years, 1690 to 1950* (New York: Macmillan, 1953), 206. For subscription numbers see Albaugh, *History and Annotated Bibliography*, xiii, and Brown, *Word in the World*, 155.

12. *CA*, 1826: 2.

13. *CA*, 1826: 50; 1828: 206.

14. *CA*, 1826: 2.

15. *CA*, 1826: 10.

16. *CA*, 1828: 189.

17. See Brown, *Word in the World*, 177.

18. Tocqueville, *Democracy in America*, 220.

19. Anderson, *Imagined Communities*, 25, 63.

20. Brown, *Word in the World*, 173.

21. *CA*, 1827: 76.

22. Nancy F. Cott, *The Bonds of Womanhood: "Woman's Sphere" in New England, 1780–1835* (New Haven, CT: Yale University Press, 1977), 63–64; Barbara Welter, "The Cult of True Womanhood: 1820–1860," *American Quarterly* 18, no. 2 (1966): 151–74.

23. See Barbara J. Harris, *Beyond Her Sphere: Women and the Professions in American History* (Westport, CT: Greenwood, 1978), 33.

24. Lindley, *"You Have Stept,"* 53.

25. *CA*, 1832: 52.

26. Schmidt, *Grace Sufficient*, 79.

27. These works are discussed in Schmidt, *Grace Sufficient*, 80–82.

28. Cott, *Bonds of Womanhood*, 159.

29. *CA*, 1826: 52; 1828: 192; 1832: 20; 1826: 8.

30. *CA*, 1830: 116.

31. See *CA*, 1826: 28.

32. *CA*, 1826: 24.

33. *CA*, 1826: 24.

34. *CA*, 1826: 64.

35. *CA*, 1827: 120.

36. Emphasis is mine, *CA*, 1827: 108.

37. Ibid.

38. *CA*, 1832: 12.

39. See *CA*, 1827: 104; 1831: 196.

40. *CA*, 1826: 28.

41. *CA*, 1827: 104.

42. Barbara Leslie Epstein, *The Politics of Domesticity: Women, Evangelism, and Temperance in Nineteenth-Century America* (Middletown, CT: Wesleyan University Press, 1981), 77.

43. *CA*, 1829: 4.

44. *CA*, 1830: 140.

45. Lindley, *"You Have Stept,"* 63.

46. Epstein, *Politics of Domesticity*, 76.

47. *CA*, 1826: 8; 1830: 136.

48. Schneider, *Way of the Cross*, 175.

49. *CA*, 1828: 168.

50. Sarah Robbins, *Managing Literacy, Mothering America: Women's Narratives on Reading and Writing in the Nineteenth Century* (Pittsburgh: University of Pittsburgh Press, 2004), 72.

51. Welter, "Cult of True Womanhood," 152.

52. *CA*, 1828: 196; 1827: 112.

53. See Mary P. Ryan, *Cradle of the Middle Class: The Family in Oneida County, New York, 1790–1865* (Cambridge: Cambridge University Press, 1981), 98–104.

54. Lori D. Ginzberg, *Women in Antebellum Reform* (Wheeling, IL: Harlan Davidson, 2000), 8–9.

55. See Karin J. Bohleke, "Americanizing French Fashion Plates: *Godey's* and *Peterson's* Cultural and Socio-Economic Translation of *Les Modes Parisiennes*," *American Periodicals* 20, no. 2 (2010): 120–55.

56. Carol Mattingly, *Appropriate[ing] Dress: Women's Rhetorical Style in Nineteenth-Century America* (Carbondale: Southern Illinois University Press, 2002), 12.

57. Patricia Bizzell, "Frances Willard, Phoebe Palmer, and the Ethos of the Methodist Woman Preacher," *Rhetoric Society Quarterly* 36, no. 4 (2006): 388.

58. *CA*, 1826: 44.

59. *CA*, 1830: 76.

60. 1 Tim. 2:9; 1 Peter 3:3. Throughout, I reference the King James Version because this is the version nineteenth-century audiences would have read.

61. *CA*, 1830: 76.

62. *CA*, 1828: 180.

63. *CA*, 1827: 104.

Chapter 4. Stepping Outside the Ladies' Department

1. *CA*, 1828: 165.

2. Mountford, *Gendered Pulpit*, 33.

3. Carole Pateman, *The Disorder of Women: Democracy, Feminism, and Political Theory* (Stanford: Stanford University Press, 1989), 118.

4. Sibley, *Geographies of Exclusion*, 33.

5. Epstein, *Politics of Domesticity*, 87.

6. *CA*, 1830: 87.

7. *CA*, 1832: 37.

8. *CA*, 1829: 15; 1830: 108; 1829: 64; 1826: 6.

9. *CA*, 1827: 106 and 1828: 162.

10. *CA*, 1830: 130; 1829: 59; 1832: 54; 1832: 6.

11. *CA*, 1830: 70; 1831: 142.

12. *CA*, 1830: 139; 1826: 2.

13. *CA*, 1826: 10.

14. *CA*, 1830: 107; 1829: 54; 1829: 15; 1830: 131; 1830: 131.

15. Paul Lewis, "'Lectures or a Little Charity': Poor Visits in Antebellum Literature and Culture," *New England Quarterly* 73, no. 2 (2000): 250–51.

16. Amy Gilman, "From Widowhood to Wickedness: The Politics of Class and Gender in New York City Private Charity, 1799–1860," *History of Education Quarterly* 24, no. 1 (1984): 59–74. Susan M. Ryan similarly notes that women were often given more latitude in legitimizing their destitution in *The Grammar of Good Intentions: Race and the Antebellum Culture of Benevolence* (Ithaca, NY: Cornell University Press, 2005), 21.

17. Luke 21:4.

18. *CA*, 1826: 38.

19. *CA*, 1827: 102.

20. *CA*, 1830: 133.

21. *CA*, 1826: 49.

22. Lewis, "'Lectures or a Little Charity,'" and Tompkins, *Sensational Designs*, 151–52.

23. *CA*, 1826: 5.

24. *CA*, 1827: 101.

25. Lori D. Ginzberg, *Women and the Work of Benevolence: Morality, Politics, and Class in the Nineteenth-Century United States* (New Haven, CT: Yale University Press, 1990), 5. In the first chapter, Ginzberg describes the ideology of female benevolence and the way in which women used this ideology to their advantage (11–35).

26. See Daniel S. Wright, *"The First of Causes to Our Sex": The Female Moral Reform Movement in the Antebellum Northeast, 1834–1848* (New York: Routledge, 2006), 35; and Mary P. Ryan, "Gender and Public Access: Women's Politics in Nineteenth-Century America," in *Habermas and the Public Sphere*, ed. Craig Calhoun (Cambridge: MIT Press, 1992), 284.

27. *CA* 1826: 2; 1827: 134; 1828: 170; 1830: 86, 131; 1832: 19, 34.

28. Anne Firor Scott, *Natural Allies: Women's Associations in American History* (Chicago: University of Illinois Press, 1991), 2.

29. Historian Nancy Cott notes how women's prayer groups; charities; and missionary, education, and Sabbath school societies grew exponentially at the beginning of the nineteenth century. And unlike men's associations, which addressed secular, civic, and political concerns, women's associations remained closely tied to the church through the first third of the nineteenth century. *Bonds of Womanhood*, 132–33.

30. See Ryan, *Grammar of Good Intentions*, 12–14.

31. *CA* 1828: 186; 1826: 58.

32. *CA*, 1832: 39. All the societies mentioned in the *CA* were not necessarily connected to the Methodist church. Reports in the *CA* reflect how members of Methodist churches often participated in ecumenical charities, organizations sponsored by other churches, or efforts to address community needs such as the New-York Magdalen Society, which tried to assist prostitutes.

33. *CA*, 1826: 54; 1832: 52.

34. See Bruce Dorsey, *Reforming Men and Women: Gender in the Antebellum City* (Ithaca: Cornell University Press, 2002), 31.

35. *CA*, 1832: 9.

36. Barbara F. Reskin and Patricia A. Roos, *Job Queues, Gender Queues: Explaining Women's Inroads into Male Occupations* (Philadelphia: Temple University Press, 1990), 11–15.

37. Catharine Beecher, *A Treatise on Domestic Economy* (1841; repr. New York: Schocken, 1977), 9.

38. Johnson, *Gender and Rhetorical Space*, 144.

39. In discussing the business side of benevolence, Ginzberg describes many of the business skills women honed and enacted within benevolent organizations, and how women's acquisition of those skills was obscured. *Women and the Work of Benevolence*, 36–66.

40. *CA*, 1830: 94.

41. *CA*, 1830: 139.

42. Anne Ruggles Gere, *Intimate Practices: Literacy and Cultural Work in U.S. Women's Clubs, 1880–1920* (Urbana: University of Illinois Press, 1997), 115. In her examination of women's clubs, Gere similarly notes that these clubs offered women an opportunity to assume leadership and managerial roles rarely available to them in society.

43. *CA*, 1823: 62.

44. Ginzberg, *Women and the Work of Benevolence*, 39–40.

45. *CA*, 1830: 77; 1828: 162.

46. Mattingly, *Well-Tempered Women*.

47. *CA*, 1828: 142.

48. *CA*, 1826: 54.

49. *CA*, 1832: 52.

50. *CA*, 1826: 50.

51. See Anne M. Boylan, "Women in Groups: Analysis of Women's Benevolent Organizations in New York and Boston, 1797–1840," *Journal of American History* 71, no. 3 (1984): 497–523.

52. See Jacqueline Jones Royster, *Traces of a Stream: Literacy and Social Change among African American Women* (Pittsburgh: University of Pittsburgh Press, 2000), 103.

53. *CA*, 1828: 158.

54. *CA*, 1829: 22.

55. See Wright, *"The First of Causes to Our Sex,"* 38.

56. *CA*, 1829: 42.

57. Bruce David Forbes, "'And Obey God, Etc': Methodism and American Indians," in *Perspectives on American Methodism: Interpretive Essays*, ed. Russell E. Richey, Kenneth E. Rowe, and Jean Miller Schmidt (New York: Abingdon, 1993), 209–27.

58. In nineteenth-century missions' materials, the term "heathen" was commonly used to reference non-Christians.

59. *CA*, 1830: 138; 1828: 165.

60. Joan Jacobs Brumberg, "The Case of Ann Hasseltine Judson: Missionary Hagiography and Female Popular Culture, 1815–1850," in *Women in New Worlds*, vol. 2, ed. Rosemary Skinner Keller, Louise L. Queen, and Hilah F. Thomas (Nashville: Abingdon, 1982), 234–48.

61. For information about the Methodist Woman's Foreign Missionary Society and Woman's Home Missionary Society, see Rosemary Skinner Keller, "Creating a Sphere for Women: The Methodist Episcopal Church 1869–1906," in *Perspectives on American Methodism: Interpretive Essays*, ed. Russell E. Richey, Kenneth E. Rowe, and Jean Miller Schmidt (New York: Abingdon Press, 1993), 332–36. For information about the broader American Woman's Foreign Mission movement, see Patricia R. Hill, *The World Their Household: The American Woman's Foreign Mission Movement and Cultural Transformation, 1870–1920* (Ann Arbor: University of Michigan Press, 1985), 3, 8.

62. This article likely came from a religious weekly newspaper that John Holt Rice published in Richmond, Virginia, from 1822 to 1827 titled the *Family Visitor*. A. J. Morrison, "Presbyterian Periodicals of Richmond, 1815–1860," *Tyler's Quarterly Magazine* 1 (1920): 175.

63. Ecclesiastes 12:1 (King James Version).

64. *CA*, 1828: 185.

65. Anne M. Boylan, *Sunday School: The Formation of an American Institution* (New Haven, CT: Yale University Press, 1988), 101.

66. *CA*, 1827: 93.

67. See Philip B. Cliff, *The Rise and Development of the Sunday School Movement in England, 1780–1980* (Nutfield, Redhill, Surrey: National Christian Education Council, 1986).

68. In her discussion of British Sunday Schools, Vicki Tolar Burton discusses the controversy surrounding the question of whether Sunday schools should teach students to write. *Spiritual Literacy*, 285.

69. Today, this book is referred to as *The Book of Discipline*, and it contains the doctrine and the administrative and organizational guidelines for the Methodist denomination.

70. Addie Grace Wardle, *History of the Sunday School Movement in the Methodist Episcopal Church* (New York: Methodist Book Concern, 1918), 46.

71. Boylan, *Sunday School*, 61–63.

72. *CA*, 1827: 130.

73. *CA*, 1827: 93.

74. Boylan, *Sunday School*, 14–15.

75. Schneider, *Way of the Cross*, 204.

76. *CA*, 1830: 105.

77. Wigger, *Taking Heaven by Storm*, 186.

78. James E. Kirby, Russell E. Richey, and Kenneth E. Rowe, *The Methodists* (Westport, CT: Greenwood, 1996), 180.

79. *CA*, 1832: 14; 1830: 134.

80. *CA*, 1830: 85.

81. *CA*, 1828: 146.

82. Daniel P. Kidder, ed., *The Sunday-School Teacher's Guide* (New York: Lane and Tippett, 1848).

83. Kirby, Richey, and Rowe, *Methodists*, 180–82.

84. *CA*, 1828: 158.

85. *CA*, 1827: 121.

86. *CA*, 1826: 37.

87. See Boylan, *Sunday School*, 119–22.

88. Kirby, Richey, and Rowe, *Methodists*, 182. In 1844, Methodists in the North and South separated over the issues of slavery and episcopacy, with Southern Methodists forming the Methodist Episcopal Church South. In 1939, ninety-five years later, the two churches reunited.

89. *CA*, 1830: 88.

90. *CA*, 1829: 68.

91. Leonard I. Sweet, *The Minister's Wife: Her Role in Nineteenth-Century American Evangelicalism* (Philadelphia: Temple University Press, 1983), 3–11.

92. Wigger, *Taking Heaven by Storm*, 64–69.

93. Julie Roy Jeffrey, "Ministry Through Marriage," in *Women in New Worlds: Historical Perspectives on the Wesleyan Tradition*, ed. Hilah F. Thomas and Rosemary Skinner Keller (Nashville: Abingdon, 1981), 143–160, see especially 143–44.

94. *CA*, 1828: 144; 1830: 76; 1827: 121.

95. *CA*, 1831: 204.

96. *CA*, 1829: 16.

97. In this context, mourners likely refer to penitent sinners. Often at Methodist Camp meetings, mourners' benches were designated as a place for those seeking salvation.

98. *CA*, 1831: 175, 204.

99. Jeffrey, "Ministry Through Marriage," 153–56.

100. *CA*, 1826: 21–22; 1827: 102; 1827: 134.

101. See Lindley, *"You Have Stept,"* 72

102. Brumberg, "The Case of Ann Hasseltine Judson." For a discussion about the rich print culture that emerged out of the women's foreign mission movement in the late nineteenth century, see Robbins, "Woman's Work for Woman."

103. Nathan Bangs, *An Authentic History of the Missions Under the Care of the Missionary Society of the Methodist Episcopal Church* (New York: Methodist Episcopal Church, 1832), 27.

104. Wade Crawford Barclay, *Missionary Motivation and Expansion*, vol. 1 of *History of Methodist Missions* (New York: The Board of Missions of the Methodist Church, 1957), 210, 267–79.

105. Wade Crawford Barclay, *Widening Horizons, 1845–95*, vol. 3 of *History of Methodist Missions* (New York: The Board of Missions of the Methodist Church, 1957), 148.

106. *CA*, 1831: 144.

107. *CA*, 1828: 186. The United Brethren joined with the Evangelical Church in 1946 to form the United Evangelical Church; that church then joined with the Methodists in 1968 to form the United Methodist Church.

108. *CA*, 1830: 81–82.

109. *CA*, 1828: 195; 1830: 89; 1830: 118.

110. *CA*, 1830: 122, 138–39.

111. Elizabeth Gillan Muir, *Petticoats in the Pulpit: The Story of Early Nineteenth-Century Methodist Women Preachers in Upper Canada* (Toronto: The United Church Publishing House, 1991), 108, 114.

112. Brekus, *Strangers and Pilgrims*, 299.

113. Hill, *World Their Household*, 25.

Chapter 5. A Magazine of Their Own

1. *LR*, 1845: 166. *The Ladies' Repository and Gatherings of the West* (1841–1848), found in American Periodical Series Online II (Ann Arbor, MI: ProQuest, PMID 41624); *The Ladies' Repository* (1849–1876), found in American Periodical Series Online II (Ann Arbor, MI: ProQuest, PMID 41620). *The Ladies' Repository and Gatherings of the West* shortened its name to *The Ladies' Repository* in 1849. I consistently use this shorter title, and for future references to *The Ladies' Repository*, I will use the abbreviation *LR* and provide the year followed by the page number. This thirty-two-page monthly magazine used continuous pagination for each yearly volume.

2. Amy Beth Aronson, *Taking Liberties: Early American Women's Magazines and Their Readers* (Westport, CT: Praeger, 2002), 2.

3. Mary Ellen Zuckerman, *A History of Popular Women's Magazines in the United States, 1792–1995* (Westport, CT: Greenwood, 1998), xv.

4. Joanna Bowen Gillespie, "The Emerging Voice of the Methodist Woman: *The Ladies' Repository*, 1841–61," in *Perspectives on American Methodism: Interpretive Essays*, ed. Russell E. Richey, Kenneth E. Rowe, and Jean Miller Schmidt (Nashville: Kingswood, 1993), 248; Kathleen L. Endres and Therese L. Lueck, eds., *Women's Periodicals in the United States: Consumer Magazines* (Westport, CT: Greenwood, 1995), 182–83.

5. Norwood, *Story of American Methodism*, 214.

6. *LR*, 1855: 126.

7. *LR*, 1844: 28.

8. Frank Luther Mott, *A History of American Magazines, 1850–1865* (Cambridge, MA: Harvard University Press, 1938), 301.

9. The *LR* began before *Godey's* produced its first "Americanized" fashion plate in 1846, see Bohleke, "Americanized French Fashion Plates," 121.

10. Endres and Lueck, *Women's Periodicals in the United States*, 182.

11. *LR*, 1841: 7.

12. *LR*, 1841: 3–4.

13. Drawing on Barbara Welter's concept of true womanhood, Jean Miller Schmidt uses the terms "true woman" and "new woman" to distinguish antebellum women, for whom their households were the primary responsibility, from post–Civil War women, who began to define broader spheres of influence. See Welter, "The Cult of True Womanhood," 151–52; Schmidt, *Grace Sufficient*, 79–80.

14. Catherine Hobbs, "Introduction: Cultures and Practices of U.S. Women's Literacy," in *Nineteenth-Century Women Learn to Write*, ed. Catherine Hobbs (Charlottesville: University Press of Virginia, 1995), 6.

15. *LR*, 1841: 10–11.

16. *Godey's*, 1841: 236, 293. *Godey's Lady's Book and Ladies' American Magazine* (1840–1843), found in American Periodical Series II (Ann Arbor, MI: ProQuest, PMID 41727).

17. Welter, "Cult of True Womanhood," 165.

18. Aronson, *Taking Liberties*, 100.

19. *LR*, 1845: 255–56; 1841: 121, 146.

20. *LR*, 1841: 51.

21. *LR*, 1846: 280; 1844: 12.

22. *LR*, 1846: 305.

23. *LR*, 1841: 66. Italics appear in the original text.

24. Averil Evans McClelland, *The Education of Women in the United States* (New York: Garland, 1992), 123–25.

25. Patricia Smith Butcher, *Education for Equality: Women's Rights Periodicals and Women's Higher Education, 1849–1920* (New York: Greenwood, 1989), 35.

26. Thomas Woody, *A History of Women's Education in the United States*, vol. 1 (New York: Octagon, 1980), 399.

27. Ibid, 366.

28. *LR*, 1846: 288; 1845: 255.

29. *LR*, 1846: 320.

30. Butcher, *Education for Equality*, 16–20.

31. *LR*, 1842: 196.

32. *LR*, 1849: 351; 1846: 371.

33. Aronson, *Taking Liberties*, 18–19.

34. *LR*, 1842: 159; 1842: 222; 1847: 127; 1843: 319; 1845: 189.

35. *LR*, 1846: 286–87; 1846: 288.

36. Brown, *Word in the World*, 66, 76.

37. *LR*, 1861: 128.

38. *LR*, 1846: 285.

39. *LR*, 1845: 169–70. Although no additional information is given about Ross or her school, this essay predates the Indian boarding schools instituted in the late nineteenth century, so she was likely attending a female seminary or a church mission school. Also, asking a student to publicly read an essay defending her Indian heritage runs counter to the program of "mainstream assimilation" often pursued by Indian boarding schools.

40. *LR*, 1845: 191.

41. Gillespie, "Emerging Voice of the Methodist Woman."

42. *LR*, 1843: 359.

43. Paula Bernat Bennett, ed., *Nineteenth-Century American Women Poets: An Anthology* (Malden, MA: Blackwell, 1998), xxxv.

44. Bennett, *Nineteenth-Century;* Janet Gray, ed., *She Wields a Pen: American Women's Poetry of the Nineteenth-Century* (Iowa City: University of Iowa Pres, 1997); Cheryl Walker, ed., *American Women Poets of the Nineteenth Century: An Anthology* (New Brunswick: Rutgers University Press, 1992).

45. Bennett, *Nineteenth-Century*, xl.

46. Kristina K. Groover, ed., *Things of the Spirit: Women Writers Constructing Spirituality* (Notre Dame, IN: University of Notre Dame Press, 2004), 2–3.

47. This line references Psalm 61:2: "From the ends of the earth I call to you, I call as my heart grows faint; lead me to the rock that is higher than I."

48. *LR*, 1844: 22. I considered whether this writer might be Julia Ward Howe, but I was unable to find any connection with Howe, who resided in New York and Boston, and the midwestern *LR*. Moreover, the previous year, four poems were published in the *LR* by a Mrs. Howe. One of these appeared in the April issue, which is the same month that Julia Ward married Samuel Howe, so I believe the *LR*'s Mrs. Howe was another female poet.

49. *LR*, 1850: 201; 1843: 198.

50. *LR*, 1849: 351; 1849: 319; 1847: 127; 1849: 319.

51. *LR*, 1841: 372.

52. Marion Ann Taylor and Heather E. Weir, *Let Her Speak for Herself: Nineteenth-Century Women Writing on Women in Genesis* (Waco, TX: Baylor University Press, 2006), 15.

53. For information about Morgan's life, see *Poems by Mrs. Lyttleton F. Morgan: With a Memoir by Her Husband* (Baltimore: D. H. Carroll, 1888). To read Poe's stinging review of Morgan's novel, see *Edgar Allan Poe, "The Swiss Heiress; or The Bride of Destiny—A Tale,"* in *The Complete Works of Edgar Allan Poe: Literary Criticism*, vol. 2, ed. James Harrison (New York: George Sproul, 1902), 185–91.

54. *LR*, 1843: 232.

55. Royster, *Traces of a Stream*, 83.

56. In the *LR*, the title of the article is "Rebecca's Nurse," but in the Bible the name is usually spelled "Rebekah."

57. Gen. 24:59; 35:8.

58. *LR*, 1847: 175.

59. *LR*, 1844: 78.

60. *LR*, 1845: 140.

61. Miriam conspires against Moses, and the Lord afflicts her with leprosy (Num. 12:1–14). Delilah betrays her husband by revealing the source of his strength, his uncut hair, to his enemies, the Philistines (Judg. 16).

62. Gillespie, "Emerging Voice of the Methodist Woman," 251.

Epilogue: Ambiguous and Liminal Spaces

1. Hardesty, *Women Called to Witness*, 134.

2. Lindley, *"You Have Stept,"* 116.

3. Phyllis Mack, "Religion, Feminism, and the Problem of Agency: Reflections on Eighteenth-Century Quakerism," *Signs* 29, no. 1 (2003): 155.

4. See Hardesty, *Women Called to Witness*.

5. Initially established as the New York Female Moral Reform Society, the organization changed its name to American Female Moral Reform Society in 1839 to better reflect the national reach of the organization.

6. *Advocate of Moral Reform*, 1835: 4 (New York: New York Female Moral Reform Society).

7. Sarah Grimké, "Letters on the Equality of the Sexes and the Condition of Woman," in *Letters on the Equality of the Sexes and Other Essays*, ed. Elizabeth Ann Barlett (1837; repr., New Haven: Yale University Press, 1988), 34; Angelina Grimké, "Letters to Catherine Beecher," in *Women's Rights in the United States: A Documentary History*, ed. Winston E. Langley and Vivian C. Cox. (1828; repr., Westport, CT: Greenwood, 1994), 64.

8. Mattingly, *Well-Tempered Women*, 50.

9. The two verses from Paul's preaching often used to justify women's preclusion from preaching and public speech are 1 Cor. 14:34 and 1 Tim. 2:11–12.

10. Mack, "Religion, Feminism, and the Problem of Agency," 157.

11. See Lindley, *"You Have Stept,"* 86.

12. Women's involvement in missions moved them into the problematic space of religious and cultural imperialism.

13. Braude, "Women's History *Is* American Religious History," 92.

14. Feminist theologians generally advocate a view that because God is not literally male, all language about God is metaphorical or symbolic. See Lindley, *"You Have Stept,"* 428.

Bibliography

Advocate of Moral Reform, 1835. New York: New York Female Moral Reform Society.

Albaugh, Gaylord P. *History and Annotated Bibliography of American Religious Periodicals and Newspapers Established from 1730 through 1830.* Worcester, MA: American Antiquarian Society, 1994.

Anderson, Benedict. *Imagined Communities: Reflections on the Origin and Spread of Nationalism.* London: Verso, 1991.

Andrews, Dee E. *The Methodists and Revolutionary America, 1760–1800: The Shaping of an Evangelical Culture.* Princeton: Princeton University Press, 2000.

Arminian Magazine (Philadelphia), 1790. American Periodical Series I, reel 8. Ann Arbor, MI: University Microfilm.

Aronson, Amy Beth. *Taking Liberties: Early American Women's Magazines and Their Readers.* Westport, CT: Praeger, 2002.

Baker, Frank. *From Wesley to Asbury: Studies in Early American Methodism.* Durham, NC: Duke University Press, 1976.

Bangs, Nathan. *An Authentic History of the Missions under the Care of the Missionary Society of the Methodist Episcopal Church.* New York: Methodist Episcopal Church, 1832.

Barclay, Wade Crawford. *Missionary Motivation and Expansion.* Vol. 1 of *History of Methodist Missions.* New York: Board of Missions and Church Extension of the Methodist Church, 1957.

―――. *Widening Horizons, 1845–95.* Vol. 3 of *History of Methodist Missions.* New York: Board of Missions and Church Extension of the Methodist Church, 1957.

Beecher, Catharine. *A Treatise on Domestic Economy.* 1841. Reprint, New York: Schocken Books, 1977.

Bennett, Paula Bernat, ed. *Nineteenth-Century American Women Poets: An Anthology.* Malden, MA: Blackwell, 1998.

Biesecker, Barbara. "Coming to Terms with Recent Attempts to Write Women into the History of Rhetoric." *Philosophy and Rhetoric* 25, no. 2 (1992): 140–61.

Bizzell, Patricia. "Frances Willard, Phoebe Palmer, and the Ethos of the Methodist Woman Preacher." *Rhetoric Society Quarterly* 36, no. 4 (2006): 377–398.

Bizzell, Patricia, and Bruce Herzberg, eds. *The Rhetorical Tradition: Readings from Classical Times to the Present.* 2nd ed. Boston: Bedford/St. Martin's, 2001.

Bohleke, Karin J. "Americanizing French Fashion Plates: *Godey's* and *Peterson's* Cultural and Socio-Economic Translation of *Les Modes Parisiennes.*" *American Periodicals* 20, no. 2 (2010): 120–55.

Boylan, Anne M. *Sunday School: The Formation of an American Institution, 1790–1880.* New Haven, CT: Yale University Press, 1988.

————. "Women in Groups: Analysis of Women's Benevolent Organizations in New York and Boston, 1797–1840." *Journal of American History* 71, no. 3 (1984): 497–523.

Brandt, Deborah. *Literacy in American Lives.* Cambridge: Cambridge University Press, 2001.

Braude, Ann. "Women's History *Is* American Religious History." In *Retelling U.S. Religious History*, edited by Thomas A. Tweed, 87–107. Berkeley: University of California Press, 1997.

Brauer, Jerald C. "Conversion: From Puritanism to Revivalism." *Journal of Religion* 58, no. 3 (1978): 227–43.

Brekus, Catherine A. "Female Evangelism in the Early Methodist Movement, 1784–1845." In *Methodism and the Shaping of American Culture*, edited by Nathan O. Hatch and John H. Wigger, 135–73. Nashville: Kingswood, 2001.

————. *Strangers and Pilgrims: Female Preaching in America, 1740–1845.* Chapel Hill: University of North Carolina Press, 1998.

Brereton, Virginia Lieson. *From Sin to Salvation: Stories of Women's Conversions, 1800 to the Present.* Bloomington: Indiana University Press, 1991.

Brown, Candy Gunther. *The Word in the World: Evangelical Writing, Publishing, and Reading in America, 1789–1880.* Chapel Hill: University of North Carolina Press, 2004.

Brown, Earl Kent. *Women of Mr. Wesley's Methodism.* New York: Edwin Mellen, 1983.

Brumberg, Joan Jacobs. "The Case of Ann Hasseltine Judson: Missionary Hagiography and Female Popular Culture, 1815–1850." In *Women in New Worlds: Historical Perspectives on the Wesleyan Tradition.* Vol. 2, edited by Rosemary Skinner Keller, Louise L. Queen, and Hilah F. Thomas, 234–48. Nashville: Abingdon, 1982.

Buchanan, Lindal. *Regendering Delivery: The Fifth Canon and Antebellum Women Rhetors.* Carbondale: Southern Illinois University Press, 2005.

Burton, Vicki Tolar. *Spiritual Literacy in John Wesley's Methodism: Reading, Writing, and Speaking to Believe*. Waco, TX: Baylor University Press, 2008.

Butcher, Patricia Smith. *Education for Equality: Women's Rights Periodicals and Women's Higher Education, 1849–1920*. New York: Greenwood, 1989.

Campbell, Karlyn Khors, ed. *Man Cannot Speak for Her*. Vol. 1. New York: Greenwood, 1989.

Carey, James W. *Communication as Culture: Essays on Media and Society*. Boston: Unwin Hyman, 1988.

Casper, Scott E. *Constructing American Lives: Biography and Culture in Nineteenth-Century America*. Chapel Hill: University of North Carolina Press, 1999.

Christian Advocate (New York), 1826–1832. American Periodical Series II, reels 1749–1750. Ann Arbor, MI: University Microfilm.

Cliff, Philip B. *The Rise and Development of the Sunday School Movement in England, 1780–1980*. Nutfield, Redhill, Surrey: National Christian Education Council, 1986.

Collins, Vicki Tolar. "The Speaker Respoken: Material Rhetoric as Feminist Methodology." *College English* 61, no. 5 (1999): 545–73.

———. "Women's Voices and Women's Silence in the Tradition of Early Methodism." In *Listening to Their Voices: The Rhetorical Activities of Historical Women*, edited by Molly Meijer Wertheimer, 233–54. Columbia: University of South Carolina Press, 1997.

Connors, Robert. *Composition-Rhetoric: Backgrounds, Theory, and Pedagogy*. Pittsburgh: University of Pittsburgh Press, 1997.

———. "Dreams and Play: Historical Method and Methodology." In *Methods and Methodology in Composition Research*, edited by Gesa Kirsch and Patricia A. Sullivan, 15–36. Carbondale: Southern Illinois University Press, 1992.

Cott, Nancy F. *The Bonds of Womanhood: "Woman's Sphere" in New England, 1780–1835*. New Haven, CT: Yale University Press, 1977.

Crowley, Sharon, and Debra Hawhee. *Ancient Rhetorics for Contemporary Students*. 2nd ed. Boston: Allyn and Bacon, 1999.

Daniell, Beth. *A Communion of Friendship: Literacy, Spiritual Practice, and Women in Recovery*. Carbondale: Southern Illinois University Press, 2003.

Dorsey, Bruce. *Reforming Men and Women: Gender in the Antebellum City*. Ithaca, NY: Cornell University Press, 2002.

Douglas, Ann. *The Feminization of American Culture*. New York: Anchor, 1988.

Eaton, Rev. H. M. *The Itinerant's Wife: Her Qualifications, Duties, Trials, and Reward*. 1851. Reprinted in *The Nineteenth-Century American Methodist Itinerant Preacher's Wife*, edited by Carolyn De Swarte Gifford. New York: Garland, 1987.

Eliot, George. *Adam Bede*. 1859. Reprint, New York: Modern Library, 2002.

Endres, Kathleen L., and Therese L. Lueck, eds. *Women's Periodicals in the United States: Consumer Magazines.* Westport, CT: Greenwood, 1995.

Epstein, Barbara Leslie. *The Politics of Domesticity: Women, Evangelism, and Temperance in Nineteenth-Century America.* Middletown, CT: Wesleyan University Press, 1981.

Forbes, Bruce David. "'And Obey God, Etc': Methodism and American Indians." In *Perspectives on American Methodism: Interpretive Essays,* edited by Russell E. Richey, Kenneth E. Rowe, and Jean Miller Schmidt, 209–27. Nashville: Kingswood, 1993.

Foucault, Michel. "Space, Knowledge, and Power." In *The Foucault Reader,* edited by Paul Rabinow, 239–56. New York: Pantheon, 1984.

Genette, Gérard. *Narrative Discourse: An Essay in Method.* Translated by Jane E. Lewin. Ithaca, NY: Cornell University Press, 1980.

———. *Paratexts: Thresholds of Interpretation.* Translated by Jane E. Lewin. Cambridge: Cambridge University Press, 1997.

Gere, Anne Ruggles. *Intimate Practices: Literacy and Cultural Work in U.S. Women's Clubs, 1880–1920.* Urbana: University of Illinois Press, 1997.

Gillespie, Joanna Bowen. "'The Clear Leadings of Providence': Pious Memoirs and the Problems of Self-Realization for Women in the Early Nineteenth Century." *Journal of the Early Republic* 5, no. 2 (1985): 197–221.

———. "The Emerging Voice of the Methodist Woman: *The Ladies' Repository,* 1841–61." In *Perspectives on American Methodism: Interpretive Essays,* edited by Russell E. Richey, Kenneth E. Rowe, and Jean Miller Schmidt, 248–64. Nashville: Kingswood, 1993.

Gilman, Amy. "From Widowhood to Wickedness: The Politics of Class and Gender in New York City Private Charity, 1799–1860." *History of Education Quarterly* 24, no. 1 (1984): 59–74.

Ginzberg, Lori D. *Women and the Work of Benevolence: Morality, Politics, and Class in the Nineteenth-Century United States.* New Haven, CT: Yale University Press, 1990.

———. *Women in Antebellum Reform.* Wheeling, IL: Harlan Davidson, 2000.

Godey's Lady's Book and Ladies' American Magazine (1840–1843). American Periodical Series II. Ann Arbor, MI: ProQuest, PMID 41727.

Gray, Janet, ed. *She Wields a Pen: American Women's Poetry of the Nineteenth-Century.* Iowa City: University of Iowa Press, 1997.

Grimké, Angelina. "Letters to Catherine Beecher." 1838. Reprinted in *Women's Rights in the United States: A Documentary History,* edited by Winston E. Langley and Vivian C. Cox, 63–65. Westport, CT: Greenwood, 1994.

Grimké, Sarah. "Letters on the Equality of the Sexes and the Condition of Woman." 1837. Reprinted in *Letters on the Equality of the Sexes and Other Essays*, edited by Elizabeth Ann Bartlett, 31–103. New Haven, CT: Yale University Press, 1988.

Groover, Kristina K., ed. *Things of the Spirit: Women Writers Constructing Spirituality*. Notre Dame, IN: University of Notre Dame Press, 2004.

Haines, Michael. "Fertility and Mortality in the United States." *EH.Net Encyclopedia*, edited by Robert Whaples. June 26, 2005. http://eh.net/encyclopedia.

Hardesty, Nancy A. *Women Called to Witness: Evangelical Feminism in the Nineteenth Century*. 2nd ed. Knoxville: University of Tennessee Press, 1999.

Harris, Barbara J. *Beyond Her Sphere: Women and the Professions in American History*. Westport, CT: Greenwood, 1978.

Hart, James D. *The Popular Book: A History of America's Literary Taste*. New York: Oxford, University Press, 1950.

Hatch, Nathan O. *The Democratization of American Christianity*. New Haven, CT: Yale University Press, 1989.

———. "The Puzzle of American Methodism." In *Methodism and the Shaping of American Culture*, edited by Nathan O. Hatch and John H. Wigger, 23–40. Nashville: Kingswood, 2001.

Hatch, Nathan O., and John H. Wigger. "Introduction." In *Methodism and the Shaping of American Culture*, edited by Nathan O. Hatch and John H. Wigger, 11–22. Nashville: Kingswood, 2001.

Heyrman, Christine Leigh. *Southern Cross: The Beginnings of the Bible Belt*. New York: Knopf, 1997.

Higginbotham, Evelyn Brooks. *Righteous Discontent: The Women's Movement in the Black Baptist Church, 1880–1920*. Cambridge, MA: Harvard University Press, 1993.

Hill, Patricia Ruth. *The World Their Household: The American Woman's Foreign Mission Movement and Cultural Transformation, 1870–1920*. Ann Arbor: University of Michigan Press, 1985.

Hobbs, Catherine. "Introduction: Cultures and Practices of U.S. Women's Literacy." In *Nineteenth-Century Women Learn to Write*, edited by Catherine Hobbs, 1–33. Charlottesville: University Press of Virginia, 1995.

Jeffrey, Julie Roy. "Ministry through Marriage." In *Women in New Worlds: Historical Perspectives on the Wesleyan Tradition*, edited by Hilah F. Thomas and Rosemary Skinner Keller, 143–60. Nashville: Abingdon, 1981.

Johnson, Nan. *Gender and Rhetorical Space in American Life, 1866–1910*. Carbondale: Southern Illinois University Press, 2002.

Journals of the General Conference of the Methodist Episcopal Church. Vol. 1, *1796–1836*. New York: Carlton and Phillips, 1855.

Juster, Susan. *Disorderly Women: Sexual Politics and Evangelicalism in Revolutionary New England.* Ithaca, NY: Cornell University Press, 1994.

Keller, Rosemary Skinner. "Creating a Sphere for Women: The Methodist Episcopal Church 1869–1906." 1981. Reprinted in *Perspectives on American Methodism: Interpretive Essays,* edited by Russell E. Richey, Kenneth E. Rowe, and Jean Miller Schmidt, 332–42. Nashville: Kingswood, 1993.

Kidder, Daniel P., ed. *The Sunday-School Teacher's Guide.* New York: Lane and Tippett, 1848.

Kirby, James E., Russell E. Richey, and Kenneth E. Rowe. *The Methodists.* Westport, CT: Greenwood, 1996.

Knowles. James D. *Memoir of Mrs. Ann H. Judson, Late Missionary to Burmah: Including a History of the American Baptist Mission in the Burman Empire.* Boston: Lincoln and Edmands, 1829.

The Ladies' Repository and Gatherings of the West (1841–1848). American Periodical Series Online II. Ann Arbor, MI: ProQuest, PMID 41624.

The Ladies' Repository (1849–1876). American Periodical Series Online II. Ann Arbor, MI: ProQuest, PMID 41620.

Latham, Sean, and Robert Scholes. "The Rise of Periodical Studies." *PMLA* 121, no. 2 (2006): 517–30.

Lerner, Gerda. *Why History Matters: Life and Thought.* New York: Oxford University Press, 1997.

Lewis, Paul. "'Lectures or a Little Charity': Poor Visits in Antebellum Literature and Culture." *New England Quarterly* 73, no. 2 (2000): 246–73.

Lindley, Susan Hill. *"You Have Stept Out of Your Place": A History of Women and Religion in America.* Louisville, KY: Westminster John Knox, 1996.

Lobody, Diane H. "'That Language Might Be Give Me': Women's Experience in Early Methodism." In *Perspectives on American Methodism: Interpretive Essays,* edited by Russell E. Richey, Kenneth E. Rowe, and Jean Miller Schmidt, 127–44. Nashville: Kingswood, 1993.

Lunsford, Andrea A. "On Reclaiming Rhetorica." In *Reclaiming Rhetorica: Women in the Rhetorical Tradition,* edited by Andrea A. Lunsford, 3–8. Pittsburgh: University of Pittsburgh Press, 1995.

Lyerly, Cynthia Lynn. *Methodism and the Southern Mind, 1770–1810.* New York: Oxford University Press, 1998.

Mack, Phyllis. "Religion, Feminism, and the Problem of Agency: Reflections on Eighteenth-Century Quakerism." *Signs* 29, no. 1 (2003): 149–77.

Mattingly, Carol. *Appropriate[ing] Dress: Women's Rhetorical Style in Nineteenth-Century America.* Carbondale: Southern Illinois University Press, 2002.

———. *Well-Tempered Women: Nineteenth-Century Temperance Rhetoric*. Carbondale: Southern Illinois University Press, 1998.

McClelland, Averil Evans. *The Education of Women in the United States*. New York: Garland, 1992.

Methodist Magazine (New York), 1818–1828. American Periodical Series Online. Ann Arbor, MI: ProQuest, 2000.

Morgan, Mrs. Lyttleton F. *Poems by Mrs. Lyttleton F. Morgan: With a Memoir by Her Husband*. Baltimore: D. H. Carroll, 1888.

Morrison, A. J. "Presbyterian Periodicals of Richmond, 1815–1860." *Tyler's Quarterly Magazine* 1 (1920): 174–76.

Mott, Frank Luther. *American Journalism: A History of Newspapers in the United States through 260 Years, 1690 to 1950*. New York: Macmillan, 1953.

———. *A History of American Magazines, 1850–1865*. Cambridge, MA: Harvard University Press, 1938.

Mountford, Roxanne. *The Gendered Pulpit: Preaching in American Protestant Spaces*. Carbondale: Southern Illinois University Press, 2003.

Muir, Elizabeth Gillan. *Petticoats in the Pulpit: The Story of Early Nineteenth-Century Methodist Women Preachers in Upper Canada*. Toronto: The United Church Publishing House, 1991.

Norwood, Frederick A. *The Story of American Methodism: A History of the United Methodists and Their Relations*. Nashville: Abingdon, 1974.

Pateman, Carole. *The Disorder of Women: Democracy, Feminism and Political Theory*. Stanford, CA: Stanford University Press, 1989.

Pilkington, James Penn. *The Methodist Publishing House: A History*. Vol. 1. Nashville: Abingdon, 1968.

Poe, Edgar Allan. "The Swiss Heiress; or The Bride of Destiny—A Tale." In *The Complete Works of Edgar Allan Poe: Literary Criticism*. Vol. 2, edited by James Harrison, 185–91. New York: George Sproul, 1902.

Prentiss, Elizabeth. *Stepping Heavenward: One Woman's Journey to Godliness*. 1869. Reprint, Ulhrichsville, OH: Barbour, 1998.

Reskin, Barbara F., and Patricia A. Roos. *Job Queues, Gender Queues: Explaining Women's Inroads into Male Occupations*. Philadelphia: Temple University Press, 1990.

Richey, Russell E. *Early American Methodism*. Bloomington: Indiana University Press, 1991.

Ritchie, Joy, and Kate Ronald. "Introduction: A Gathering of Rhetorics." In *Available Means: An Anthology of Women's Rhetoric(s)*, edited by Joy Ritchie and Kate Ronald, xv–xxxi. Pittsburgh: University of Pittsburgh Press, 2001.

Robbins, Sarah. *Managing Literacy, Mothering America: Women's Narratives on Reading and Writing in the Nineteenth Century*. Pittsburgh: University of Pittsburgh Press, 2004.

———. "Woman's Work for Woman: Gendered Print Culture in American Mission Movement Narratives." In *Women in Print: Essays on the Print Culture of American Women from the Nineteenth and Twentieth Centuries*, edited by James P. Danky and Wayne A. Wiegand, 252–80. Madison: University of Wisconsin Press, 2006.

Rose, Gillian. *Feminism and Geography: The Limits of Geographical Knowledge*. Minneapolis: University of Minnesota Press, 1993.

Royster, Jacqueline Jones. *Traces of a Stream: Literacy and Social Change among African American Women*. Pittsburgh: University of Pittsburgh Press, 2000.

Ryan, Mary P. *Cradle of the Middle Class: The Family in Oneida County, New York, 1790–1865*. Cambridge: Cambridge University Press, 1981.

———. "Gender and Public Access: Women's Politics in Nineteenth-Century America." In *Habermas and the Public Sphere*, edited by Craig Calhoun, 259–88. Cambridge: MIT Press, 1992.

Ryan, Susan M. *The Grammar of Good Intentions: Race and the Antebellum Culture of Benevolence*. Ithaca, NY: Cornell University Press, 2005.

Schmidt, Jean Miller. *Grace Sufficient: A History of Women in American Methodism, 1760–1939*. Nashville: Abingdon, 1999.

Schneider, A. Gregory. *The Way of the Cross Leads Home: The Domestication of American Methodism*. Bloomington: Indiana University Press, 1993.

Scott, Anne Firor. *Natural Allies: Women's Associations in American History*. Urbana: University of Illinois Press, 1991.

Sibley, David. *Geographies of Exclusion: Society and Difference in the West*. London: Routledge, 1995.

Sinor, Jennifer. *The Extraordinary Work of Ordinary Writing: Annie Ray's Diary*. Iowa City: University of Iowa Press, 2002.

Smith, George G. *The Life and Letters of James Osgood Andrew*. Nashville: Southern Methodist Publishing House, 1882.

Soja, Edward W. *Postmodern Geographies: The Reassertion of Space in Critical Social Theory*. London: Verso, 1989.

Stansell, Christine. *City of Women: Sex and Class in New York, 1789–1860*. New York: Knopf, 1986.

Sweet, Leonard I. *The Minister's Wife: Her Role in Nineteenth-Century American Evangelicalism*. Philadelphia: Temple University Press, 1983.

Sweet, William Warren. *Religion on the American Frontier 1783–1840*. Vol. 4, *The Methodists*. Chicago: University of Chicago Press, 1946.

Taylor, Marion Ann, and Heather E. Weir. *Let Her Speak for Herself: Nineteenth-Century Women Writing on Women in Genesis.* Waco, TX: Baylor University Press, 2006.

Tocqueville, Alexis de. *Democracy in America.* Translated by Henry Reeve. Revised by Francis Bowen. 1835, 1840. Reprint, Ware, Hertfordshire: Wordsworth, 1998.

Tompkins, Jane P. "An Introduction to Reader-Response Criticism." In *Reader-Response Criticism: From Formalism to Post-Structuralism,* edited by Jane P. Tompkins. Baltimore: John Hopkins University Press, 1980.

———. *Sensational Designs: The Cultural Work of American Fiction, 1790–1860.* New York: Oxford University Press, 1985.

Tucker, Mary Orne. *Itinerant Preaching in the Early Days of Methodism by a Pioneer Preacher's Wife.* 1872. Reprinted in *The Nineteenth-Century American Methodist Itinerant Preacher's Wife,* edited by Carolyn De Swarte Gifford. New York: Garland, 1987.

Walker, Cheryl, ed. *American Women Poets of the Nineteenth Century: An Anthology.* New Brunswick: Rutgers University Press, 1992.

Walton, Douglas N. *On Defining Death: An Analytic Study of the Concept of Death in Philosophy and Medical Ethics.* Montreal: McGill-Queen's University Press, 1979.

Wardle, Addie Grace. *History of the Sunday School Movement in the Methodist Episcopal Church.* New York: Methodist Book Concern, 1918.

Warner, Laceye. *Saving Women: Retrieving Evangelistic Theology and Practice.* Waco, TX: Baylor, 2007.

Welter, Barbara. "The Cult of True Womanhood: 1820–1860." *American Quarterly* 18, no. 2 (1966): 151–74.

———. "The Feminization of American Religion: 1800–1860." In *Religion in American History: A Reader,* edited by Jon Butler and Harry S. Stout, 158–78. New York: Oxford University Press, 1998.

Westerkamp, Marilyn J. *Women and Religion in Early America, 1600–1850: The Puritan and Evangelical Traditions.* London: Routledge, 1999.

Wigger, John H. *Taking Heaven by Storm: Methodism and the Rise of Popular Christianity in America.* New York: Oxford University Press, 1998.

Woody, Thomas. *A History of Women's Education in the United States.* Vol. 1. New York: Octagon, 1980.

Wright, Daniel S. *"The First of Causes to Our Sex": The Female Moral Reform Movement in the Antebellum Northeast, 1834–1848.* New York: Routledge, 2006.

Zuckerman, Mary Ellen. *A History of Popular Women's Magazines in the United States, 1792–1995.* Westport, CT: Greenwood, 1998.

Index

African Methodist Episcopal Church, 8, 49

advocacy, women's public, 4, 10, 15, 80, 82

American Female Moral Reform Society, 129, 153n5

American Sunday School Union, 91

Anderson, Benedict, 11, 22, 59, 137n34

Andrews, Dee, 1, 9, 141n11

Anglican, 8, 20, 22, 48

Arminian Magazine (American), 21

Arminian Magazine (British), 19, 21

Aronson, Amy Beth, 106, 111, 116

Asbury, Francis, 21, 56, 139n12

assistant ministers, 4, 96–99

awakening, 27–29

Bangs, Nathan, 56–57, 92

Beecher, Catherine, 65, 82, 113, 130

benefactors, 4, 71, 76; bequests, 74; material donations, 73–74

benevolent organizations, 10, 16, 77, 80, 87, 95, 103–4, 131–32, 146n29; business/leadership skills, women's acquisition of, 46, 83–84, 86, 147n39; reports, 80, 84–86

benevolent organizers, 4, 16, 54, 80, 88, 109; and benevolent/charitable endeavors, 73–74, 76, 80–82, 86, 95; and careers, 86

Bennett, Paula, 119

Bible society, 57, 76, 95

Bizzell, Patricia, 2, 7, 68

Boylan, Anne, 16, 89, 92

Braude, Ann, 6, 132

Brekus, Catherine, 2, 7, 9, 16, 48, 103

Brown, Candy, 23, 25, 59–60

Buchanan, Lindal, 50

Burton, Vicki Tolar, 19, 45, 137n28, 142n25, 148n68

Campbell, Karlyn Kohrs, 7

camp meetings/revivals, 5–6, 22, 54, 59, 72, 99

Carey, James, 24

Cary, Alice, 106–7, 119

charitable organizations/societies. *See* benevolent organizations

Christian Advocate (*CA*): audiences/popularity, 53, 56–58, 72, 137n35; columns, 54, 58–59; contents, 58–59; editors, 57, 61, 107; inception, 55–56;

space: discursive, 52; gendered, 7, 38–39, 52, 55, 71–72, 84; private/public, 39, 55, 71–72, 82; sacred, 11, 38, 53, 55

spatial assignments, 9, 14, 54–55, 62–63, 71

spiritual diaries/journals/letters, 39, 45–46, 142n25

sponsors of literacy, 10, 122

sponsors of women's rhetorical development, 7, 10, 16, 81, 85–86, 88, 109, 125, 132–33

Stanton, Elizabeth Cady, 83, 128

Stepping Heavenward (Prentiss), 19

Stowe, Harriet Beecher, 40, 106; *Uncle Tom's Cabin*, 40

Sunday schools: 72, 88; administrators, 4, 42, 95; conversions, 92–95; early English and American, 90–91; as evangelical enterprises, 90–92; teachers, 4, 13, 10, 16, 71, 86, 89, 93–96

Taylor, Marion Ann, 122

temperance, 17, 73, 84, 104, 125, 128–29, 131

textual communities, 11–12

tract and Bible societies, 57, 72, 74, 80–81

transmission of information, 24

traveling preachers. *See* itinerant ministers

tropes: for death, 34–35; "eloquent mother," 83; poverty, 76; woman on

her deathbed, 40; "a woman's place," 38

true woman, 60, 109, 122, 126, 132 151n13

virtue, feminine, 45, 51, 60, 67–69, 108, 111

Weir, Heather, 122

Welter, Barbara, 40, 60, 111

Wesley, John, 4, 8–9, 44, 49, 97, 137n28, 140n55

widow's mite, 76–77

Wigger, John, 5, 8–9, 44, 49, 97

Willard, Frances, 6, 68, 83, 107, 128

Woman's Foreign Missionary Society, 6, 88

Woman's Home Missionary Society, 88

women preachers, 2, 7, 9 48–49, 128; women's ordination, 7, 136n16

Women's Christian Temperance Union, 128, 131

women's education, 105, 110–15, 122, 125; connection between intellect and piety, 110–13

women's magazines, 40, 60, 105–7, 109–10, 116–17, 125

women's rhetorical development, 7, 10, 16, 81, 85–86, 88, 109, 125, 132–33

women's rights, 127–131

Woody, Thomas, 114

Zuckerman, Mary Ellen, 106